Sarbanes-Oxley and the Board of Directors

Sarbanes-Oxley
and the Board
of Directors

Techniques and Best Practices for
Corporate Governance

SCOTT GREEN

WILEY

John Wiley & Sons, Inc.

Library of Congress Cataloging-in-Publication Data:
Green, Scott, 1962-
  Sarbanes-Oxley and the board of directors: techniques and best practices for corporate governance / Scott Green.
     p. cm.
  Includes index.
  ISBN-13 978-0-471-73608-0 (cloth)
  ISBN-10 0-471-73608-2 (cloth)
   1. Boards of directors—United States.   2. Corporate governance—United States.
  3. Corporations—Accounting—Law and legislation—United States.   I. Title.
  HD2745.G74 2005
  658.4'22—dc22
  2005010214

Printed in the United States of America

10 9 8 7 6 5 4 3 2 1

In memory of my grandfather who instilled in me the notion that we owe it to the next generation to leave the world better than when we entered it. I also dedicate this book to Nicholas and Christina, who sustain me and represent that bright and better future.

Contents

Preface

Nearly three years ago, as the Sarbanes-Oxley Act became law, I recognized that there would be a need for accessible but detailed guidance to help managers implement certain sections of the Act. Additionally, it was clear that related social systems must also be addressed if the time and money spent on internal controls was to be effective. These beliefs motivated me to write *Manager's Guide to the Sarbanes-Oxley Act* (John Wiley & Sons, 2004) for medium and small public companies as an aid to compliance. (The guide has since then found an audience in large organizations as well.) The procedural aspects of Sarbanes-Oxley have indeed been burdensome, particularly on smaller companies. As I sat down to write *Manager's Guide*, I was tempted to expand the scope of the book to include other audiences. After its publication, my focus on the needs of our nation's corporate managers was validated by the book's acceptance in the marketplace. Nevertheless, other stakeholders were still left without a text that enables quick, easy assimilation of the important compliance criteria emanating from Sarbanes-Oxley. One such group encompasses the thousands of directors who sit on the boards of every corporation and those who support their activities.

I was constantly reminded of this need. At conferences at which I was invited to participate—and radio, television, and online "webinar" appearances relating to *Manager's Guide to the Sarbanes-Oxley Act*—questions frequently moved beyond purely management concerns to the broader role of the Act and governance in the U.S. business model. Over time, I have tried to address many of these questions through my academic and professional writings.* These

---

*These include "The Limitations of the Sarbanes-Oxley Act," *USA Today Magazine*, (March 2005); "Abolish the Imperial CEO," *Journal of Corporate Accounting and Finance* (September 2004); "The Ripple Effect," *Internal Auditor Magazine* (February 2005); "The Causes, Impact and Future of the Sarbanes-Oxley Act," *Journal of International Business and Law* (Spring 2004); and "Take Seven Key Actions Before You Certify," *Journal of Corporate Accounting and Finance* (May 2004).

articles dispensed useful advice to the nation's directors and gate-keepers. However, each by nature is narrowly focused and cannot independently quench the incredible thirst for knowledge on the subject. Therefore, I have written a book in which much of this advice has been excerpted and included together with the other important issues of our day.

There is little doubt that the risks from sitting on a board, including not-for-profits, has risen exponentially, leaving directors and related stakeholders searching for answers. This necessitates a clearly written book that helps new or potential directors understand how boards operate, detail the special risks of board committees, identify best practices, and recognize the red flags of board governance. Such a book is also useful to sitting directors for understanding governance trends, evaluating their own practices, and understanding what needs to be done if things go wrong. This type of analysis helps directors to properly represent the company's shareholders and limit their own liability.

The problem with many books on corporate governance is that they are narrowly focused, addressing a segment of governance such as director liability, board independence, culture, risk assessment, and so on, or are written at a highly theoretical level that lacks practical guidance on application. I have set out to provide a book that assists potential, new, and sitting directors in understanding and meeting the word and spirit of the Sarbanes-Oxley Act and beyond. This is accomplished not only by citing the requirements of the Sarbanes-Oxley Act, but also by exploring best practices found around the world. These practices are then packaged into five discrete governance factors to help directors think about governance as a process, one that can be followed, the results analyzed, and the implications of conclusions determined. Numerous real world examples, vignettes, case studies, surveys, and other data are presented to bring context to the discussion.

My beliefs regarding board operations is similar to the one that I hold for company management—that is, simply implementing procedural rules will not be effective if social issues are ignored. The boards of Enron and WorldCom met the checklist criteria for acceptable governance practices of their day, and yet the companies melted down on their watch. The culture of the company and social interaction of the board make a difference, and a workable framework weaves this important concept into the new procedural changes required by legislation, regulators, and even best practice.

Once you have completed this book, you will:

- Understand how current governance practices developed
- Appreciate your potential liability as a director
- Recognize the red flags of governance
- Be conversant in issues surrounding director selection and evaluation
- Understand the strengths and weaknesses of certain board structures
- Grasp the additional responsibilities associated with committee assignments
- Know what steps to take when a potential crisis threatens the company

You will also have the tools to implement best governance practices even when there are few serious threats to the company. The complexity of a directorship requires supervisory ability, emotional intelligence, and attention to procedural details. These skills are important not only for the health of the company and its stockholders. They also protect a director's reputation and financial well-being. Risks to a serving director are real and must be managed. Those who sit idle as events unfold around them will be held accountable. The best way to protect yourself is to be aware of the risks, remain engaged, and actively work for the stockholders of the company.

Acknowledgments

This book is truly a collaborative effort. Without the help of many, it is likely that the topics raised in this book would be impenetrable to all but the most dogged readers. These topics are usually technical; nevertheless, the goal here is to present them in a highly accessible manner. (The initial drafts could quite possibly be classified as torture under international law!) To that purpose, several individuals dedicated substantial time reading my work-in-progress and challenging and helping me to refine the text so that we could benefit from their knowledge and expertise. They include Mark Chimsky, Harold Gibson, Jim Balsillie, Rich Davis, Dr. Cliff Green, Dane Bonn, Scott Foushee, Susan Foushee, Allan Shaw, Julie Daum, Arnold Ross, Mike Wilson, Les Zuke, Kevin Curtin, Lori Leach, and Gabriella Green.

While the opinions contained herein are my own, and not necessarily those of Weil, Gotshal & Manges, I would nevertheless like to express gratitude to those colleagues and coworkers who support my writing activities. Without their help, my books would remain unpublished. They include Stephen Dannhauser, Norman LaCroix, and Robert Messenio.

I would like to thank Sheck Cho, my editor, who believed me when I preached that Section 404 of the Sarbanes-Oxley Act would result in the need for literary support. He has helped John Wiley & Sons, Inc., dominate the fulfillment of that need. He has also thrown his considerable support behind the needs of our nation's boards of directors faced, as they are, with the ever-changing world of corporate governance. Sheck and the entire Wiley team are first rate. I also appreciate the efforts of my agent, Richard Curtis. His advice is always "top shelf."

A special thanks to the fine companies that have contributed their years of collective knowledge and experience to this book is also due. Johnson & Johnson's Credo, General Motors Audit Committee Charter, TIAA-CREF's Principles for Fund Governance and Practice, National Association of Corporate Directors Board Evaluation Tool, and Champion Enterprises, Inc.'s CEO Evaluation Form are all examples of best practice. I also thank General Metrics International for sharing their corporate governance ratings, Spencer Stuart for contributing key findings from their annual board survey, and AuditAnalytics.com for their research on U.S. accounting firms. We can now all benefit from their research, hard work, and effort perfecting these documents and related standards.

Sarbanes-Oxley
and the Board
of Directors

A Sturdy Framework

You have worked hard your entire career, reached the pinnacle of your profession, obtained the respect of your peers and community, assured yourself financial success, and are recognized as an outstanding alumni by your alma mater. Then you get a call to take on a new job that is time consuming, will test your character, and can destroy your reputation and wealth. As unappealing as that sounds, it happens every day and many do not hesitate to answer the call.

The offer of sitting on the board of directors for a public company is often viewed as the culmination of a successful career. The self-esteem, social recognition, and business networking opportunities might be all that come to mind when such an offer is made. Smart executives will also carefully consider the risks. They assess the health of both the business and the board. They evaluate whether they can truly contribute as a director. They recognize that if they accept, the job will require homework to make certain that they are prepared to perform their duties according to the highest principles and implement practices that will protect their reputation and ensure their professional survival.

The problem, however, is that newly appointed directors typically have not prepared themselves for this role. As successful executives, many believe that they have all the requisite tools and knowledge necessary (and could likely teach others a thing or two). In reality, a directorship is a job that takes preparation, requires a thorough understanding of governance practices and responsibilities, and requires a different mindset than that of management. Directors are representing stockholders and, as such, must possess a certain amount of professional skepticism in executing their duties. Failure to do so is a breach of the most sacred business covenants: duty of care, good faith, and independence. The purpose of this chapter is to introduce a framework that will enable directors to approach their job in a way that minimizes their risk and maximizes their impact.

There are certain board facts that all potential directors should grasp, namely, that being a director is:

- **Time consuming.** Most boards in the S&P 500 hold just under eight meetings per year on average.[1] Some board committees meet frequently. Audit committees not only meet more frequently than other committees, they also carry more responsibility.
- **Risky.** If the company comes under attack for illegal or even unethical behavior, a director's reputation could be forever tarnished. If related decisions are deemed to lack good faith, they can be financially damaging as well.
- **Not as profitable as you might think.** While compensation at larger companies can be significant (and is increasing to attract reluctant candidates), the amounts usually pale in comparison to the individual's net worth. For smaller company directors, their net worth may not be comparable, but neither is the compensation.

Nevertheless, there are benefits to becoming a director. Most of these are quite obvious. There is the respect and other psychic rewards associated with being selected to serve a company. An invitation to be a director is often viewed by many as reaching the pinnacle of the business world—your acceptance to the "club." A directorship can result in business and social networking contacts not otherwise available. Many directors enjoy the mentor role involved in helping to guide a company to greater prosperity. This is not to suggest that these rewards are not worth the liability associated with becoming a director. In fact, there are legitimate concerns that many qualified candidates conclude outweigh the rewards. It is suggested that potential directors need to do their homework to make certain that they are joining a healthy board that supports transparency and acts in the best interests of stockholders.

It is critical for the health of our public companies that quality directors continue to provide them with the benefit of their experience.

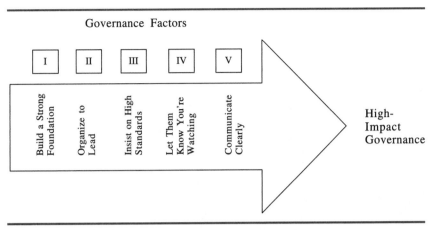

Governance Factors

High-Impact Governance

EXHIBIT 1.1   High-Impact Governance Framework

As such, directors not only need information, but a framework that will help guide and provide confidence that they are doing all that they can to reduce their personal risk by championing rock-solid governance practices. The High-Impact Governance Framework is such a device designed with a view toward providing the power tools that conscientious directors seek. The framework contains the strongest concepts currently available and is unapologetically black-belt grade with the director's well-being at heart. It consists of five governance factors: Build a Strong Foundation, Organize to Lead, Insist on High Standards, Let Them Know You Are Watching, and Communicate Clearly (see Exhibit 1.1).

GOVERNANCE FACTOR I: BUILD A STRONG FOUNDATION

We begin our journey by placing our initial focus on building a strong governance foundation. This includes a brief legislative history to put current events into proper context. Having the right board structure can be important to good process, so "board basics" will be introduced to serve as the bedrock for the governance structure. In this section, we also cover director "independence," "good faith," and the "business judgment rule" as it relates to director liability and ways a board can mitigate risk.

GOVERNANCE FACTOR II: ORGANIZE TO LEAD

Once our foundation is established, Factor II will help us organize to lead. A board can lead without proper organization, but it only makes the job more difficult. We will evaluate the role of the audit committee and explain why an intelligent director candidate should interview the CFO and the outside auditor among others before taking on such a responsibility. Even if you do not intend to sit on the audit committee or consider yourself a financial expert, this is a critical step. It is important to form an opinion regarding the aggressiveness of management's financial policies. A high-level discussion regarding the company's revenue recognition, reserve, and financing policies can tell a director much about management's approach to business. Motivated candidates should also interview the general counsel regarding any pending legal or regulatory issues. For instance, you do not want to learn at your first board meeting that the company's sole product is being contested for violating a patent. We will explore a number of red flags that directors can familiarize themselves with prior to interviewing the external auditor and general counsel.

There has been no shortage of compensation scandals. Directors are coming under increasing fire for their lack of oversight and understanding of the compensation plans covering their executives. Given the amount of recent litigation and negative press, a potential director should always attempt to determine if there are any compensation issues forming. We will examine both faulty remuneration plans and the components of a strong plan.

Most director nominees understand how they were selected for board service. Nevertheless, we will study components of a strong nomination process and the risks of directors selected through the good old boy network. One of the country's best corporate matchmakers will share her experiences and an action plan that helps boards identify that perfect candidate. We will examine when committees, other than audit, compensation, and governance, might be appropriate and highlight one committee to be avoided.

GOVERNANCE FACTOR III: INSIST ON HIGH STANDARDS

A board can follow all the right rules, check all of the governance boxes, and still preside over a rapid financial meltdown of stunning proportions. This happens because a premium is placed on process over culture and social systems. The path to high-impact governance requires that the board insist on high social standards. This includes establishing the right culture, not just in the company, but also in the boardroom. Building a strong culture is more than issuing a statement of values or code of ethics; it is the result of a prolonged program of communication and action that clearly delineates behavioral boundaries and rewards desired activities. This "soft subject" is worthy of even the most hard-nosed boards. A strong, ethical culture can overcome a number of governance sins, and directors have a vested interest in supporting steps to embed such a culture in order to keep their personal liability to a minimum. Together, we will explore the social characteristics of boards that work well together and how they are able to set and enforce the proper "tone from the top." Finally, we will evaluate desired board behaviors and ways to reinforce them, some structural, some not. This includes conducting executive sessions without unnecessarily upsetting the CEO and the importance of populating a balanced board with the people you need to succeed. We will further examine what qualities effective directors and their boards possess (and why a nominee should also determine who else is on the board), their background, their ownership stake in the company, and the board's relationship to management to determine if it is sufficiently independent to ensure healthy debate and decision making.

GOVERNANCE FACTOR IV: LET THEM KNOW THAT YOU ARE WATCHING

Even a well-organized and socially healthy board can falter if it does not possess strong oversight skills. Techniques for board supervision and monitoring will be reviewed in this part of the book. We will address risk analysis, operational oversight, and even monitoring management's compliance with corporate policies. We will also cover a subject that interests most directors: the issue of shareholder access and corporate defenses and what to do when hostile forces find your boardroom.

GOVERNANCE FACTOR V: COMMUNICATE CLEARLY

Boards can do all the proper things, but if they do not succeed in communication, particularly to regulators and investors, their good actions will be lost in the noise of negative perception. Governance Factor V focuses on how to comply with the new communication requirements imposed by Sarbanes-Oxley and the U.S. Securities and Exchange Commission (SEC).

What should a director do when, despite his or her best efforts and the efforts of other board members, things go wrong? Much depends on the type of crisis and the board's measured reaction. Therefore, we will cover some crisis management steps that directors can take to protect themselves and the shareholders they represent.

It will become clear that many procedures presented in this book are required, while others are considered best practice. Furthermore, some best practices are controversial. Opinions will be given on these subjects. However, it is less important that you agree with the personal position of the author on these issues than you are made aware of the vigorous debate being waged. Each side of an argument is provided to some degree so that you can begin to develop your own position if you have not already done so. I must also point out that, although I work for one of the most respected law firms in the world and a recognized leader in the field of corporate governance, the opinions contained in this book are my own and not necessarily those of Weil, Gotshal & Manges, the corporate governance group, or any other practice of the Firm. We all try to find the best approach to these heavy issues, and the more knowledgeable voices there are to join the debate, the better the opportunity to make the most informed choices.

In the end, good governance requires a team effort between honest management and a board willing to offer their experience to challenge, counsel, and guide. In the final chapter, a call to service is proposed and why you are needed is explained. After reading this book, you will be ready to answer the call. Once you are fully informed, the question becomes, will you want to serve?

A final note: at the end of each chapter, a summary of key concepts is presented. These issues and objectives may prove to be a useful reference as you perform your oversight duties. The following are the key concepts for this introductory chapter.

KEY CONCEPTS

- Learn to:
  - Build a strong governance foundation.
  - Organize to lead.
  - Insist on high standards.
  - Let them know you're watching.
  - Communicate clearly.
- Prepare to spend the time it takes to do the job.
- Understand the risks of serving.
- Serve for altruistic reasons. Do not serve solely for the monetary rewards, you may be disappointed.

ENDNOTE

1. Spencer Stuart, "Spencer Stuart Board Index 2003," *SpencerStuart.com*. http://www.spencerstuart.com/research/boards/739/ (17 November, 2004).

Building a Strong Foundation

We start our journey by constructing a strong governance base on which we can build our competency. History underpins our foundation. Understanding the legislative continuum is important for developing strategies for coping with change. Therefore, we begin by reviewing some of the more significant legislative initiatives leading up to and including passage of the Sarbanes-Oxley Act.

Knowing the basic organizational issues concerning director liability and board structure provide directors with the confidence to act. They need not second guess decisions. They have a firm handle on their duties and know what they must do to protect themselves and their shareholders. So we will also review "board basics" to establish our governance foundation.

Upon a strong foundation, we can easily organize to lead, which will be the subject of Governance Factor II.

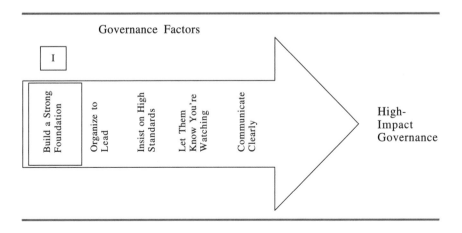

CHAPTER 2

Making of a
Governance Revolution

So here you are, nominated to join a board, with all of the respect, responsibilities, and liabilities that come with the job. Every board member has traveled a unique and personal path to arrive at a similar destination. History has shown that some arrive more prepared than others. To put this governance history into perspective, it is useful to know how governance evolved and where it is potentially headed. We will go back in time to appreciate how corporate governance developed and, based on these trends, evaluate what the future holds for serving directors. With this knowledge, each of us can make that most personal of decisions, not only whether an organization is right for us, but if serving on a board in the current environment is truly what we desire.

Corporate governance is an evolving ideal, a process of continuous improvement. This chapter provides the historical context regarding how corporate governance developed. This and an enhanced example of corporate governance will help directors recognize that they are participants in an ongoing movement and prepare them for the inevitable changes to come.

The common corporate structure, ubiquitous to both developed and developing states, is actually a relative newcomer to the business world. While the concept of a board of directors can be traced to early colonial days in this country, prior to 1840, owners generally managed companies directly. There were partnerships in which management duties were distributed; but these partners were still stakeholders in the business with joint and unlimited liability. There were also salaried managers who reported directly to the owners, primarily on plantations and estates.[1]

Modern managerial structures began to appear in the 1850s and 1860s as industrialization increased the complexity of business operations. However, the public limited liability corporation, in which a shareholder's liability was limited to their investment, took hold only in the 1900s. Since their creation, corporations have initiated the rise of the professional manager. Limited liability corporations not only met the structural needs of an organization, it freed up capital trapped under mattresses and in secret bank accounts. Individuals were willing to put their money to work now that they no longer placed their entire net worth at risk when they decided to invest in a business. Better yet, investors could easily transfer interest simply by selling their shares in the company.

REGULATORY DEVELOPMENT IN THE UNITED STATES

Since the advent of the modern corporate structure, the agents and gatekeepers of our public companies have served a vital role in the capitalist system. At the most basic level, they are the appointed guardians of a stockholder's invested capital. The agents comprise our boards of directors and executive management of our public companies. The gatekeepers are the regulators, accountants, the lawyers, and even the financial analysts whose opinions we rely on when investing capital. The vast majority of agents and gatekeepers are honest, hard working people who want to do the right thing. However, repeated instances of corruption have, from time to time, threatened to destroy public confidence in our public markets and the very system that has created unprecedented and highly distributed wealth. Congress has repeatedly responded to these threats through legislation. An overview of what is arguably the most significant corporate legislation is provided in Exhibit 2.1.

The tendency for businesses to strive for monopoly and limit competition led to the passage of the Sherman Antitrust Act of 1890. President Theodore Roosevelt (1901–1909) used the powers of the Act to effectively initiate over 40 antitrust lawsuits. In true Roosevelt fashion, he took on some of the most powerful people and organizations of the time including John D. Rockefeller's Standard Oil, James B. Duke's tobacco trust, and even J. P. Morgan's Northern Securities Company. The Clayton Antitrust Act of 1914 further strengthened the tools to fight monopolies by forbidding price fixing and preventing directors from serving on the boards of competing companies.

EXHIBIT 2.1   Significant U.S. Corporate Legislation

Year	Legislation	Primary Target	Result
1890	Sherman Antitrust Act	Monopolies	Used by President Theodore Roosevelt to break huge, monopolistic trusts
1914	Clayton Antitrust Act	Monopolies /unfair business practices	Prevented directors from sitting on competing boards. Outlawed price fixing.
1933	Securities Act	Corporate transparency	Better information for investors
1933	Banking Act	Unfair banking practices	Separation of commercial banking, investment banking, and insurance industries for 65 years
1934	Securities Exchange Act	Regulation of the securities market	Created the SEC and the regular filing of financial reports
1940	Investment Company and Investment Advisor Acts	Abusive investment company practices	Increased transparency to reduce conflicts of interest
1977	Foreign Corrupt Practices Act	Bribery	Applied antibribery and record keeping requirements on the worldwide operations of U.S. based companies
1989	Financial Institutions Reform, Recovery and Enforcement Act	Restore confidence in savings-and-loan institutions	Created the Resolution Trust Corporation to dispose of assets of failed savings-and-loan institutions
1990	Comprehensive Thrift and Bank Fraud Prosecution Act	Financial institutions	Strengthened federal regulator's authority to combat financial fraud
2002	Sarbanes–Oxley Act	Public company financial reporting	Greater agent and gatekeeper accountability for financial reporting

After the Stock Market Crash of 1929, the U.S. financial system came under unprecedented pressure as poor monetary policy assured the nation's plunge into depression. By 1933, the country was feeling the full effects of these hard times. President Franklin Delano Roosevelt was elected President, declared a bank holiday, and reassured the country during numerous fireside chats. Congress also acted by passing the Securities Act of 1933 and the Securities Exchange Act of 1934. A lack of transparency and fair dealing led Congress to pass these acts to regulate the securities markets. This legislation is perhaps the most far reaching and effective corporate legislation in U.S. history. The markets were previously regulated by a patchwork of state laws that were commonly referred to as "blue sky" laws, many of which are still in place today as yet another level of regulation. The 1933 Act was passed to meet two basic objectives: It requires that investors receive material information concerning securities being offered for public sale; and it prohibits deceit, misrepresentations, and other fraud in the sale of securities. This legislation was designed to require issuers to disclose important information to investors so that they could make informed investment decisions. The theory is that greater public disclosure is bound to discourage bad behavior or, as Supreme Court Justice Louis Brandeis stated, "sunlight is the best disinfectant."

Congress also passed the Banking Act of 1933 to address harm caused by banks to the investing public. In short, the Act was designed to prevent banks from selling securities, thereby preventing them from peddling their soured investments to the public. There were certain sections of the Act, referred to as Glass-Steagall, which prohibited commercial banks from owning investment banks and vice versa. For years, this was viewed as an overly broad approach to a specific problem, yet was not readdressed until passage of the Gramm-Leach-Bliley Act of 1999.

The Securities Exchange Act of 1934 extended regulation to securities already issued and trading. The Act also created the Securities and Exchange Commission (SEC) and empowered it with extensive regulatory authority over all aspects of the securities industry and markets. Additionally, the Act requires issuers to provide information to the marketplace by filing annual and quarterly reports. Finally, there are provisions contained in the Act that prohibit activities that defraud investors.

In response to investment company abuses, Congress acted again to minimize conflicts of interest that arise in the operations of these companies. The Investment Company Act of 1940 and Investment Advisors Act of 1940 were passed to regulate companies that exist primarily to invest in securities of other companies. Mutual funds are one type of investment company covered under these acts. Importantly, this legislation also included antifraud provisions for all those who meet the definition of an investment advisor.

In 1977, President James Earl Carter and the U.S. Congress addressed unethical business practices utilized by certain U.S. companies doing business abroad by passing the Foreign Corrupt Practices Act. The Act prohibits U.S. companies, their subsidiaries, officers, directors, employees, and agents from bribing "foreign officials" or paying excessive "fees" to do business in a foreign country.

Despite previous legislation and federal oversight, the savings and loan industry experienced a crisis in the late 1980s that led to additional regulation. The cause of the crisis is best epitomized by Lincoln Savings and Loan, a California thrift purchased by Charles Keating in 1984. When purchased, Lincoln was a $1 billion company, but by 1988 it had grown to $5 billion. The mix of business also dramatically changed during this period. When purchased, the business was comprised almost exclusively of home mortgages, but by 1988, "home mortgages were almost nonexistent while direct investments in stocks and bonds were commonplace. For example, Lincoln bought $11.8 million in Circus Circus junk bonds and, on another occasion, it invested $132 million in the stock of Gulf Broadcasting Co., which was involved in a takeover fight."[2] Lincoln, however, was not alone in experiencing deteriorating investment portfolio quality. Eventually, as investments in junk bonds and direct investments soured, savings and loans from across the country found themselves insolvent. The Financial Institutions Reform, Recovery, and Enforcement Act of 1989 was passed to "restore the public's confidence in the savings and loan industry." Deposit insurance and the system of oversight were restructured to reinforce the safety of deposits, and the Resolution Trust Corporation was created to dispose of the assets of failed institutions. Congress later added the Comprehensive Thrift and Bank Fraud Prosecution Act of 1990 to expand the authority of federal regulators to combat financial fraud.

Not all structural changes were initiated by government, however, as market pressures can also have a positive impact on corporate governance. There were many examples of shareholder activists waging battles with corporations throughout the 1990s. They fought against "poison pills" (corporate actions that prevent an unsolicited takeover) and brought about greater transparency for boards and regulators by attacking secret executive compensation.

Since their inception, boards of directors have been tasked with the responsibility to make certain that investor capital is used to maximize profit and to ensure that profits accrue to the investor. The power of the board, however, seemed to wane from the 1960s through the 1980s until decades of profitless growth finally brought shareholders to call on management and boards of directors for change. Modern shareholder activism is generally believed to have come into full bloom during the 1990s.

By the late 1980s, CEOs had become so powerful that dismissal was a rare and newsworthy event. The corporate world was shocked in 1993 when, under shareholder pressure, General Motors ousted Robert C. Stemple followed by the removal of John F. Akers from IBM. The dam then broke and heads rolled in short order at American Express, Kodak, and Westinghouse.

During 2001 and 2002, a series of financial reporting frauds again shook the public's confidence in the capital markets. Managers and directors did not always subordinate their own interests to the interests of shareholders on whose behalf they are supposed to be acting. Instead they abused their position to enrich themselves or passively allowed management's power to go unquestioned. Congress responded by passing the Sarbanes-Oxley Act in 2002. Perhaps the most comprehensive corporate legislation since the 1930s, the Act was designed to restore confidence, not only by expanding regulatory oversight and guidance of gatekeepers, but also by addressing many of the structural and cultural issues that impeded detection of the numerous financial reporting frauds. The Act also energized the efforts of the domestic private sector and governments worldwide to reevaluate and improve governance practices.

RELATIVE MATURITY OF WORLDWIDE GOVERNANCE[3]

Corporate governance as a discipline has been developing over several decades. Nevertheless, many important developments have occurred recently, primarily in the United States, as a reaction to perceived governance failings. The tectonic shift in corporate governance now being experienced began shortly after the numerous and massive frauds in the United States came to light in 2001 and 2002. At first, many saw this as strictly an American problem, but a far-reaching response by the U.S. Congress imposed new practices on many foreign-based companies whose securities are trading in U.S. financial markets. Since then, a number of countries have responded by studying, debating, and strengthening their governance practices. Importantly, the European Union (EU) has issued a phased action plan to underscore their claim to regulate the corporate governance and auditing standards of EU companies. The plan could result in profound changes for EU member states. So what began as an American response to a succession of disturbing revelations of corporate malfeasance and fraud eventually created a governance revolution that is making its way through sovereign capitols worldwide.

Governance Metrics International (GMI), the corporate governance research and ratings agency, analyzed over 3,200 global companies and evaluated them based on board accountability, financial disclosures and internal control, executive compensation, shareholder rights, ownership base and takeover provisions, and corporate behavior and responsibility. They found that, based on their criteria, the United States has the highest overall governance rating followed by Canada, the United Kingdom, and Australia. Greece and Japan were noteworthy in having the lowest scores.[4] In their most recent release, they also disclosed that 34 companies worldwide received their highest score of "10," of which 27 were U.S. based. GMI has permitted us to reprint the list of these well-governed companies in Appendix A, as well as some lessons learned from those organizations that were flagged previous to experiencing difficulties. Exhibit 2.2 provides a summary of some key corporate governance practices for different regions of the world. The status of governance development in the world's major regions is reviewed in the following sections.

United States

By Summer 2002, restoring public confidence in the U.S. markets became paramount. Congress responded to the financial reporting fraud crisis by passing the Sarbanes-Oxley Act of 2002. The Act expanded the regulatory oversight and guidance for auditors,

EXHIBIT 2.2 Comparison of Selected Governance Practices for Certain Countries[5]

Practice/Country	United States	United Kingdom (Combined Code)	Germany (Cromme)	Japan (JCGC)
Basis	Mix of mandated and voluntary.	Comply or explain.	Comply or explain.	Voluntary.
Separation of Chairman and CEO	Traditionally not separated. Trend toward separation or lead director.	Separated.	Two-tiered board structure.	Traditionally not separated.
Independent Board Majority	Listing standards require an independent majority.	At least half the board, excluding the chairperson, should comprise nonexecutive directors.	One-third to one-half of the supervisory board may be employee representatives. No more than two members of management board may sit on the supervisory board.	Recognizes that a majority should be independent.
Required Board Committees	Audit committees required by law. Nominating and compensation committees required by NYSE listing requirements, but not by NASDAQ.	There should be a nomination, remuneration, and audit committee.	Supervisory Board shall set up an audit committee. No other requirements.	The board should establish audit, nomination and compensation committees. The board may establish litigation or other committee for a specific purpose.
Board Access to Independent Advisors	Audit committee authorized by law to retain public accountant and advisors. NYSE Listing standards indicate that nominating and compensation committee charters should give committees sole authority to retain search firms and compensation consultants, respectively.	"… nonexecutive directors have access to independent professional advice at the company's expense where they judge it necessary …"	None other than the outside auditor specified.	None other than the outside auditor specified.
Auditor Independence	Mandatory audit partner rotation. All audit and nonaudit services of registered accountants approved by audit committee. Nonaudit services restricted.	The audit committee reviews and monitors auditor independence and nonaudit services supplied by the outside auditor.	Supervisory board must determine if auditor is independent based on review of all board and company relationships with the auditor and any additional services provided by the auditor that might impair independence.	Not covered.

lawyers, and analysts as well as addressed many of the structural corporate reforms necessary through interpreting rules issued by the Securities and Exchange Commission (SEC) and a new set of listing standards by the New York Stock Exchange (NYSE), and the National Association of Securities Dealers (NASD). As is common with legislation impacting U.S. financial markets, the Act provides an overall framework for regulating the markets, while leaving detailed oversight to the SEC. The SEC in turn allows the self-regulatory organizations (NYSE and NASD) to draft and implement detailed rules that address the requirements of the Act as well as the SEC.

Most are conversant with the parts of the Sarbanes-Oxley Act that require the principal executive and financial officer of public companies to certify their financial statements (Section 302) and to document their systems of internal control (Section 404); but there are other provisions of the Act, SEC implementing rules, and exchange listing requirements that also have a considerable impact on how our public companies are governed. Among other things, these provisions specify that audit committees establish procedures for bringing questionable accounting and auditing matters to light and, more importantly, provide for the confidential submission by employees of such complaints or concerns. The Act requires listed companies to adopt and disclose a code of ethics for key executives or explain why they have not done so. The SEC has also approved amendments to NYSE and NASD listing standards. Some additional NYSE requirements include:

- A board that must consist of an independent majority
- A nominating/corporate governance committee that is composed entirely of independent directors
- A compensation committee that is composed entirely of independent directors
- Additional audit committee requirements including the preparation of a charter and an annual self-evaluation
- A requirement that nonmanagement directors regularly meet in executive session without management
- That each company must have an audit department
- That each company adopt and disclose corporate governance guidelines that include director qualification standards, responsibilities, compensation, continuing education, succession, and annual performance evaluation of the board

- The adoption of a code of ethics for directors, officers, and employees and disclosure of waivers for officers and directors
- CEO certification that they are not aware of any violations of the NYSE corporate governance listing standards

The listing requirements further define "independence" to create bright line criteria regarding whether a director is and remains independent for the purpose of meeting corporate governance requirements. NASD standards are similar except that the thresholds are lower, reflecting the smaller market capitalization of many of their listings. The NASD rules also do not require compensation or nominating committees; but they do require an independent audit committee and that a majority of the full board's independent members approve compensation and nomination proposals.

These amendments address board and committee structures and processes, enhance the role of independent directors and provide a tighter definition of director independence. They are designed to better position boards to hold management accountable for the accurate portrayal of a company's financial condition. They also require disclosures designed to assist shareholders in monitoring corporate governance guidelines.[6]

While the regulatory framework in the United States continues to evolve, public companies are now focused on implementation of and compliance with the new regulations and standards. Many of these new requirements are now recognized as best practice internationally.

European Union

The discussion of modern corporate governance reform in the United Kingdom had been ongoing since the seminal Cadbury Code was published more than a decade ago. Subsequently, several other important contributions have been united with that code into a set of voluntary practices—for companies traded on the London Stock Exchange—called the Combined Code. The Combined Code works on a voluntary "comply or explain" basis. Companies must disclose whether they comply with its provisions and, if not, why. Over time, various components of the code have influenced the development of rules and regulations governing public companies in other jurisdictions. The most visible of these is the comply-or-explain methodology of compliance, which has been embraced by several other EU member states. Additionally, disclosure of compliance (or noncompliance) with national voluntary governance codes has become a component of the EU's action plan for governance reform.

In the EU, corporate governance regulation and oversight of audit firms has been conducted on a national level with little uniformity between member states. On May 31, 2003, the EU presented an action plan to improve corporate governance and audit services throughout its membership. Unlike the fast track of U.S. reforms, the European plan envisions a lengthy implementation period, stretching—for some of the reforms—to the end of the decade. Each proposal requires further development and then eventual implementation through either nonbinding recommendations or directives to each member state to achieve the result with room for national authorities to choose the form and methods.

The European plan is detailed in two communications emanating from the European Commission (EC) to the European Council and the European Parliament. The first communication addresses the modernization of company law and corporate governance presented in short- and long-term objectives. In the short term, the plan calls for:

- Creating a European Governance Forum to coordinate governance efforts of member states
- Expanding disclosure requirements for director compensation, governance policies, and related parties and reaffirming board liability for nonfinancial communications
- Strengthening independence and the role of nonexecutive directors
- Harmonizing and integrating the legal frameworks to ensure efficient shareholder communications and participation
- Simplifying the current EU directive on minimum capital maintenance requirements for listed companies
- Facilitating cross-border mergers between companies of member states

Longer-term initiatives include research and feasibility studies on institutional investor disclosures, board structures, board member accountability, shareholder voting, and company structures.

The second communication from the EC contains major elements proposed to improve statutory audits. These elements include:

- Implementation of international audit standards
- Creation of a pan-European mechanism to coordinate regulatory oversight of the audit profession
- Definition of principles for the hiring, firing, and compensation of auditors
- Further definition of auditor independence
- Examination of the auditor's role in reviewing and assessing a company's internal control system
- Harmonization of auditor ethics throughout the EU
- Implementation of quality assurance mechanisms
- Examination of EU auditor continuing education requirements
- Development of disclosure requirements concerning audit firm relationships
- Further study of auditor liability regimes

In October 2004, as a step in implementing its Corporate Governance Action Plan, the EC adopted a set of more detailed recommendations for member states relating to directors' remuneration and the role and presence of nonexecutive directors on listed companies' boards of directors. Member states are called on to adopt at a national level, whether by legislation or by a comply-or-explain approach, provisions concerning the roles of nonexecutive directors. The recommendation provides basic principles intended to strengthen the role of independent directors as well as additional guidance to assist the member states in interpreting these principles. In particular, it mandates that a unitary or supervisory board should include a sufficient number of independent nonexecutive directors to ensure that any material conflicts of interest involving directors are dealt with properly.

Even prior to its release, many member states already expressed nonexecutive director principles set forth in the recommendation in their national code. For example, the United Kingdom's Combined

Code and the Swiss Code & Directive mandate a majority of independent directors. Additionally, Spain's Olivencia Report recommends that outside directors should outnumber executive directors. The EC recommendation relating to the compensation of directors promotes transparency by inviting member states to adopt measures, including mandatory disclosure requirements and the submission of certain director remuneration policies to shareholder votes.

Beginning with the move to International Auditing Standards, the EU is starting to harmonize governance and audit regulation. The commission continues to express concern about the "unnecessary outreach effects" of Sarbanes-Oxley for European auditors and companies and the failure of the United States to "mutually recognize the equivalence of high-quality regulatory systems." It identifies certification of financial statements and internal control systems, direct U.S. access to EU audit working papers, U.S. auditor independence requirements, and audit committee requirements as areas of continuing disagreement with the U.S. regulatory approach.

Asia

The aftereffects of recent scandals have been less potent in Asia as some believe that Japan has used Enron and other large frauds as an excuse to put off real corporate governance reform. Despite evidence that the Japanese governance system needs improvement, problems in the United States seem to have retarded reforms aimed at correcting these shortcomings as critics point to the inability of U.S.-style corporate governance to prevent similar fraud. However, not long ago, in a fraud similar to Enron, Yamaichi Securities used off-balance sheet vehicles to manipulate their financials resulting in their collapse. Furthermore, some believe Japan's banking sector crises has been a partial result of poor corporate governance and shareholder accountability.[7]

Elsewhere in Asia, the China Securities Regulatory Commission has been implementing a set of globally recognized corporate governance practices. The *Code of Corporate Governance for Listed Companies in China* seeks to make listed companies in China more attractive to investors through:

- Establishing minority shareholder rights
- Restricting the power of the state
- Requiring independent directors
- Providing for board evaluation of management
- Establishing a framework for director and executive compensation
- Requiring the provision of internal control systems
- Detailing independence criteria for external auditors

Following the U.K. model, the code has been implemented on a comply-or-explain basis. Despite this important advance, some view wide-spread corruption and political interference with the judiciary as a continuing obstruction to the rule of law in China.

Africa and Latin America

In South Africa, the adoption of the *King Report on Corporate Governance for South Africa—2002* provides a governance framework for those companies listed on the Johannesburg Stock Exchange. The King Report and the United Kingdom's Combined Code have few differences. Both are applied on the comply-or-explain basis. Also of interest, the Johannesburg Stock Exchange is preparing to launch the Socially Responsible Index to measure the social, environment, and economic effects of top South African companies. Corporate governance practices will be one criterion for inclusion in the index.

In Latin America, corporate governance reforms remain elusive. It is common for companies based in Latin America to have controlling shareholders, therefore, minority shareholder rights reform remains the most visible issue in these markets. While Argentina, Brazil, Chile, and Mexico have passed laws strengthening minority shareholder rights, enforcement is inconsistent. The Organization for Economic Cooperation and Development (OECD) and World Bank sponsored the Latin American Roundtable on Corporate Governance in November of 2003 that established a blueprint for regional reform. It advocates creating stronger regulatory oversight, safeguarding minority rights, adopting international accounting standards, and limiting cronyism throughout the region.

Corporate governance has come a long ways in recent years—and it continues to evolve. Practices are still different among the many diverse countries with publicly traded companies, but they are converging in those with a mature rule of law. In one case, a director of a number of investment companies investing in emerging markets represents that he will pay a premium for those entities with good corporate governance in immature markets. A survey conducted by McKinsey & Co. supports this view as "an overwhelming majority of investors are prepared to pay a premium for companies exhibiting high governance standards. Premiums averaged 12 to 14 percent in North America and Western Europe; 20 to 25 percent in Asia and Latin America; and over 30 percent in Eastern Europe and Africa."[8] The overall result of these macro- and micro-initiatives is an overall improvement in the corporate governance of public companies. While most of the action of late has been in the United States, the more interesting changes may well occur in Europe as the EU begins to harmonize the various practices of its member countries. The unfolding story there will be worth watching.

KEY CONCEPTS

- Stay current. Governance is a process of continuous improvement. It is inevitable that we will experience change as governance evolves and matures.
- Make certain that "owners" are identified to monitor governance trends in markets where the company competes. Governance maturity and practices are uneven from country to country.
- More regulation will not stop fraud. Those that intend to defraud will find a way. Directors, management, employees, and other stakeholders need to work together to identify those that would harm our public companies.

ENDNOTES

1. Alfred Chandler and Richard Tedlow, *The Coming of Managerial Capitalism* (Homewood, IL: Irwin, 1985), 396–399.

2. James D. Stice, W. Steve Albrecht, and Leslie M. Brown, Jr., "Lessons to be learned-ZZZZ Best, Regina, and Lincoln Savings," *CPA Journal* (April 1991): accessed at http://www .nysscpa.org/cpajournal/old/10691661.htm.
3. Scott Green and Holly J. Gregory, "Global Governance Practices: International Corporations Are Experiencing the Ripple Effect of Governance Practices That Are Evolving on a Global Scale," *Internal Auditor* 62 (February 2005): 48–60.
4. Governance Metrics International, "GMI Releases New Global Governance Ratings," *GMIRatings.com.* http://www.gmiratings .com/(puwmf455mvry0z55jrozrame)/Release20040903.html (7 September 2004).
5. Green and Gregory, 51.
6. John Plender, "Tilt in the balance of boardroom power," *Financial Times* (London), 21 January 2004, 8.
7. Green and Gregory, 53.
8. McKinsey & Company, "Global Investor Opinion Survey: Key Findings," July 2002, 2. www.mckinsey.com/client service/organization leadership/service/corporate governance/pdf/global investor opinion survey 2002.pdf.

CHAPTER 3

Board Basics

Given the recent flurry of lawsuits filed and jail sentences meted out, it would be easy for potential directors to remove themselves from such risks by refusing to serve, but as the old saying goes, "Let us not look back in anger, nor forward in fear, but around in awareness." More than ever, public companies need educated, experienced directors who are aware of the risks and prepared to take on the duties and functions of the boardroom. The goal of "board basics" is to introduce the most elementary concepts in corporate governance from which we can build those skills that differentiate the solid boards from the empty suits.

According to the Business Roundtable, an association consisting of leading CEOs of U.S. companies, the board of directors has several primary oversight functions:

- Select, evaluate, and, if necessary, replace the CEO. The board should also plan for CEO and senior management succession as well as determine management compensation.
- Review, approve, and monitor the operating plans, budget objectives, major strategies, and plans of the corporation, including risk assessment and continuity planning.
- Focus on the integrity and clarity of the corporation's financial statements, including responsibility for engagement of the outside auditors.
- Provide advice and counsel to top management.
- Review and approve corporate actions.
- Nominate and recommend to shareholders for election an appropriate slate of candidates for the board of directors. Evaluate board processes and director performance.
- Review the adequacy of the systems to comply with all applicable laws and regulations.[1]

In short, it is not the responsibility of the board to run the company. That is the job of management. Instead, directors have the difficult job of ensuring that those running the company run it as effectively as possible. Even before the passage of the Sarbanes-Oxley Act, there have been important discussions from many different quarters regarding how to build the most effective board of directors. The question is how to best structure a board to effectively exercise their responsibilities. The truth of the matter is that while a well-structured board will better enable more efficient oversight, it does not guarantee quality performance. Only fully informed and engaged directors can ensure that shareholders are adequately protected. However, a poorly designed board can obstruct otherwise good directors from properly meeting their responsibilities—particularly where a board is not largely independent, there is more than one class of board members with greater powers, or the board is under the spell of a celebrity or imperial CEO.

Good board structure will take into account the following basic factors:

- Independence
- Size
- Committees and functions
- Lead director or independent chair
- Director development

Spencer Stuart, a leading executive search firm, conducts an annual survey of the boards of companies listed in the S&P 500. The survey provides valuable insights into shifts in the governance trends for these "board basics." Applicable statistics based on Spencer Stuart research will be referred to throughout this chapter, beginning with their 2004 survey shown in Exhibit 3.1.

INDEPENDENCE IS THE KEY

Independence is the key foundation to a properly functioning board of directors. If the board of a company is loaded with management, or a founder with a controlling stock interest, then it is possible that the directors are simply rubber-stamping the decisions of management

- Boards appointing lead or presiding director surged to 84% from 36% the prior year.
- Still, 74% combine the position of CEO and Chairperson, down from 80% five years ago.
- Average board size consists of 11 directors, down from 13 a decade ago.
- Only 9% of boards have 15 or more directors.
- Surprisingly, only 14% of directors have financial management and accounting backgrounds, unchanged from last year despite the new requirements for financial expertise. However, 40% of newly appointed audit committee chairpersons have a CFO or accounting background, an increase from 10% last year.
- 91% of boards have identified at least one financial expert.
- 17% of S&P 500 companies have three or more women on the board, and 87% have at least one women director.
- The average board has four committees.

EXHIBIT 3.1   2004 S&P 500 Board Statistics
Source: Data originally published in the "Spencer Stuart Board Index 2004." Copyright © 2004 Spencer Stuart. Used by permission.

rather than digging in to understand what is happening at the company.

While the Sarbanes-Oxley Act of 2002 did address board independence, lawmakers limited their focus to the board's audit committee. Specifically, the Act states that "in general—each member of the audit committee of the issuer shall be a member of the board of directors of the issuer and shall otherwise be independent." The Act then describes independence: "Criteria—In order to be considered to be independent for purposes of this paragraph, a member of an audit committee of an issuer may not, other than in his or her capacity as a member of the audit committee, the board of directors or any other board committee—(i) accept any consulting, advisory or other compensatory fee from the issuer; or (ii) be an affiliated person of the issuer or any subsidiary thereof."[2]

The Act addressed many perceived conflicts with the auditors and other service providers, but the real action occurred in the listing standards of the New York Stock Exchange and the NASD. These self regulatory organizations developed more stringent listing requirements and independence definitions which were accepted by the SEC. The New York Stock Exchange listing standards include:

- A requirement that listed companies must have a board that consists of an independent majority.
- That a company's board must make a determination regarding each director's independence and may adopt categorical standards to assist in this determination.
- Certain independence guidance that covers not only employees of the listed company, but also business relationships where a director receives more than $100,000 in compensation (other than his compensation from his board service) or a company he or she is affiliated with pays the listed company more than $1 million or 2 percent of the other such company's consolidated gross revenues. Internal and external auditors are also not considered independent. These rules extend to immediate family members and will disqualify a director from being independent until three years after the end of the affiliation, employment, or auditing relationship.

The NASD rules are similar, although some thresholds for independence are lower with compensation greater than $60,000 or business with the listed company in excess of $200,000 disqualifying a director's independence.

A useful study of director independence involves the legendary businessman Armand Hammer and Occidental Petroleum. Hammer was both the Chairperson and CEO of Occidental Petroleum until his death in 1990, friend and advisor to leaders of foreign states, famed philanthropist, and subject of a best-selling biography. His stature alone would prove formidable for any board to question his decisions or operate independently. Hammer also stacked the deck even further by hand picking his directors carefully. More than half of the board were insiders or had ties to the company that could conflict with the best interests of shareholders. Some of the outside directors had ties to other organizations that received compensation from Occidental, were paid advisors as well as directors, or sold their company to Occidental. There was also an unproven rumor that Hammer possessed signed, undated letters of resignation for every director.[3] Not surprisingly, the company committed millions of dollars for Hammer's many projects including the building and funding of an art museum, funding a second autobiography, and the purchase of a Leonardo da Vinci notebook, all of which troubled shareholders.

As an example that organizations can change their behavior, Occidental Petroleum has made substantial progress since Hammer's passing and can now be found on GMI's list of companies scoring a perfect "10" corporate governance rating (see Appendix A).

There is value to having insiders on a board. Knowing a company is important and has a worth that should not be overlooked. But a paradigm of increased independence is still what is needed. Overly dependent boards become pawns of management and cannot effectively represent shareholders.

The NYSE and NASD listing standards require that a majority of the board be independent as defined; but there is still potential for a board to be too close to management to function independently in mind and spirit. This is particularly true where the CEO is revered in the business community. How do prospective directors prevent themselves from joining a "beholden" board? The board process can be quite telling. If the CEO is also chairperson, and there is no lead director, this is a red flag of a controlling CEO. Additionally, the prospective director should determine if there is a process for selecting directors that is independent from the CEO. A good nomination process requires that an independent committee, such as a nominating or governance committee, determine what director qualities are sought and conduct a search for directors who best fits those criteria. In Chapter 7, in which governance committees are discussed, we will explore in detail how to implement best practice in the selection of new directors.

BOARD SIZE MATTERS

The size of a board can also impede good oversight. The larger the board, the harder it is to become active and engaged, and this often results in more reliance on and deference to the CEO. According to *The Report of the NACD Blue Ribbon Commission on Director Professionalism* (2001), typical large-cap company boards are in the 10- to 13-seat range, which many observers believe to be optimal. Turnaround specialist Gary Sutton goes even farther saying that "five or seven board members work best . . . more is worse since it diffuses responsibility."[4] Except for smaller companies, the substantial responsibilities placed on boards make it difficult to reduce beyond seven directors. But, in fact, boards have become smaller. The executive recruiters Spencer Stuart have found that the average board size has decreased from 14 in 1993 to 11 directors in 2004. However, this trend has been lost on some boards such as M&T bank's with 26 directors.[5]

The number of board members should be limited to allow for meaningful discussion of issues. Larger boards can become less powerful as the ability of individual directors to communicate and build consensus with a majority of the board becomes more difficult. One size does not fit all; but a boardroom filled with over 25 directors and managers prevent meaningful dialog. Even simple issues can take a large amount of board time if all present are to participate fully.

The board must be large enough to have a range of skills and experience necessary to provide value to board oversight. Additionally, if committees are to meet at the same time as regular board meetings, membership must be large enough to prevent overlap of committees. The NYSE requires audit, compensation, and governance committees. There may be other committees that add to the board's work load, such as finance/investment, safety, health and environment, and diversity if determined by the board as adding value to their oversight function. While size does matter, the social interaction and engagement of a board can overcome the obstacles inherent with large boards. GE is a good example of a company with a large (17 directors), but highly respected and active board.

COMMITTEES: SOURCE OF FUNCTIONAL SUPPORT

The concept of committees supporting the board of directors is nothing new. In fact, there is a long history of executive committees exercising board authority between board meetings and audit committees providing oversight for the preparation and communication of the company's financial results. Congress recognized the importance of audit committees, and through the Sarbanes-Oxley Act (Section 301), required public companies to have an audit committee and to document their responsibilities as well.

The NYSE went even further by requiring companies with securities listed on the big board to have independent compensation committees and nominating/governance committees. The NASD rules do not require independent compensation or nominating committees, but do require that a majority of the full board's independent members approve compensation and nomination proposals. However, the best practice is to establish audit, compensation and governance committees consisting of independent board members. Committees of three people is ideal according to Harvard Business School professors Colin Carter and Jay Lorsch.[6] Each committee should prepare a charter, establish a fair and just system of oversight, and perform regular evaluations regarding the effectiveness of the committee's policies and procedures.

Minding the Numbers: Audit Committee

The audit committee has the awesome responsibility for oversight of the financial reporting process. To make certain that accounting policies are sound and financial statements properly prepared and audited, the board should have an audit committee consisting only of outside directors and at least one financial expert. This is now a legal requirement in the United States and 91 percent of the S&P 500 companies reported that they have identified their audit committee financial expert.

The importance of the audit committee to the proper oversight of financial reporting cannot be overstated. One only has to look to the numerous financial reporting frauds recently experienced to understand that the lack of strong oversight can lead to disastrous results. Deceit is blind to industry and country as indicated by the following list of high profile financial reporting frauds: HealthSouth, World-Com, Tyco, Enron, Xerox, Global Crossing, Qwest, Sunbeam, Adelphia Communications, Waste Management, Cendant, Rite Aid, Computer Associates, AOL-Time Warner, Symbol Technologies, Parmalat, and Royal Ahold.

But as we learned with Enron, simply having an audit committee is not enough. Its tremendous responsibilities require tools that enable it to execute its mission. Its members need to be engaged and knowledgeable, have access to all of the resources necessary to meet its oversight objectives including the retention of outside advisors, hiring, termination and remuneration of the public accountants and internal auditor, and access to the results of management's own testing of assertions and key internal controls.

Question of Incentives and Wealth: Compensation Committee

While a compensation committee consisting of only outside directors will not guarantee a fair and balanced compensation program, a committee consisting of insiders can only lead to suspicion regarding a program's legitimacy. The compensation committee should be able to retain advisors as it deems necessary to ensure that the proper incentives are in place and have metrics available to assess the effectiveness of the remuneration program. Ill-conceived compensation practices can produce incentives to manipulate financial statements, enter into transactions that are not in the best interest of shareholders, or lead to abuse of corporate assets. Best practice requires that compensation be tied to long-term incentives, not short-term stock swings or the closing of transactions. Stock awards that vest over time can align the CEO's interests with that of shareholders while tying compensation to short-term stock price appreciation or option grants can create pressure to manipulate the financial statements. But simply tying compensation to long-term returns is not enough. Long-term plans can also be poorly designed. For example, a judge ordered three executives of Computer Associates to repay $550 million of stock awarded in 1998 under a five-year arrangement because it did not meet the original intent of the plan.[7] Later, a federal grand jury charged the former chairperson and chief executive officer of Computer Associates International, Sanjay Kumar, with securities fraud. According to the indictment, Mr. Kumar backdated billions of dollars of contracts to meet Wall Street's forecasts.[8] What motivation would Mr. Kumar have to do this? Consider the stock awards just discussed and the effect on Mr. Kumar's wealth if the value of the stock declined before sold.

Keeping the Board Fair and Balanced: Governance Committee

Finally, there should be an independent nominating or governance committee that has oversight of director nominations. In an interview with the *Harvard Business Review*, Eliot Spitzer is quoted as saying that "until now, the pool of board candidates has been a limited universe of people who have been playing ball with the industry, who are all from the industry—usually from management—and these people have never had sufficient incentive to rock the boat in the way an aggressive independent board member would."[9]

An independent governance or nominating committee is particularly important for those public companies that are lead by imperial CEOs. It is a natural inclination for a CEO to seek those who are like-minded for his or her board. But that might not be the best answer for the shareholders. The best boards can call on diverse backgrounds and experiences for the benefit of the company. Best practice would require a process that defines what qualities are currently lacking on the board, the profile of a candidate who would best fit that role, conducting a search for a candidate based on the profile, and selecting the most qualified candidate due to his or her credentials and the needs of the board. In a sign of increasing board diversity, 87 percent of S&P 500 companies report that they have at least one female director, and 17 percent have more than three women serving on their boards. A board selected primarily through relationships held by the CEO should be a red flag that the board may not be sufficiently independent and oversight might not be as effective as would otherwise be the case.

Special Needs Committees

According to Spencer Stuart, most boards have four committees, so, in addition to the three basic committees just mentioned, a board may require other standing or ad hoc committees due to the drivers of the business. Other possible committees might include employee safety, finance, or executive committees. For instance, Rinker Group is one of the world's largest heavy building materials companies with operations in United States, Australia, and Canada. While technically an Australian company, over 80 percent of Rinker's earnings originate in the United States. Given its focus on heavy building materials, safety is an important success factor for the company. A poor safety record can lead to regulatory penalties, make recruiting good employees difficult, and increase operating costs due to downtime. To provide oversight of this important driver, the board established a

Safety, Health, and Environment Committee, led by an independent, nonexecutive director, in addition to their audit, remuneration, and nominations committees.[10] These company/industry-specific committees can help a board provide important focus and supervision to critical operations not covered by the standard board committees.

THE IMPERIAL CEO[11]

The Sarbanes-Oxley Act addressed many of the perceived causes of corporate abuses exposed during 2001 and 2002. New implementing rules from the SEC and listing standards issued by the New York Stock Exchange and the NASDAQ further strengthened corporate governance practices by improving the independence of public company boards. Arguably the most comprehensive public company legislation since the 1930s, Congress nevertheless left undone one of the most contentious issues of our day: the problem of a single individual holding the conflicting roles of CEO and Chairperson of the Board of a public company or what many refer to as the "imperial CEO."

This unfinished business was not due to a lack of visibility. Academics, corporate governance experts, and shareholder activists have ensured that both Congress and corporate America are well aware of this conflict of interest. However, it appears that these combined roles are so pervasive in the nation's public companies that many believe it would be too disruptive to summarily demand separation. Yet shareholder activists are not waiting for corporate boards or Congress to begin reform. They are taking the fight to the boardrooms of some of our largest corporations. Smart executives, who currently hold both positions, will take the initiative to make certain that change will occur on their terms.

In his book *Boards at Work: How Corporate Boards Create Competitive Advantage* (1998), Ram Charan, a highly respected board consultant, argues against an independent chairperson or the creation of a lead director. He suggested that separate positions dilute accountability, diffuse communications, and lead to personal rivalries.[12]

Granted, these dynamics exist, however, they can also be driven by issues unrelated to the identification of a lead director. The chairperson of the board sets the board agenda and administers its workings. The CEO manages the company. These roles are clear. Both sit on the board, so there should not be a communication problem unless there are other underlying problems that could lead to personal rivalries. In such circumstances, the board must identify the true genesis of the conflict and clear the way.

Others also make effective arguments against splitting the position of chairperson and CEO. Some warn it could create gridlock if there is not a consensus between the CEO and chairman regarding how to move the company forward. In my view, this is healthy conflict reflecting a possible weakness with the competitive strategy or other issue dividing the board. Once again, the board must debate the issues, arrive at the appropriate conclusions, and enable action. If personalities continue to get in the way after a course of action has been agreed, the board has the hard task of removing the obstacle. Many also argue that the imperial CEO model, which is prevalent in the United States, has served this country well over time. However, while we have done well, we can and will do better.

Best practice is to separate the chairperson and CEO positions. The role of chairperson conflicts with that of CEO because the CEO often is, or should be, the subject of board discussions and will be directly affected by decisions on matters such as who joins the board, management team performance, and compensation. An imperial CEO who has unfettered control of the board can discourage discourse and implement a range of policies that serve only management as opposed to the shared needs of management and shareholders. This increased risk must be assessed by a director.

Today, approximately 74 percent of U.S. public companies run under the imperial CEO model. While not uniquely an American problem, of the major Western economies, only France combines the roles of chairperson and CEO more frequently. The United Kingdom, along with the United States, is often cited as having some of the strongest corporate governance practices in the world. Over 95 percent of the FTSE 350 companies split the duties of chairperson and CEO. Germany and the Netherlands maintain a split board structure with a nonexecutive supervisory board exerting general oversight and governance rights and a management board consisting of company executives that provide operational supervision.[13] This structure, by definition, precludes the creation of the imperial CEO.

But will splitting the role of chairperson and CEO really make that much of a difference in corporate performance? There have been a number of studies that question whether good governance is profitable. A recently published work by Yale economist Paul W. MacAvoy and corporate governance guru Ira M. Millstein, however, makes a compelling argument that good corporate governance does in fact lead to better returns for shareholders. Their study of corporate governance practices, compiled by the California Public Employees' Retirement System (CalPERS) and related Economic Value Added[TM][14] for public companies, found a causal link between good governance and shareholder return. The authors' most important recommendation culminating from their work is to separate the roles of chairperson and CEO and designate an independent director as chairperson.[15]

Other countries are doing it, and it seems to be a profitable practice, so why have the boards of our public companies not embraced this governance initiative? The most obvious reason is that imperial CEOs are loath to easily give up the power they have achieved, and boards are unwilling to upset a CEO they view as important to the company. Some also argue that separating the roles will not ensure good operating performance. Furthermore, some believe that any benefits to a company are short lived as a director's independence of mind degrades the longer they are in the role since they begin to identify themselves with some of the decisions made.[16]

Regardless of the counterarguments, shareholder activists are not waiting for debate to settle the question. As Michael Eisner found out the hard way, institutional shareholders are banding together to force change. Years of underperformance, rich paychecks, and a reputation for forcing out talented managers who might one day take the company reigns moved some of Disney's largest shareholders to action. CalPERS, the nations largest and, arguably, the most influential public pension fund refused to support Eisner's reelection; and many other public pension funds followed suit.[17] A remarkable 43 percent voted no confidence in Eisner. Under shareholder pressure, he was forced to resign his role as chairperson in order to continue as the company's CEO. He eventually decided to retire. The year after Eisner resigned as chairperson and announced his pending retirement, 92 percent of shareholders voted to reelect the Disney board. Robert A. Iger, the only viable internal candidate who could succeed

Eisner, received almost 95 percent approval. However Disney is not the only company facing challenges from shareholder activists. TIAA-CREF, another pension fund behemoth, has targeted 50 companies that they have identified as having independence issues.

Companies with strong share price appreciation may be able to keep activists at bay for a time, but any turn in fortune will leave a CEO vulnerable. A smart management team will take steps to address this issue now on their own terms rather than waiting for the inevitable market downturn. They will not wait for their largest shareholders to raise the issue; instead they will work with their board to adopt a roadmap or plan that takes concrete steps to aid board independence and create a succession plan that eventually leads to the creation of an independent chairperson.

The first action is to appoint an independent lead director to develop and run executive session meetings where management is not present. The CEO may still be chairperson of the board, but the lead director will guide discussion of management performance, compensation and other sensitive issues with the other independent directors. This intermediate step demonstrates the board's commitment to independence while buying some time to prepare a succession plan in a deliberate fashion. Many companies appear to be adopting this approach as a first step. Spencer Stuart reports that 84 percent of S&P 500 companies have appointed a lead or presiding director, up from just 36 percent last year.[18]

The second necessary action to take is the preparation of succession plan for both the CEO and chairperson positions to be implemented on the retirement or unavailability of the current CEO. The most difficult aspect of a succession plan is not preparing the plan itself, but identifying successor candidates. The successor to the CEO should ideally be developed from the management ranks. The importance of this concept was recently underscored by the untimely death of McDonald's Corporation's CEO followed by the resignation of his successor for health reasons. Due to the foresight of former CEOs and directors, a succession plan was in place at the company that resulted in the transfer of power in a manner that assured the least possible impact on the company's strategy and operations. Despite the turnover, the company was able to post a first quarter increase in earnings of 42 percent a year later. Compare that to Disney, where very talented managers have left over the years—leaving the board to consider outside contenders in addition to a single inside candidate to replace Michael Eisner.

The choice for the chairperson role, however, should not originate from within the company, rather it should be an independent director that the board begins to prepare immediately for the duties of the job. Some CEOs have successfully moved into the chairperson role and became a tremendous asset for the company. Herb Keller of Southwest Airlines and Bernie Marcus at Home Depot come to mind. But more often the chairperson can create dissention and deadlock as the "new guy" attempts to put his stamp on the corporation.

Finally, the board should designate the conditions under which the succession plan will be implemented. Retirement, incapacitation, untimely death, or a successful vote of no confidence from shareholders all seem to qualify.

Most imperial CEOs are good people and great managers. They got to where they are by creating value for shareholders. Accepting the chairperson role along side their everyday CEO duties was likely conferred as recognition for a job well done. Smart executives will see that the governance model in the United States is changing and will take steps to be out in front of it. It is always better to be a change agent rather than be the subject of change. By addressing these valid concerns now, CEOs and boards can manage this coming evolution while meeting the interests of both shareholders and the management team.

Is your board impaired by an imperial CEO? In Exhibit 3.2, the signs a director should pay attention to are presented. How does your board stack up?

DIRECTOR DEVELOPMENT

Training is a word some directors publicly deride, but secretly want to embrace. Never was this point more clear than during the financial reporting crisis of 2001 and 2002 as directors flocked to accounting courses and financial reporting symposiums. We can discard the word "training" if that makes it easier to digest. Setting our egos aside, however, there is not a single living human that could not benefit in some way from additional development.

Does an Imperial CEO impair the effectiveness of your board? Here are some signs that, alone or in combination with other symptoms, might indicate that the inherent conflict between that of CEO and chairperson of the board is affecting your board.

- There is no independent lead director or presiding outside director.
- There is a lack of open dialog at board meetings.
- The board does not retain their own outside experts to counsel them on important issues such as compensation, risk management, governance, and so on.
- Meeting materials are not sent sufficiently ahead of time to properly assimilate.
- Nonexecutive directors are overly reliant on management for setting meeting agendas.
- The size of the board is overly large, retarding effective communication among directors and independent consensus building.
- Nonexecutive director contact with line managers is not encouraged.
- Director terms are staggered preventing the removal of a full board by a single election.
- There are excessive antitakeover provisions in place that disadvantage active shareholders and unfairly protect management.
- There is little consideration of shareholder proxy requests.
- A significant number of company executives are directors who could be expected to follow the lead of the CEO.

EXHIBIT 3.2 Symptoms of a Board Impaired by an Imperial CEO

One nonprofit board I served on had a problem so basic and obvious that no one wanted to be the first to raise it. Despite being a not-for-profit, the board was debating heavy issues with real potential for director liability. The exchanges, at times, could become heated, and the more aggressive directors would not hesitate to interrupt others who had the floor. Still other directors would ramble on for an eternity, seemingly verbalizing some stream of consciousness, sometimes changing subjects and continuing on without providing any clue as to when they might run out of gas. What many of us finally agreed on was that the board needed basic parliamentary training. We had no control of our meetings and could not arrive at important decisions. Having these decisions drag on only divided the board as the issues were allowed to fester. As silly and embarrassing as it sounds, we bit the bullet and spent approximately an hour and a half during one meeting sitting through a presentation on basic parliamentary protocol. A summary of procedures was handed out together with a more detailed guide for director reference. A year later, you would not recognize that it was the same board. Meetings ran smoothly, difficult decisions were made on an informed and timely basis, and board relationships improved as opposing views on certain matters were not allowed to loiter long and became irrelevant as the organization moved forward.

The threat of this happening on the boards of larger corporations is unlikely as there is much more structure, support, and formality for the boards supervising companies of significant size. But you might recognize the situation described in the previous paragraph if you sit on the board of a small public or not-for-profit company. However, even directors at larger companies need development. While certain board committees are tasked with developing compensation recommendations, reviewing the financial statements, or nominating directors, their work does not absolve other directors for decisions made in these areas. It is important that directors have a firm grounding in these subjects and understand the underpinnings of committee recommendations.

As there are more demands on a board's time, development is likely to be the first victim of a crowded agenda. Best practice is to set aside time, at least once a year, for board development. It may be a presentation on director liability, the red flags of financial reporting, or pros and cons of different compensation schemes. Whatever it is, *make the time* and put it on the schedule. If there is an annual offsite to discuss strategy and other white board issues (see Chapter 7) this would be a perfect opportunity to invite experts to make a presentation regarding current issues of interest to the board.

New director training is also a basic tool utilized by well-functioning boards. This also does not have to be an overly formal affair. A technique that works effectively is to invite new directors to a long working lunch. At the lunch, a few longer-serving directors take the new ones through the board book (which normally contains bylaws, committee charters, board procedures, and the like). Each committee chair describes what their committee does, and the company strategy and significant issues addressed over the past year are discussed together with any significant board objectives for the coming year. The informality of the lunch allows for give and take, and new directors are much more open to asking questions in a non-threatening environment.

KEY CONCEPTS

- Be engaged, but refrain from managing the company.
- Effective boards are largely independent under regulatory definitions and in spirit.
- Keep board size reasonable, large boards inhibit engagement.
- Strong boards have separate audit, compensation and governance committees consisting entirely of independent directors to do the heavy lifting.
- Appoint a lead director where the roles of chairperson of the board and CEO are combined.
- Make director development a board priority.

ENDNOTES

1. The Business Roundtable, *Principles of Corporate Governance,* May 2002, 4–8.
2. *Sarbanes-Oxley Act of 2002,* Pub. L. No. 107-204, 116 Stat. 745, 107 H. R. 3763, § 301.
3. Robert A. G. Monks and Nell Minow, *Corporate Governance,* 3rd ed. (Cambridge, MA: Blackwell, 2004), 420.
4. Gary Sutton, "Rules for Rock-solid Governance," *Directors & Boards* 25 (Spring 2004): 19.
5. Spencer Stuart, *Spencer Stuart Board Index 2004,* 6; and *Spencer Stuart Board Index 2003,* 6.
6. Colin B.Carter and Jay W. Lorsch, *Back to the Drawing Board: Designing Corporate Boards for a Complex World* (Boston: Harvard Business School Press, 2004), 107.
7. John Geralds, "Judge orders CA execs to repay half of last year's stock compensation," *vnunet.com* 11 November 1999. http://www.vnunet.com/news/103230 (29 September 2004).

8. *SEC v. Sanjay Kumar and Stephen Richards,* 04 Civ. 4104 (E.D.N.Y.) (Glasser, I.L.), *FindLaw.com.* http//:findlaw.com (6 October 2004).

9. Louise O'Brien, "The HBR Interview Eliot Spitzer: How to Restore the Fiduciary Relationship," *Harvard Business Review* 82 (May 2004): 70–77.

10. Rinker Group LLC, *Rinker Concise Annual Report 2004,* 27.

11. Scott Green, "Unfinished Business: Abolish the Imperial CEO!" *Journal of Corporate Accounting & Finance* 15 (September 2004): 19–22. Note: Special Sarbanes-Oxley issue.

12. Ram Charan, *Boards at Work: How Corporate Boards Create Competitive Advantage* (San Francisco: Jossey-Bass, 1998), 49–52.

13. Paul Coombes and Simon Chiu-Yin Wong, "Chairman and CEO: One Job or Two?" *McKinsey Quarterly,* No. 2 (2004): 43–44.

14. Economic Value Added™ and EVA™ are registered trademarks of Stern Stewart & Co.

15. Paul W. MacAvoy and Ira M. Millstein, *The Recurrent Crisis in Corporate Governance* (London: Palgrave MacMillan, 2003), 114.

16. Coombes and Wong, 44.

17. Tim Arango, "CalPERS Piles On: Biggest Pension Fund Urges Disney to Boot Eisner," *New York Post,* 26 February 2004, 33.

18. Spencer Stuart, 8.

CHAPTER 4

Dealing with Your Liability Up Front

The potential for liability or exposure to prosecution that accompanies a position on the board of directors is a grave concern for directors. Many cite New York Attorney General Eliot Spitzer's prosecution of Kenneth Langdon for his involvement in the compensation package of Dick Grasso, the former head of the New York Stock Exchange. In reality, directors are fairly well insulated from personal liability under three widely recognized protections built into governance systems: judicial protections predicated on the business judgment rule, indemnification, and Directors and Officers (D&O) insurance, although some see these protections weakening. This chapter presents strategies to best limit your risk while serving as a director.

BUSINESS JUDGMENT "BUNKER"

Judicial protections are usually predicated on *duty of care, duty of loyalty,* and *duty of good faith*—legal terms often referred to collectively as the "business judgment rule." The business judgment rule holds that decisions made by directors who are fully informed and free from conflicts of interest should not be second guessed by the courts. This rule is the best defense that a director has against opportunistic allegations. Any long-serving director eventually hears a lawyer refer to these terms, so it is helpful to understand what they mean.

Duty of care requires that a director be informed and make decisions based on a deliberative documented process. *Smith v. Van Gorkom* is a commonly cited case where it was held that directors breached their duty of care.[1] In short, the board agreed to sell the company without informing themselves of the CEO's motive to support the sale or role in establishing the purchase price, determining the intrinsic value of the company, and unnecessarily rushing the approval of sale without reviewing the proposed terms of the merger agreement. Even though the company was sold at a substantial premium, the speedy approval process (a matter of hours not days) illustrated that the board did not take the time necessary to diligently consider the offer or any conflicts that might entice the CEO to support the sale.

Duty of loyalty generally speaks to a director's potential conflict of interest. A director is required to act in good faith and in a manner reasonably and honestly believed to be in the best interests of the corporation and its shareholders to the exclusion of personal gain. Where a conflict of interest exists, a director should recuse themselves from deliberation and decision making. A case that exemplifies this duty can be found in the recent battle between Conrad Black and his board at Hollinger. A special investigative report commissioned by the board of directors accused Black of misappropriating company assets. After the headline grabbing accusations, Lord Black entered into an agreement with Hollinger to repay several million dollars in unauthorized payments. He also agreed that he would sell control of the company only if such a transaction was equally beneficial to other stockholders among other things. Despite this agreement, Lord Black privately entered negotiations to sell control of the company. The courts held that Black breached his duty of loyalty to the company by failing to tell the board about this suitor's interest in buying the company, misleading the board about his dealings with the suitor, using confidential information to aid the transaction, and in attempting to subvert the loyalty of a financial advisor to a special committee of the board. He also tried to amend the company bylaws covering asset sales. It seems that the court found it difficult to accept the argument that these actions were made in the best interests of Hollinger's shareholders.[2]

Incorporating the duty of care and duty of loyalty, Delaware's business judgment rule provides protection if a director " . . . acted on an informed basis, in good faith and in the honest belief that the action taken was in the best interest of the company."[3] Most boards are covered under Delaware law, which allows corporations to include a provision in their charter restricting or eliminating a director's personal liability for breach of fiduciary duty except for "acts or omissions not in good faith or which involve intentional misconduct or a knowing violation of law."[4] In short, as long as a director acts in good faith for (or not opposed to) the best interests of the corporation, they should be shielded from personal liability, even if the decisions made result in losses to the shareholders. It is recognized that, in hindsight, every decision will not necessarily benefit the corporation. As long as the board makes informed and rational decisions, which they believe are in the best interests of the corporation, the courts usually avoid second guessing them. Having said that, "conscious inaction" by a board can result in exposure for a director.

The board of Abbott Laboratories, a pharmaceutical giant, was not protected under Delaware's business judgment rule because, despite warning letters from the Federal Drug Administration, and published articles in the *Wall Street Journal* and other publications disclosing Abbott's regulatory problems, the board took no corrective action. Where directors are aware of red flags or material decisions that exclude the board, they must take action to address these known issues and ensure there is proper deliberation by the board and appropriate oversight of corrective measures. Indifference to a material decision or red flag indicating potential harm to the company can give rise to a finding of bad faith by the courts.[5]

There are other holes developing in traditional protections. In the *Emerging Communications, Inc. Shareholders Litigation*, the Delaware Chancery court determined that a director with "specialized" expertise or knowledge can be held to a higher standard than other directors.[6] In this case, a director with extensive investment banking experience did not bring his knowledge to bear in evaluating a going-private transaction. The court held that the fact that the director, who did not object to the valuation provided by an outside advisor retained by the board given his intimate knowledge of valuation, was a violation of his duty of loyalty. To come to this conclusion, the court had to determine that the price paid was too low and that the director did not provide a satisfactory explanation for his failure to object. To laypeople, it sounds a bit like second guessing a business decision. Regardless, directors must now take special care when considering matters pertaining to their area of expertise. Unfortunately, it is also a case where outside consultants cannot be of very much help.

NEXT LINE OF DEFENSE: INDEMNITY AND INSURANCE

While Delaware law allows companies to indemnify their directors, a director must make certain that the company charter or bylaws specifically provide that protection. If not, it is imperative a director obtain individual indemnification for costs and exposure beyond those covered by insurance. Defense costs alone can be staggering. The director needs to ensure that either the company or insurer covers these costs as incurred.

The twin dangers of exhausted Directors & Officers (D&O) liability insurance combined with a bankrupted company that can no longer pay for a director's legal defense must also be contemplated. Make certain that coverage is both adequate and updated often to reflect the risk of serving. Some directors are shocked to find that insurance companies do not pay attorneys fees directly, rather they reimburse such legal expense at some point in time. These fees can also eat into the overall coverage limit so your exposure grows the longer a case is litigated.

Independent insurance brokers or attorneys with relevant experience can help determine the amount of coverage a director needs based on actual defense costs for directors of companies of comparable size. Do your research on the financial stability of the insurer and revisit it often. From 1996 to 2001, the number of companies sued due to securities litigation increased 300 percent and settlement values rose 150 percent. Likewise, D&O insurance claims rose from $9.6 million to over $23 million in 2002. As a result, insurance premiums rose over 500 percent.[7] Insurers who do not charge enough quickly find themselves in financial difficulty. Two large insurers became insolvent in 2000 and the balance sheets of many D&O insurers remain alarmingly weak.[8] A director can find the insurance coverage worthless if the company standing behind the promise becomes insolvent.

REPUTATION: A PRICELESS ASSET

Often, the biggest threat to a director is the potential damage to his or her reputation. Directors are frequently chosen based on their standing as successful and respected businesspeople. The damage to a director's reputation from association with a company experiencing unethical or illegal behavior, or worse yet, fraudulently bankrupt as were a number of our largest corporations in 2001 and 2002, can be terminal. Directors can protect their reputation and further limit their liability by making certain that they spend the time in the right areas to properly supervise management. We will get into some detail later regarding how a director can best supervise, but to begin with, a few rules can be useful to help focus a director's attention:

- Keep communication lines open to company managers and employees, even the constant whiners (which we often tend to avoid). They can be important sources of information. Doggedly follow up issues as they arise and get back to your sources with what you found, even if it does not support their accusations.
- When issues are raised, bring needed resources to bear. You will read this advice several times throughout this book, but it is worth repeating. Do not hesitate to hire investigators and consultants. Spend the money to protect you and the company.
- Enforce a zero tolerance standard on management. This advice, unfortunately, is frequently reasoned away. The strongest cultures take a hard line—one infraction of a material ethical mandate and you are shown the door. Do not consider explanations or excuses; it only muddles the message to the rest of the organization.
- Avoid related party transactions and other conflicts. Related-party transactions increase your exposure, even if initially they make sense. If there are related-party transactions, which the board determines are in the best interest of the company, then the board is responsible to ensure the relationship is monitored and terminated the minute it is no longer favorable to the organization.
- Aggressively disclose any conflicts of interest, perceived or real. The board should have written conflict of interest procedures. Know and follow them at the first blush of a possible conflict. It may mean that you simply refrain from participation in a discussion, or if more substantial, resignation from the board. Ensure that there is a robust dialog by the board to determine the proper disposition and revisit the decision if circumstances change.
- Understand all aspects of your CEO's compensation. Structure it in the long-term best interests of the company (see Chapter 6).

- Ensure the minutes reflect the result of every vote taken. Keep unnecessary language out of the minutes. If there are concerns raised in the minutes, then they should also be considered for public disclosure. Be careful overriding previous decisions made by the board as it may increase exposure to liability. Obtain independent counsel where necessary.
- Make certain that there is a policy for the retention and destruction of board materials and that it is rigorously followed. Destroying documents under routine procedures consistently applied in accordance with company policy is an acceptable practice.

   However, a company does not want to be viewed by regulators or a court as enforcing a destruction policy only when it suits them. Both Nancy Temple, former counsel for Arthur Andersen, and the Credit Suisse First Boston investment banker Frank Quattrone found this out the hard way. Both reminded employees of their respective destruction policies after they were aware that their organizations were about to come under federal scrutiny. Ms. Temple sent an October 12, 2001 e-mail that reminded executives about the firm's policy on retaining documents knowing that the firm's audit of Enron was going to come under intense analysis. For Andersen, it resulted in an obstruction conviction that, despite being overturned by the U.S. Supreme Court, caused its demise. Quattrone knew of an imminent federal investigation concerning allegations of client kickbacks paid to gain access to hot stock issues. In an e-mail sent on December 5, 2000, Quattrone encouraged employees to "clean up" their files. He was sentenced to 18 months for obstruction of justice and witness tampering.

Adherence to good process is becoming ever more important. An emerging financial threat to directors is the insistence of prosecutors and shareholder activists that directors personally suffer financial pain for corporate failures. A recent example is the proposed settlement by the directors of WorldCom. Eleven former directors agreed to pay one-fifth of their net worth (not counting their homes and pensions) to settle charges. A twelfth director agreed to pay $5.5 million which represented substantially more than the 20 percent collected from the others.[9] In this case, the New York State Trustee of the Common Retirement Fund, Alan Hevesi, insisted that directors be held personally liable rather than letting their insurance companies pay their penalties. It is likely that these types of director settlements will become more common.

By example, 10 of 18 former outside directors of Enron agreed to pay $13 million out of their own pockets as part of a $168 million agreement. The settlement reflected 10 percent of each director's pre-tax proceeds from their stock trading during the period that false financial information were disseminated by the company. One director contributed over $5 million, other directors, who did no trading during the period, paid nothing. This is on top of $1.5 million paid

KEY CONCEPTS

- Stay informed. Directors are fairly well protected as long as they are fully informed and free of conflicts.
- Be engaged. Passive directors will be held liable.
- Bring your expertise to bear. Directors with specialized expertise are held to a higher standard than other directors.
- Review insurance providers, coverage, and costs often. Indemnity and D&O insurance are worthless if the company and insurer do not have the financial ability to stand behind the pledge.
- Understand you are still exposed. Even with the protections provided by indemnity and D&O insurance, prosecutors and plaintiffs are requiring directors to personally participate in financial settlements.
- Listen to whiners as they are an important source of information.
- Do not hesitate to bring in independent advisors.
- Take a hard line on ethical lapses.
- Avoid related-party conflicts and aggressively disclose conflicts of interest.
- Understand CEO compensation issues.
- Make certain that there is a good process for preparing board minutes including review for unnecessary language or concerns that require disclosure.
- Ensure that a written retention and destruction policy for board documents exists and is consistently followed.

by Enron directors to settle with the Department of Labor a lawsuit claiming breach of fiduciary duty with regards to the company's pension plans.[10]

Despite the many protections afforded directors under law, this new threat must be considered by all director candidates. While director protections are robust, they will not protect passive boards. Boards must implement procedures that enable them to engage in oversight activities, many of which are discussed in the remainder of this book.

ENDNOTES

1. *Smith v. Van Gorkum*, 488 A. 2d 858 (Del. Supr. 1985).
2. *Hollinger Int'l, Inc. v. Black,* C.A. No. 183-N, Strine, V.C. (Del. Ch. Feb. 26, 2004).
3. *Aronson v. Lewis*, 473 A.2d 805, 812 (Del. 1984).
4. *Del. C. § 102(b)(7).*
5. *In Re Abbott Laboratories Deriv. Shareholders Litig.*, 325 F.3d 795 (7th Cir. 2003); and *In Re The Walt Disney Co. Derivative Litig.*, 825 A.2d 275 (Del. Ch. 2003).
6. *Emerging Communications Shareholders Litigation*, C.A. No. 16415 (Del. Ch. May 3, 2004)
7. Holly Isdale, "Directors: Protect Your Personal Assets," *Directors & Boards* 26 (First Quarter [Winter] 2005): 55.
8. William Cotter and Christopher Barbee, "2002 D&O Insurance White Paper," *GeoCities.com.* www.geocities.com/jroycma/pdf/DOWPF3x.pdf (5 April 2005), 17.
9. Bloomberg News, "Former WorldCom Chairman To Pay $5.5 Million Settlement," *New York Times*, 3 March 2005, C4.
10. Kurt Eichenwald, "Ex-Directors of Enron to Chip in on Settlement," *New York Times*, 8 January 2005, C1.

Organize to Lead

As the old saying goes, "The devil is in the details." Now that we have established our board basics, we can focus on the detailed operations that create an engaged and dynamic board. In the next chapters, we build on our foundation to take performance to the next level.

This includes implementing the proper processes at both the board and committee levels, which allow the board to execute its duties efficiently and help it focus its limited time on the issues that count. In this section we also look at specific board operations and issues associated with the various board committees such as audit, compensation, and governance.

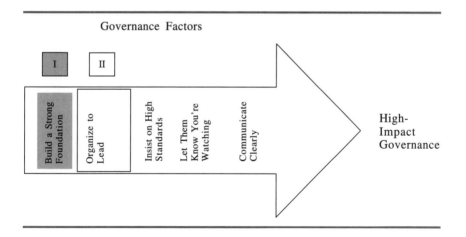

Governance Factors

I   II

Build a Strong Foundation | Organize to Lead | Insist on High Standards | Let Them Know You're Watching | Communicate Clearly | High-Impact Governance

CHAPTER 5

Minding the Numbers: The Audit Committee

Often overshadowed by the noise surrounding implementation of the Sarbanes-Oxley Act, are the increased strength and visibility provided audit committees. Congress understands the vital importance of audit committees in the governance framework and paid particular attention to their role when drafting the Sarbanes-Oxley Act. Audit committees add value to board operations by bringing powerful oversight authority to the organization's financial reporting, internal control, and audit processes. This becomes more challenging as financial engineering grows more sophisticated, financial systems more complex, and opportunities for financial reporting fraud multiply. The goal of this chapter is to provide directors with the information they need to organize the audit committee and focus their time on those financial reporting areas that need the most attention.

To effectively execute their function, audit committees need structural support in the form of a strong charter. Additionally, they need directors with the time, the professional skepticism, and the well-developed financial, accounting, and control skills necessary to carry out this critical oversight function. In this chapter, we review the contents of a strong, empowering audit committee charter. We will also discuss other audit committee requirements such as the need for a financial expert, an operational complaint procedure, a process for the hiring and firing of advisors, and an approach for providing financial reporting oversight.

A STRONG CONSTITUTION: THE AUDIT COMMITTEE CHARTER

The foundation for audit committee activities is formed by the audit committee charter. The NYSE listing standards (approved by the SEC) requires every audit committee to have at least three members, consist solely of independent directors, and have a charter that details the committee's mission, duties, and responsibilities. The audit committee charter must, at a minimum, address the following.

Purpose:
- Assist board oversight of the:
  - Integrity of the company's financial statements
  - Company's compliance with legal and regulatory requirements
  - Independent auditor's qualifications and independence
  - Performance of the company's internal audit function and independent auditor
- Prepare the report that SEC rules require be included in the company's annual proxy statement

Duties and Responsibilities:
- Retain and terminate the independent auditor (subject to shareholder ratification)
- At least annually, obtain and review a report provided by the independent auditor describing:
  - Its internal quality control procedures
  - Any material issues raised by the most recent internal quality control review, or peer review, of the firm, or by any inquiry or investigation by governmental or professional authorities, within the preceding five years, respecting one or more of the firm's audits, and any steps taken to deal with any such issues
  - All relationships between the independent auditor and the company
- Discuss with management and the independent auditor the annual and quarterly financial statements, including disclosures in Management's Discussion and Analysis (MD&A)
- Discuss earnings press releases, as well as financial information and earnings guidance provided to analysts and rating agencies

- As appropriate, obtain advice and assistance from outside legal, accounting, or other advisors
- Discuss policies with respect to risk assessment and risk management
- Periodically, meet separately with management, with internal auditors, and with the independent auditor
- Review with the independent auditor any audit problems or difficulties and management's responses
- Set clear hiring policies for employees or former employees of the independent auditor
- Report regularly to the board of directors
- Conduct an annual performance evaluation of the audit committee[1]

While extensive, charters that are best practice contain additional information such as the membership criteria, minimum number of meetings to be held each year, responsibilities for the receipt, retention and treatment of financial reporting and internal control complaints together with the anonymous receipt of such concerns, and committee education and orientation. The audit committee should periodically assess the committee's performance against this charter.

General Motors (GM) has long been recognized as leading the way for improvement in corporate governance, having received a perfect score from Governance Metrics International and also recently named the winner of Treasury & Risk Management's Corporate Governance Award. (The GM board's audit committee charter, which represents best practice, can be examined in Appendix B.) Directors who sit on the audit committee can be well served using this charter as a guide for evaluating the charter of their company.

YOUR FINANCIAL EXPERTS

While the audit committee charter is the foundation of a quality structure, the financial expert or experts are what give it functional integrity. Without at least one member with highly develop financial dexterity, the committee cannot hope to function effectively in an increasingly sophisticated corporate world. Section 407 of the

Sarbanes-Oxley Act introduced the concept of requiring financial skills on a board. The Act requires an audit committee to have at least one financial expert, as defined by the SEC. Accordingly, the full board must make the determination regarding whether a director qualifies as an audit committee financial expert. The SEC, in turn, has provided guidance by defining an "audit committee financial expert" as having the following attributes:

- An understanding of generally accepted accounting principles and financial statements
- The ability to assess the general application of such principles in connection with the accounting for estimates, accruals, and reserves
- Experience preparing, auditing, analyzing, or evaluating financial statements that present a breadth and level of complexity of accounting issues that are generally comparable to the breadth and complexity of issues that can reasonably be expected to be raised by the registrant's financial statements, or experience actively supervising one or more persons engaged in such activities
- An understanding of internal controls and procedures for financial reporting
- An understanding of audit committee functions[2]

Under the SEC's final rules, a person must have acquired these attributes through education and experience as a principal financial officer, principal accounting officer, controller, public accountant, or auditor experience in one or more positions that involve the performance of similar functions or supervision of these personnel or functions. SEC rules also require that the name of the audit committee financial expert be disclosed in the annual report, normally Form 10-K. (We discuss this disclosure further in Chapter 14.)

Concern about additional liability for directors designated the audit committee financial expert led the SEC to include a safe harbor provision in its rules designed to prevent the courts from inferring that such a designation affected the duties, obligations, or liability as an audit committee member or board member. Alternatively, the safe harbor does not reduce the liability of the audit committee financial expert from that of any other board member. While the rules only require one audit committee financial expert, all members should be financially literate. How can a director ask penetrating questions of management and the auditors without a grounding in accounting, finance, or management controls? The board can reduce the risk of aggressive financial reporting or fraudulent practices by recruiting and assigning the best financial minds available to the audit committee.

LISTEN TO THE WHINERS

For many of the recent financial reporting frauds, there existed a person of conscience who tried to alert gatekeepers to a problem. Congress set out to formalize a process for capturing these complaints at the board level. Under Section 301 of the Sarbanes-Oxley Act, the audit committee is required to "establish procedures for the following:

■ The receipt, retention, and treatment of complaints received by the issuer regarding accounting, internal accounting controls, or auditing matters
■ The confidential, anonymous submission by the employees of the issuer of concerns regarding questionable accounting or auditing matters[3]

Corporate leaders who disregard ethical and legal conduct often devise incentives to encourage those around them to push the envelope and discourage or even punish those that resist or report questionable activities. For corporate governance systems to identify such behavior, there must be a strong culture that rewards appropriate behavior and provides an effective means for reporting those it wishes to discourage. Employees must trust their efforts to "do the right thing" will be supported and should they report problems, that their actions will be welcomed. Establishing trust requires that whistle-blowing not lead to punitive measures; rather evidence that it is valued. To encourage this culture, the Sarbanes-Oxley Act and SEC rules require companies to adopt a code of ethics for senior financial officers. Stock exchange rules and Federal Sentencing Guidelines further require that companies adopt codes of business conduct for all employees to assist them in avoiding illegal and unethical conduct.

Section 806 of the Sarbanes-Oxley Act gives these codes teeth, protecting employees of publicly traded companies that provide evidence of fraud, by prohibiting actions to "discharge, demote, suspend, threaten, harass or in any other manner discriminate against an employee . . . because of a lawful act done by the employee . . ."[4] and provides remedies in the form of compensatory damages.

Amendments to the Federal Sentencing Guidelines for Organizations became effective on November 1, 2004. Importantly, the guidelines provide that if a compliance and ethics program is deemed to be "effective" it will not only protect a corporation in the penalty phase of a criminal proceeding; it also should help lessen the likelihood that a criminal proceeding—or an SEC civil enforcement action—is initiated in the first place.

Effective whistle-blower protections are critical to directors. Without them, important sources of information may be reticent to come forward out of fear that their job is on the line. A sound compliance and ethics program may go even further in helping protect the corporation. It is in every director's interest to ensure that whistle-blower mechanisms are effective and that their efforts visibly contribute to the enforcement of their company's compliance program.

MANAGING THE AUDITORS

An interesting and unexpected development arising from implementation of certain sections of the Sarbanes-Oxley Act is auditor rotation. The extra work required of the independent auditors under the Act have strained their resources. The "Big Four" accounting firms have responded by shedding clients at an accelerating rate and raising fees for those they choose to keep. AuditAnalytics.com is an independent research firm that tracks the accounting industry and provides access "to detailed audit information on over 1,500 accounting firms and 20,000 publicly registered companies." They track "who is auditing whom, issues surrounding the audit, and how much the registrants are paying for what services." According to AuditAnalytics.com, the Big Four resigned 70 clients in 2001, 78 in 2002, 152 in 2003, and 210 in 2004, which is illustrated in Exhibit 5.1. National firms have benefited the most from the clients shed from the Big Four, but these firms are also resigning more clients. Some see auditor resignations accelerating through 2005 as smaller public companies prepare for their Section 404 deadline.

The more aggressive a company's accounting policies, the more likely they will be on their auditor's short list of clients they are prepared to eject. Immediately after the passage of the Sarbanes-Oxley and prior to 2004, clients that had going concern issues were the most likely to be shed by the Big Four. In 2004, with the focus shifting to the internal control provisions of the Act, those companies with internal control issues were the most likely to be shed as illustrated in Exhibit 5.2. Fully 74 percent of the affected companies had revenues of less than $100 million (96 percent less than $500 million in market capitalization), therefore, mid-cap and small-cap companies are bearing the brunt of these resignations.

Losing a large accounting firm can be negatively viewed by the investment community. It can also leave a company scrambling to fill the void left by an auditor's resignation. Auditor resignation is a risk that the boards of midsized and smaller public companies should evaluate and monitor as finding a suitable replacement will not be easy for some companies.

The audit committee now has the expressed power to hire and fire the independent auditors, subject to the approval of shareholders.

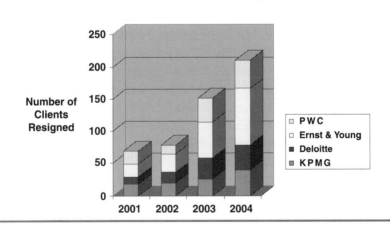

Big Four Resignations

EXHIBIT 5.1   Auditor Resignations
Source: Used with permission. Courtesy of AuditAnalytics.com.

Issues Disclosed — Big Four Departures

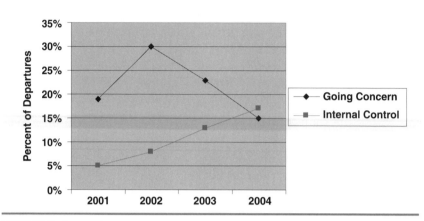

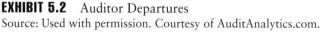

EXHIBIT 5.2   Auditor Departures
Source: Used with permission. Courtesy of AuditAnalytics.com.

This authority is supported by the Act's requirement that the company provide the funding the committee needs to hire outside advisors. To execute this duty, procedures for evaluating the independence and effectiveness of the outside auditors must be well defined. Prior to Enron, the possible conflicts that occur from the delivery of consulting services by a company's external auditors was largely tolerated within the accounting profession. The cross-selling of services was the Holy Grail, and big firms were willing to accept lower margins on their audits if there were consulting opportunities available. Despite these economic entanglements, the firms were expected to self-police these potential conflicts. For several years, Arthur Andersen performed Enron's internal audit function and served as an advisor for the financial structuring of the company in addition to providing audit services. The last year before Enron filed for bankruptcy, Andersen collected over $25 million in audit fees, but consulting and other fees totaled more that $27 million.[5]

Congress responded to these potential conflicts in Section 201 of the Sarbanes-Oxley Act. It specifically identifies which nonaudit services are not allowed:

- Bookkeeping or other services related to the accounting records or financial statements of the audit client
- Financial information systems design and implementation services

- Appraisal or valuation services, and services involving the issuance of fairness opinions or contribution-in-kind reports
- Internal audit outsourcing services
- Management functions or human resources services
- Broker-dealer, investment advisor, or investment banking services
- Legal services
- Expert services unrelated to the audit
- Any other service that the Public Company Accounting Oversight Board determines, by regulation, is impermissible[6]

Expert services unrelated to the audit are a very broad concept, so the SEC's proposed rules refer to certain principles for use in assessing whether a service could impair independence. Independence is impaired if there is a shared mutuality of interests with the client and/or an auditor:

- Audits their own work
- Performs management functions
- Acts as an advocate for an audit client

The prohibition on expert services speaks to the role of advocacy. An auditor may help an audit committee perform its own investigation of potential accounting impropriety as long as the auditor does not take on an advocacy role. Auditors may also provide tax services.

To further aid auditor independence, the Sarbanes-Oxley Act Section 203 mandates that the lead audit partner and concurring partner rotate every five years and Section 206 bars a firm from auditing a company if the CEO, controller, CFO, chief accounting officer, or similar person worked for the firm and participated in the audit one year or less before the start of the current audit. These sections aim to break down the strong personal relationships that can develop between auditors and their clients. To maintain transparency, the Act also requires that retention, resignation, or dismissal of the independent accountant must be publicly disclosed via SEC form 8-K. Detailed disclosure requirements can be found in item 304 of Regulation SK.

Form 8-K communications are not the only new or revised audit committee disclosures. Transparency is key to good governance and the SEC has moved to improve disclosure by providing more information about audit committee composition and operations. Public companies must discuss the audit committee in the annual report. The result is that investors will have increased knowledge regarding how an audit committee executes their responsibilities. This disclosure will include such information as the committee's members, the number of meetings held, and the functions it performs. A company is also obliged to disclose in its proxy statement whether the "audit committee has reviewed and discussed the audited financial statements with management and discussed certain matters with the independent auditors" as well as "disclose whether the audit committee is governed by a charter and, if so, to provide a copy of the charter as an appendix to the proxy statement once every three years."[7] The company must also disclose if the audit committee members are independent. There are specific exemptions afforded the audit committees for certain issuers under SEC rules. For instance, some countries have a practice of including employees on their supervisory boards and audit committees. These employees do provide an independent check on management and the SEC does not want to discourage this practice. A company utilizing this exemption, and others, is required to disclose this to shareholders in the annual report and proxy statements. Some other independence exemptions include representation from controlling shareholders, government representatives, and boards of auditors. (We discuss this requirement further in Chapter 14.)

CASE STUDY: FRANKLIN RAINES AND THE FANNIE MAE ACCOUNTING DEBACLE

Even in the absence of fraud, financial reporting can create headaches for a company and its management. Consider what happened to Franklin D. Raines, the chairperson and CEO of the giant financial services company Fannie Mae.

The Federal government established Fannie Mae in 1938 to expand the flow of mortgage money by creating a secondary market. Fannie Mae would buy conforming loans from lenders so that the lenders could turn around and loan out the money again. In 1968, Fannie Mae became a private company, effectively "spun-off" from the government. Today, Fannie Mae operates under a congressional charter and is one of the largest financial services corporations in the world with approximately 5,055 employees.[a]

Fannie Mae was led by Franklin D. Raines, a man of considerable standing. One of seven children of a Seattle janitor and cleaning women, he pulled himself up to the pinnacle of American business and financial security. Prior to leading Fannie Mae, Mr. Raines served as the Director of Management and Budget for President Clinton, was a former partner at Lazard Freres & Company, a director on the boards of Pfizer and PepsiCo, and was a past President of the Board of Overseers of Harvard University. A former Rhodes Scholar, he graduated magna cum laude from Harvard University, and received his J.D. cum laude from Harvard Law. Mr. Raines achieved all of this from his humble beginnings.

How does a man with such accomplishments find himself ousted from the company he is, by most accounts, capably leading? By rigorously defending aggressive accounting. Under pressure from their regulator, the Office of Federal Housing Enterprise Oversight (OFHEO), Raines and his CFO defended their accounting practices in Congressional testimony. KPMG, the public accountants, also backed the company's accounting. According to regulators, however, Fannie Mae's treatment of prepaid mortgages and derivatives artificially propped up the company's minimum capital requirement.

It all came undone when the SEC's chief accountant agreed with OFHEO and ruled that the company had in fact violated accounting rules. The resulting $9 billion restatement meant the company did not meet minimum capital requirements and needed to take steps to restore capital accounts to mandated levels. Although the SEC had not found that senior management did anything improper, OFHEO demanded changes in senior management. Under pressure, the board finally acceded and replaced not only Raines, but the CFO and KPMG.[b]

---

[a]Fannie Mae, "Understanding Fannie Mae," *FannieMae.com* 18 January 2005 http://www.fanniemae.com/aboutfm/understanding/index.jhtml?p=About+Fannie+Mae&s=Understanding+Fannie+Mae (6 April 2005).
[b]Stephen Labaton, "Chief Is Ousted At Fannie Mae Under Pressure," *New York Times,* 22 December 2004, A1.

In the wake of accounting frauds of 2001 and 2002, there is little regulatory tolerance for aggressive accounting tactics. A management team that adopts accounting policies that push boundaries does so at its peril. The audit committee needs to monitor financial policies with the help of their advisors. That would be difficult in this case, as the outside auditors also found themselves on the wrong side of the issue, perhaps because of their close relationship to the company. However, questioning alternative treatments and having a full discussion about the merits of each will help a director identify which interpretations are aggressive and those that are conservative. Choose conservative. As represented by Fannie Mae, you do not have to have fraudulent accounting to cause harm to the company. The company's accounting problems have opened an opportunity for their critics in Congress to revisit their mission and structure. Combined with a continuing Department of Justice investigation, Fannie Mae's problems are just beginning.

RED FLAGS OF FINANCIAL REPORTING[8]

The audit committee plays a vital role in communicating financial results to the general public. They represent shareholder interests and must diligently query management, external auditors, and the Chief Audit Executive, while bringing to bear the resources necessary to execute their duties. A director must gauge the aggressiveness of accounting policies and adequacy of disclosures in order to obtain comfort regarding the reliability of the financial statements. Although the number of possible disclosure omissions and financial presentation errors are many, directors can focus their activities where they will be most effective. While auditors look at all accounting policies, there are certain areas where financial reporting problems continually surface. These include unsupported large top-side entries, aggressive revenue recognition; regular recognition of nonrecurring charges; regular changes to reserve, depreciation, amortization, or comprehensive income policy; related party and off balance sheet transactions; complex products that few understand; under-funded defined benefit plans and footnote disclosures.

Unsupported Top-Side Entries

Top-side adjustments are entries not automatically produced from the company's accounting system; instead they are manually booked adjustments added "on top" of automated results by management. These entries would fall under the category of nonroutine transactions. In distinguishing between these classes of transactions, routine transactions are generally subjected to a more formalized control structure in order to handle the anticipated volume efficiently and accurately. Routine transactions might include payroll, cash disbursements, procurement, and so on. Nonroutine data and estimates tend to be less common and more subjective, such as the calculation of income tax expense and estimating the allowance for doubtful accounts. Controls over these types of transactions are typically less formal. Many of these adjustments are appropriate and ensure business activities are accounted for in the correct period; however, they can also be used to increase reported income or hide inappropriate actions. Directors need to question material top-side entries and be assured management and the auditors have performed sufficient work to gain director comfort. Much of the financial manipulation conducted at WorldCom was the result of top-side entries shifting expenses to the balance sheet. Whether the board knew or not is irrelevant. They needed to know—and, as a director, so would you. If you or any other director is not comfortable with the answers to questions posed to managers and auditors, get an internal auditor or other accounting expert independent of finance to summarize material top-side entries and the strength of the supporting documentation. Then discuss it with management or the external auditor. Directors should insist that explanations be kept simple. Finance professionals can easily bury a person with data. If they cannot explain an entry easily, then the adjustment is likely aggressive or improper. In other words, directors need to keep digging.

Aggressive Revenue Recognition Policies

Understanding when revenues are recognized is the first step to comprehending the quality of the revenue stream. Revenues of the highest quality are those that are booked after the customer has received, accepted, and is obligated to pay for the product or service without any further performance requirement or contingency. A typical red flag for an auditor is revenue that is matched to future performance or expenses. For example, Qwest Communications has stated that, between 1999 and 2001, it incorrectly accounted for more than $1.1 billion in transactions. Revenues were contingent on the purchase of fiber capacity and future services, but they were improperly booked as earned. A director should evaluate alternative revenue recognition methodologies available to the company and ask the CFO why these were rejected in favor of the current practice. The revenue policy applied must have a sound business rationale that is easily understood.

Ever-Present Nonrecurring Charges

Companies are continually making provisions for future expenses, even if they are not sure of their exact amount. There has been an epidemic of merger, product return, lawsuit, obsolete inventory, and bad loan expenses that usually give rise to reserves or nonrecurring charges. There are many legitimate nonrecurring expenses—due to acts of nature, mergers, and asset sales. If the company regularly reverses reserves, such as reorganization expenses, back into operating income, it is likely that this activity has created inflation in reported results. A director should question his financial officers regarding:

- Why are the charges nonrecurring and not a part of normal operations?
- How was the amount of the charge determined and how accurate is it?
- What's the likelihood that all or a portion of the charge will not be used?
- What disclosures will be made regarding the charge in the financial statements?

These questions should be asked repeatedly until the director is comfortable with the answers. Confusing or hesitant answers in themselves are an indicator that, at a minimum, the charge has not been well vetted and understood.

Regular Changes to Reserve, Depreciation, Amortization, or Comprehensive Income Policy

Frequent changes in accounting guidance can also mask real financial performance. It is to be expected that the dollar amount of reserves will change with the business climate, but the method used to calculate reserves should not. If an increase in sales results in an increase in accounts receivable, then a corresponding and proportional increase in reserves and bad debt expenses would be expected. If there does not seem to be a direct correlation, director's should challenge the consistency of the reserve calculation. Any change in methodology should be justified by long-term trends, not short-term needs. The fraudulent financial reporting at WorldCom took many forms, but $3.3 billion of bogus profits was partially due to the reversal of bad debts expense.

Likewise, capital costs are an area of frequent abuse. A company can improve its bottom line by simply deferring expenses by recording them as assets on the balance sheet. Between 1989 and 1990, Chambers Development Company, Inc. capitalized significant amounts of landfill development costs based on targeted profit margins. The aggressive treatment created the illusion of profitability when an SEC accounting revealed that it was indeed losing money. A properly implemented policy recognizes a true but conservative estimate of the asset's useful life and limits the types of assets that can be capitalized to large, long lived items such as a new factory, piece of machinery, or information systems. True capital costs should be recorded as an asset and depreciated over the productive life of the asset to better match revenues to expenses, but directors serving on an audit committee must make certain that the assets capitalized and the related useful life assumption are both reasonable.

Related-Party Transactions

Related parties are entities whose management or operating policies can be controlled or influenced by another party. A "conflict of interest occurs when an individual's private interest interferes in any way, or even appears to interfere, with the interests of the corporation as a whole."[9] Such arrangements might benefit the company and may not be detrimental per se. Where conflicts arise, they must be well communicated, managed, and subjected to detailed and unimpeachable oversight to ensure that stockholders benefit from doing business with the related party. The board should be able to demonstrate this oversight. What is clear is that "employees, officers and directors should be prohibited from (1) taking for themselves personally opportunities that are discovered through the use of corporate property, information or position; (2) using corporate property, information, or position for personal gain; and (3) competing with the company.[10] A board needs to show that the company will not tolerate such actions through words and deeds. All executives and directors should be polled regarding their knowledge of related party transactions, personal or otherwise. Oversight of transactions identified should be reviewed, determination made regarding the benefit to the company, and a disclosure in the notes to the financial statements produced. This would be best accomplished by a committee consisting of independent directors to demonstrate unimpeachable due process and reasonable assurance that such transactions are well controlled and monitored. Such a process might have revealed the self-serving enrichment of Enron's CFO from managing the special purpose vehicles he created. No reasonable director would approve the multimillion dollar payouts experienced where little to no risk was involved for the administrator of these entities.

Complex Products

Some companies provide complex financial products, such as structured financial instruments containing derivatives, or use multifaceted hedging strategies that few understand. When a star performer produces complex products, few want to challenge this success or reveal that they do not understand how they work. In the early 1990s, neither Procter and Gamble nor Gibson Greetings could price complex options sold by Banker's Trust and, therefore, were experiencing unknown yet material losses on their positions. It is important that a director insist that management map out complex products or strategies and that the strengths, weaknesses, opportunities, and the risks of the product or strategy are well understood. Importantly, the capability to determine the market value of the product *must* exist in the company.

Underfunded Defined Benefit Plans

Although defined benefit plans are being replaced by defined contribution pensions such as 401(k) plans, there are still many in existence. These plans can have a huge effect on a corporation's net income and in some cases, the ability of the company to survive. By example, airline companies are declaring bankruptcy and shedding their pension plans, thereby leaving them in government hands. This strategy improves an airline's chances of survival, but the government pension insurance program caps benefits, so this will often mean significantly lower benefits for retired employees. Even so, the Pension Benefit Guarantee Corporation itself is viewed by many to be in a financial crisis, with the concern that it will run out of funds to pay benefits over the long-run.

Under a defined benefit plan, a sponsor guarantees a specific payout to participants. Contributions are made to the plan based on assumed future investment returns. For example, if it is known that in 10 years, when you retire, the company will need to pay you $100, it must contribute $61.39 today, assuming a 5 percent return, or only $46.31, assuming an 8 percent return. If actual gains exceed assumed returns in the current year, they can be reported as income by the company. IBM, for instance, recorded $1.27 billion of net pension income in 2000 and $1.45 billion in 2001 due to excess returns over their assumptions.

Director's need to understand the financial condition of any defined benefit plans currently sponsored by the company and, importantly, review plan assumptions. Companies can boost income and cash levels by increasing the expected return on plan assets, thereby reducing the company's liability to the plan. Expected returns on plan assets in excess of 8 percent should be challenged. Only a plan that is 100 percent invested in stocks would have a chance of exceeding an 8 percent return over time, and that is if past financial performance holds. The fact is that many pension funds have exposure to bonds and other lower-yielding instruments and will do well to earn 8 percent. Even with the recent turnaround in the stock market, defined benefit plans continue to lose ground as obligations to workers have increased faster than stocks have risen. This could be due to more claims from an aging population or low interest rates magnifying the present value of benefits. If a plan is underfunded, the assumptions used should be well understood by the finance staff and independent actuaries and a plan for addressing this liability in place to ensure there are not undue shocks to the company's cash flow.

There may be other postretirement benefits that a director should have investigated. At Lucent Technologies, postretirement health care costs comprised nearly 10 percent of their revenue and remain a significant issue for that company.[11] It is well worth a director's time to determine what commitments the company has made to its workers, and if these commitments are funded.

Footnote Disclosures

Not long ago, I received a call from a respected, but frustrated journalist from *USA Today*. He was writing a story on a company that had experienced a high profile loss in a segment of their business, yet the financial statement disclosures were silent on this piece of business. The company claimed the lack of disclosure was acceptable given the overall profitability of their business and lack of materiality for this segment. This lack of transparency can, indeed, be frustrating to investors who might view this segment as the emerging driver of future growth for the company. While the SEC requires certain segment disclosure, companies try to keep this type of disclosure to a minimum for competitive reasons. Shareholder-friendly companies, however, will do all that is reasonable to disclose important information so that investors can make informed decisions. In this case, the visibility of the loss-making business makes a case for disclosure. While the company may have been in compliance with existing disclosure rules, they were not complying with its spirit.

All executives and directors should be polled to determine if they know of any information that should be considered for disclosure in the financial statements. Human resources might know of a possible diversity suit that the general counsel has not yet been made aware, the COO might know of a possible worker grievance gaining steam, or the CIO may have just learned that important technology utilized by the entity will not be supported next year. Accumulating this data is more important than identification of the source. Such communications should be encouraged rather than punished and, ideally, a committee of knowledgeable executives and board members convened to evaluate them and determine which should be disclosed. A thoughtful process where management is properly informed and uses business judgment will go along way to demonstrating "reasonable assurance."

INTERNAL CONTROL: SIX SMART PRECERTIFICATION STEPS

Beginning in 2005, CEOs and CFOs will certify that their system of internal controls will provide reasonable assurance regarding the reliability of financial reporting and the preparation of the financial statements for external purposes. Most companies prepared for this by hiring consultants, convening project teams, documenting and evaluating processes, and addressing control weaknesses. But what happens after the project team disbands, consultants leave and the regulatory focus on Section 404 of the Sarbanes-Oxley Act gives way to other priorities? How does a director know that controls continue to operate? Where should a director focus his or her limited time to ensure the company's internal controls will continue to provide reasonable assurance of financial reporting reliability? In addition to repeatedly challenging financial reporting and disclosure policies—particularly those associated with traditional red flags—the audit committee can require management to perform six best practice actions to demonstrate the existence of a strong control environment. These actions are to require:

- Regular management reports communicating key control metrics
- Executives to identify and assess changes to key systems, processes, and people
- Business managers to sign off on their financial statements as accurate
- The identification and evaluation of material nonroutine processes
- Support for strong internal audit and control self assessment functions
- Require all employees to attest to their understanding of a code of conduct

Step 1: Require Regular Management Reports Communicating Key Control Metrics

Controls have a way of failing if no one is watching. For every assertion in the financial statements, there should be an indicator, automated alert, or other procedure designed to help a manager determine how well the related control is working. The indicator might be a simple factor, such as the number of days lost to injury; a metric (such as the percentage of product defects); a list that details unavailable materials; an exception report that points out threats to a system (such as when an attempt is made to circumvent system controls; or even periodic reviews and testing in which an inventory count is made or system capacity tests are performed).

One kind of control report is a listing of all reconciliations performed, who is responsible for the reconciliation, the last time the reconciliation was completed, and the gross amount of reconciling items. This should not be just cash reconciliations, but also system-to-system comparisons and physical inventory of assets to the books and records. Reconciliations are a powerful detective control, and if done properly, can provide a great deal of comfort that the accounts are correct.

A listing of all critical controls supporting financial statement assertions should already exist if the company's preparations for complying with Section 404 are nearing completion. Management should have a report prepared that lists the critical controls identified during this comprehensive review, a description of the metric that measures performance for each significant control, the frequency of measurement, the current performance of that metric, and the benchmark or targeted performance. A review of this report will tell the CFO, CEO, or audit committee what is being measured, where, how often, and how well the control is working. Benchmarking is a terrific management tool that can help bring perspective to this raw data. There are many sources on which management can draw, both internal and external to your organization (which we delve into in Chapter 11). Since inaccurate information can be dangerous, the report should also be periodically audited either by internal audit or some other qualified person independent from those preparing the report to ensure it's reliable.

Step 2: Require Executives to Identify and Assess Changes to Key Systems, Processes, and People

Change is the most significant threat to a recently completed control documentation project. Change, whether to processes, people, or systems, must be monitored, evaluated and, where necessary, have action taken to ensure controls continue to operate. Segregation of duties is a common and basic control lever often deployed in organizations. This lever divides tasks into discrete bits so that no single person can make a transaction without the help of others. This is done by separating the *custody*, *recording*, and *approval* functions for any process. But if the process changes, that segregation may be lost. Likewise, if a supervisor with unique and specific knowledge about a particular operation is no longer available, the approval function may become compromised.

Changes to systems can also unintentionally alter or eliminate controls. A well-designed change-control testing program will validate that controls are operating before the change is migrated into production. Under such a program, no changes can be made to an active system without testing on a separate test server. And then, the migration of new code into production is closely supervised.

The audit committee should require that managers document all changes to key processes, people, and systems since the last certification. This should include an evaluation of the impact of the change on the control structure. For instance, was the change planned? Does the change impact who performs the custody, recording, and approval functions? Is there still an independent reconciliation done to ensure all is operating as intended? Were replacement personnel identified and trained prior to the change or after? How does the manager know that controls are still operating? Has process documentation been updated? These and similar inquiries will help the CEO and the audit committee gauge how well the transition was managed and the risk that controls have been compromised.

Step 3: Require Managers to Sign Off on Their Financial Statements as Accurate

Requiring that managers at all levels to approve periodic financial reports for their area of responsibility is a simple but powerful tool. Rather than relying solely on financial personal to determine if everything is booked appropriately, why not include the analytical eye of those that run these businesses? By requiring ownership of items booked to their area of influence, managers take a closer look at what is there and ensure that it appears correct. The CEO should make it clear that he or she holds each manager responsible for the content of their financials. Their signature represents ownership and accountability.

Step 4: Identify and Evaluate Material Nonroutine Processes

Financial systems normally handle a high volume of transactions from multiple sources, which must be captured, classified, and reported. Distinguishing between routine transactions and nonroutine transactions or estimates can help a CFO, CEO, and audit committee focus on those areas that are at greater risk for error. Controls over these types of transactions are typically less formal. More care needs to be given to the nonroutine and estimation transaction control structure. Not only should the sources of data be mapped and evaluated, but assumptions, models, and advisors used to develop the estimates should be challenged and the results documented. Have the financial team develop a list of nonroutine sources of material information. Understand the sources of this information, whether assumptions are aggressive or conservative, and if derived from a spreadsheet or other model, ensure a qualified person independent from the model's operator has reviewed it from a technological and data quality standpoint.

Step 5: Support Strong Internal Audit and Control Self-Assessment Functions

The role of the internal audit department became more important with the passage of the Sarbanes-Oxley Act. Organizations can no longer afford weak audit functions. The audit committee should play a key role in hiring, evaluating, and if necessary, replacing the Chief Audit Executive (CAE). While there is a clear trend to have the CAE report to the audit committee, many still report directly to the CFO. Unfortunately, CFOs have been at the center of the largest financial reporting frauds. They can be deeply conflicted regarding the CAE's opinion regarding the status of financial reporting controls. Best practice would leave oversight of the internal audit department to the audit committee, and if an administrative reporting line is needed, it should be to the CEO.

Internal audit departments can add comfort regarding the competency of the control environment by independently performing risk analysis, control testing, and corroborating much of the information discussed in this book. They can also effectively aid the implementation of a company-wide control self-assessment program, thereby transferring control assessment knowledge to managers throughout the entity. The more eyes you have evaluating the control structure, the better.

Step 6: Require All Employees to Attest to Their Understanding of a Code of Conduct

Executives need to ensure that all employees understand not only their responsibility to adhere to good ethical principals, but also their obligation to report any related party transactions, conflicts of interest, or other compliance issues through appropriate channels. By having all employees annually attest to a code of conduct, management demonstrates that it takes the code seriously. Protocol for reporting suspected fraudulent behavior or grievances should be spelled out in the code of conduct as well as employee protections. This will aid the flow of information to the CEO and the board.

The business of audit committees has always been important and has never been easy. The importance of this work is recognized by the attention given to it by Congress, the SEC, and the NYSE. We have reviewed these new requirements, such as creating an audit charter, and appointing a financial expert to the audit committee. We have discussed the issues surrounding complaint monitoring and managing outside advisors. The red flags of financial reporting have been unveiled and six smart precertification actions revealed. But these tools are only effective if implemented and utilized. The charter must reflect audit committee activities, the red flags need to be carefully vetted, and the six smart actions diligently pursued. These steps will not guarantee the prevention or detection of financial fraud, but it will greatly increase the odds that fraud is deterred or uncovered. Admittedly, properly serving on an audit committee is hard work, but the shareholders depend on this committee to be informed and engaged.

Audit committees now play the starring role in the financial reporting governance of our public companies. They have never been stronger or more empowered. Recognizing the importance of audit committee financial oversight responsibilities, Congress mandated

KEY CONCEPTS

- Audit committees must have at least three members, consist solely of independent directors and have a charter that details the committee's mission, duties, and responsibilities.
- The audit committee must have a qualified "audit committee financial expert." Ensure that more than one is developed.
- The audit committee is required to establish procedures for receipt, retention and treatment of complaints, and confidential, anonymous submission of concerns regarding accounting or auditing matters.
- The audit committee is responsible for the hiring, retention, and release of the public accountants. The Big Four auditors are resigning engagements at an accelerated rate. Make certain that this risk is managed.
- Familiarize yourself with the Red Flags of Financial Reporting:
  - Question the aggressiveness of revenue recognition policies.
  - Have independent eyes review and explain material topside entries.
  - Challenge nonrecurring charges that keep recurring.
  - Question changes to reserve, depreciation, amortization, or comprehensive income policies.
  - Resist related-party transactions, and if allowed, ensure the board has a credible process in place to monitor it.
  - Have management map out complex products.
  - Assess assumptions used to determine the pension liability.
  - Support a robust footnote disclosure process such as a formal committee to poll the organization and vet what is to be disclosed.
- Determine how aggressive or conservative each of the company's accounting policies is and support conservative treatment.
- Make certain that the Chief Audit Executive reports directly to the audit committee. Leverage the audit department by having them corroborate management's assertions.

- Determine if the six smart steps have been taken before management certifies the financial statements. These include:
  - Reviewing key metrics
  - Assessing changes to key systems, processes and people
  - Requiring managers at all levels to sign off on financial statements as accurate for their area of influence
  - Identifying and reviewing nonroutine transactions
  - Reviewing internal audit and controling self assessment functions
  - Requiring employee attestation to their understanding of the code of conduct

that they have the independence, financial expertise, and the resources they need to get the job done. The insistence by shareholder activists for personal director liability will also result in greater attention to financial reporting issues. Better disclosure will help investors monitor the audit committee's role in a company's corporate governance structure. This does not mean that shareholders will never again feel the sting of financial reporting fraud, but strong oversight produces a meaningful deterrent and greatly improves the company's detection capabilities. While incidents of fraud will undoubtedly surface from time to time, these reforms should help prevent a re-run of the numerous and massive financial reporting frauds recently experienced.

ENDNOTES

1. New York Stock Exchange, *Final Corporate Governance Rules* (4 November 2003), 10–14. This Section 303A compliance document can be viewed at http://www.nyse.com/pdfs/finalcorpgovrules.pdf.
2. Securities and Exchange Commission, *Disclosure Required by Sections 406 and 407 of the Sarbanes-Oxley Act,* 17 CFR Parts 228, 229 and 249, Release nos. 33-8177; 34-47235; File No. S7-40-02.
3. *Sarbanes-Oxley Act of 2002,* Pub. L. No. 107-204, 116 Stat. 745, 107 H. R. 3763, § 301.

4. *Sarbanes-Oxley Act of 2002*, § 806.
5. Arthur L. Berkowitz, *Enron: A Professional's Guide to the Events, Ethical Issues, and Proposed Reforms* (Chicago: CCH Inc., 2002), 9.
6. *Sarbanes-Oxley Act of 2002*, § 201.
7. Securities and Exchange Commission, *Final Rule: Standards Relating to Listed Company Audit Committees*, 17 CFR Parts 228, 229, 240, 249 and 274, Release Nos. 33-8220; 34-47654; IC-26001; File No. S7-02-03, 37.
8. Scott Green, *Manager's Guide to the Sarbanes-Oxley Act: Improving Internal Controls to Prevent Fraud* (Hoboken, NJ: John Wiley and Sons, 2004), 122–133.
9. New York Stock Exchange, *Final Corporate Governance Rules*, 16–17.
10. Ibid.
11. Lucent Technologies, *2004 Annual Report, Notice of 2005 Meeting and Proxy Statement*, 2.

CHAPTER 6

How Much Is Fair?: The Compensation Committee

Warren Buffet says that expecting clubby boards to challenge out-sized compensation packages is like expecting well-mannered guests to begin "belching at the dinner table."[1] Compensation practices seems to be another of those intractable issues that only receive more scrutiny as pay packages balloon to ever greater heights. In this chapter, we identify different compensation components and understand how their use in the overall remuneration structure can lead to shareholder rewards or, alternatively, to high pay for poor performance.

While not required by the Sarbanes-Oxley Act, an independent compensation committee is compulsory under NYSE listing standards and is a best practice. The compensation committee is tasked with the increasingly difficult duty of developing a scheme that properly motivates executives, thereby rewarding shareholders. This is not as easy as it sounds as there are numerous studies that show little link between executive pay and company performance. However, the compensation committee must obtain the knowledge necessary to gain comfort that executive remuneration schemes are well designed and will yield expected results. Most committees hire consultants to aid with plan design, calculation processing, and reporting. The solicitation of outside compensation design and analysis experts is vital if those skills do not exist on the board. Even if experts are retained, however, it is critical that the committee fully understand the drivers of the compensation scheme, how they will be measured, the maximum and minimum payouts, when disbursements will occur, and how the plan will be monitored and reported back to the board. Presented in the following sections are the key success factors for good compensation plan design and execution.

DESIGNING THE PLAN

Compensating executives is still an art, but smart compensation committees are increasingly turning to science for more appropriate compensation policy design. The importance of designing fair compensation programs was highlighted recently with the highly visible compensation squabble between the former NYSE head Dick Grasso, New York Attorney General Eliot Spitzer, and SEC Chairperson William Donaldson. This we explore further in this chapter's case study, "Dick Grasso's Compensation Woes." If we have learned anything from what happened to Grasso, it is that compensation plans need to be carefully designed, fully understood, and monitored for fairness.

Subsequent to many of the recent compensation scandals, George B. Paulin, president of Fredrick W. Cook & Company, a leading pay consultant, stated that "consultants bore part of the responsibility for excesses because they did not fully warn of how stock options, restricted stock, and other devices could be exploited by executives. . . . [T]he focus now should be on adopting best practices to make sure shareholders do not pay more than necessary for executive talent."[2] Too many consultants simply benchmark an organization and recommend similar compensation. At the most simplistic level, this creates inflation because all companies believe their CEO is above average and, therefore, should receive above-average compensation. On the other extreme, the compensation is tied to the wrong benchmark or investment vehicle. Grasso's pay was set at a level commensurate with the CEO of an investment bank. But he was running a self-regulated exchange with corresponding financial results, not an investment bank that exhibits different risk/reward ratios. This fact made the general public recoil at compensation that would be spectacular, but more accepted for example, if earned by the CEO of one of the world's largest investment banks reporting billions in shareholder profits.

Components of executive compensation generally consist of salary, bonus, long-term, equity-based awards and, for some executives, deferred benefit plans. Base salary is compensation that reflects the complexity and responsibilities of the position. It may be benchmarked against the market when the CEO is hired, but otherwise should be treated like all other employee salaries that experience annual cost of living adjustments. In general, annual performance will be reflected by the variable annual bonus and attainment of long-term objectives recognized in the long-term equity component. To be effective, annual bonus must reflect performance. If the bonus is to be paid, regardless of performance, then the officer will consider it salary and an expected part of total annual remuneration.

To recognize a salary disguised as a bonus, find a board that pays executives a bonus even though they have not achieved established objectives. Typically, the payment will be preceded by one of the following excuses:

- If we don't pay, we will lose the team to a competitor.
- The market was bad for everyone and our team did great under the circumstances.
- We need to take into consideration that we are in a turnaround situation.

Let us take these one at a time. First, if an executive or their team is not performing, are we really in danger of losing them? If we do, are we really losing since they are not performing? Second, if the market was bad for everyone, then everyone else's compensation will also likely be lower. If not, the company that is out of line with everyone else is throwing away their shareholders' money. Third, if your company is in a turnaround situation, and your compensation plan did not contemplate that, then you must not have been in a turnaround situation when you began the process. How did you find yourself here?

If you want to identify a salary masquerading as a long-term equity award, look for a board that resets the strike price (the price at which the underlying stock can be bought) for option awards after the stock has tumbled. The excuse that usually precedes this action is that the market movement was systemic or industry-wide and we want to provide management incentive to grow the company. That is fine, but investors do not get to reset the price of their stock or option purchases, so neither should management. Real losses have occurred and management needs to reverse those losses to obtain value from awards already granted. Having said this, it would be appropriate for the compensation committee to issue new options in the current year with a lower strike, but these awards should be issued as a part of the regular compensation program and not of an amount designed to replace options issued in prior years. Such excuses are heard a lot—and people get paid on them. There are many other kinds of excuses, too, and compensation committees should approach them with a jaundiced eye.

By way of example, consider the pay package for management of the Union Pacific Corporation. The company's directors approved a long-term compensation plan that consisted of stock units and cash if performance goals related to the company's stock price or earnings were obtained. The compensation would be earned three years later if the stock traded above $70 for 20 consecutive days or if cumulative earnings over the period exceeded $13.50 a share. Three years later, the stock did not trade near $70 a share and earnings fell just short of the established target. So the compensation committee changed the metric. They included a nonrecurring gain from discontinued operations in the definition of earnings that activated the payout. Shareholders rightly question why the rules of the game had been changed to include other than operating earnings. If the goals were a stretch, then perhaps a better plan design could have been initially considered with tiered rewards. Even if these were stretch goals, the metrics should not have been changed or the compensation paid. It was simply not earned.[3]

Equity plans should be built to reward long-term growth of the company. Equity generally consists of restricted stock, stock options, or other long-term equity-like instruments. The trick to long-term incentives is to establish the timeframe and proper equity instrument. Most option plans will vest over a period of three to five years, and can be exercised over a 10-year period. Likewise, stock awards will vest over time and should reflect the growth of the company.

Most experts agree that total shareholder return is usually a good proxy on which to base a portion of an executive's compensation. How is it, then, that what was intended as fair equity compensation to reward a CEO for producing, instead results in massive rewards for failure? One answer to this complicated question may lie in the possibility that many boards do not recognize that the equity plan that they are approving might reward poor performance. If a current price is used to set the strike or starting value for computing gains, and a company's stock goes up, but underperforms every other peer, the management team will still make money, even though it is likely they destroyed shareholder value. And in a bull market, even poor performing managers can reap huge rewards, thus leaving the board to explain to irate shareholders how they could allow such a thing to happen.

An alternative to using the current price as a basis for computing gains is to issue stock options with a strike at a price greater than the current market price. For example, if the compensation committee wanted to reward 10 percent growth over three years, then the strike price could be set at 33 percent above (roughly 10 percent compounded over three years) the current market price for the stock. If the board wanted to provide even more reward for even better performance, they could issue significantly more options at 52 percent above market (roughly 15 percent compounded over three years) in addition to the first set. The strike and term combinations are unending. The downside, however, is that this program design is still static. Perhaps the overall market and peer groups return just 5 percent over the next three years. If our team returned 9 percent, then they will have outperformed and created shareholder value, but received no reward. However, if the market returned 15 percent year over year, our team would have underperformed the market by a wide margin, but still stand to collect huge gains. Compensation committees need to be aware of this shortcoming.

Some experts argue that equity compensation—either through shares or options—should be indexed to a company's competitors or to a broader market index, and management paid for superior performance relative to the index. Although more complex than issuing stock options with a strike at or above market, this would effectively reward the management of a company that performed better than average, and penalize those that do not. Under this scenario, the strike price of the options would be reset each year. If the company's peer group index increased 10 percent, then the exercise price of the options would also increase 10 percent. The options would only have value if the company's shares had gone up more than 10 percent. Besides its complexity, the downside to this approach is that the cost of indexed options would need to be reported as an expense while fixed-price stock options only need to be disclosed in the footnotes to the financial statements. While still under debate in Congress (see Unspoken Cost: Stock Options later in this chapter), best practice is to include these costs in a company's financial results as an expense, regardless of the type of option awarded. It is more transparent and better reflects the true economics of the compensation program.[4]

Deferred compensation usually consists of a portion of a bonus or other compensation retained, or supplemental retirement benefits invested on the executive's behalf to be paid at a later date. While normally a smaller piece of the compensation puzzle, as we learned with the public disclosure of Dick Grasso's deferred compensation, these benefits can be quite large. Executive benefit plans can be the overlooked time bomb that explodes at the most inopportune moment. The outcome can damage the company and even the reputation of the executives the plans are designed to protect. In some cases, these retirement plans are vehicles used to hide outsized compensation. It was recently revealed that Charles K. Gifford, the former chairperson of Bank of America, will receive, in addition to his $38 million in company stock accumulated over the years, a $16 million cash payment, an additional $8 million in possible incentive compensation, and $3.1 million a year for life. Better yet, if he dies before his wife, she will receive $2.3 million a year for life. Now, one can be sure that Mr. Gifford's wife has been very supportive of his career, but you have to stretch reason to determine that she contributed value to the company that entitles her to over $2 million a year. The company also guaranteed Mr. Gifford over $50,000 a year in consulting fees, an office staffed with a secretary, and liberal use of a corporate jet. Ironically, many pundits believe Mr. Gifford as a manager was fair at best. Not surprisingly, the SEC has indicated that they intend to look more closely at retirement compensation disclosure.[5]

On the other hand, deferred compensation can provide long-term corporate protection, as every year the CEO has more to lose from making conflicted or unethical decisions (which also increases pressure on the CEO to call for disbursement of the benefits). The Sarbanes-Oxley Act effectively put such compensation into play by forcing disgorgement of compensation earned during a period of fraudulent activity. Furthermore, income deferral plans are a terrific vehicle for tax effective wealth accumulation for senior executives. It is important that the compensation committee continue to monitor the full value of deferred compensation plans to make sure they are fair and will not produce reputational damage to the company. A wise committee will reallocate the mix of current and deferred compensation if the deferred component threatens to approach levels experienced at the New York Stock Exchange.

CASE STUDY: DICK GRASSO'S COMPENSATION WOES

It was May 2, 2001, a day etched in my memory if only because I met Dick Grasso, the head of the New York Stock Exchange. He had not yet led the NYSE to recovery from the attacks of September 11, 2001 or fallen from grace for his compensation woes. ABN AMRO had just bought the U.S. domestic brokerage business of ING Barings. As a Managing Director in the New York offices of ING, I too was sold and destined to become part of ABN AMRO. To honor the closing of the transaction, the senior management of the new ABN AMRO was invited down to the New York Stock Exchange to ring the closing bell. We were received at the NYSE boardroom, which is across the street from the Exchange. It is a beautiful room with high ceilings, oversized windows, and wonderfully ostentatious furnishings that ooze history and power. On cue, shortly before the close, a diminutive Dick Grasso walks in and addresses those present in what felt like a somewhat forced but effective speech extolling the virtues of the exchange and its superiority above other means of trading. Before we all walked over to the exchange for the close, he handed each of us a heavy bronze medallion in an understated red presentation box. The medallion, notable for its relief of a bull and bear locked in battle, had been struck with the company name and date to remember the day. In a way, this personal memento reflected everything Dick Grasso represented. It was classic marketing, nothing over the top, yet it required a well-oiled internal factory to churn out the gifts for every opening and closing of the exchange. You appreciated the work and the thought that went into it.

I had often heard from the old guard how hard Grasso worked to make it to the top. He started as a clerk in the listing department, earning $81 a week, and diligently studied its internal workings. I can find no one who will argue that he knew the nuances of the exchange better than anyone. Presentation seemed to be a weakness, but you could see he was passionate about the exchange, which made his somewhat stiff public-speaking style endearing. Perhaps because of where he came from, he was able to speak to people, and they would understand, no matter how complicated the subject. And he ran the exchange successfully.

Since taking over the exchange as chairman in 1995, Grasso saw the NYSE increase its share of the nation's stock trading from 70 percent to 90 percent taking business from the regional exchanges, and even the NASDAQ after the technology bubble burst. This was in the face of increasing competition from the NASDAQ and electronic trading. Over half of the companies trading on the NYSE were recruited while Grasso was chairman. The man could sell and that was critically important to the exchange. Every new listing brought in fees and more business for the specialists that made their living making the market. Additionally, the value of a NYSE seat tripled during his tenure.

You cannot talk about Dick Grasso without also considering September 11, 2001. Who can forget the hard work that went into getting the exchange open after his assurance that the NYSE would reopen a week later, which it did. He stood at the podium, surrounded by Governor Pataki, U.S. Senator Schumer, SEC Commissioner Pitt, New York Mayor Guiliani, and others before the opening bell and, after a moment of silence, led the floor in singing "God Bless America." To the approval of many, he did not allow Al-Jazeera, the Arabic news network based in Qatar, access to the Exchange due to their perceived support of Al-Qaeda. He had become an American icon.

So how could the hardworking boy in the listing department who rose to chairman end his career ignominiously? Was it the result of "absolute power corrupts absolutely?" There have been accusations that Grasso used his regulatory powers as a weapon and made enemies. Some say he unfairly used his position to pressure specialists to maintain market share that drove his bonus. Still more say that he had undue influence over his board of directors regarding nomination and compensation issues. Whether any of these accusations are accurate, what is clear is the payout of $140 million in deferred compensation set off the firestorm, and the resulting public battle with New York's Attorney General sealed his fate.

In a letter to the chairman of the Human Resources and Compensation Committee, H. Carl McCall, SEC Chairman William Donaldson called into question the distribution of nearly $140 million in deferred compensation to Mr. Grasso. In Mr. Donaldson's words "the approval of Mr. Grasso's pay package raises serious questions regarding the effectiveness of the NYSE's current governance structure."[a] Commissioner Donaldson knew what he was talking about. Before Dick Grasso, he was chairman and CEO of the NYSE and deeply understood the role. One defense put forward by the exchange was that Grasso's pay was similar to the CEOs of those companies he regulated. An internal exchange report, however, determined that Mr. Grasso was overpaid by as much as $156 million from 1995 to 2002. The report concludes that the benchmarks used (large financial institutions) was inappropriate, that Mr. Grasso's own evaluation of the exchange's performance directly impacted his pay, and that his final compensation often exceeded even the inappropriate benchmarks by a wide margin.[b]

Few would doubt that the chairman of the exchange is entitled to a retirement plan, but the amount left most Americans shocked and dismayed. How does a self-regulatory agency head make that kind of money? It is one thing if a corporate chieftain reaps huge rewards because the stock markedly appreciates also enriching his stockholders, but the NYSE paid Grasso $12 million in cash in a year where the exchange made $28 million. To receive such a large portion of earnings itself raises questions. The chairman was also able to defer bonuses and receive a guaranteed 8 percent return. Over time, his deferred compensation just exploded. Perhaps Grasso knew that he had a time bomb on his hands, which is why he wanted to cash out prematurely. According to an internal exchange report, the head of human resources at the exchange reported that Mr. Grasso "believed that there would be a strong reaction to the magnitude of his retirement package." The report also quoted Mr. Grasso telling a director of his concerns that a subsequent board might reconsider his pension benefits.[c]

Mr. Spitzer brought legal action against Mr. Grasso and a former director of the NYSE, Kenneth Langone. Mr. Spitzer seeks over $100 million in reimbursement from Mr. Grasso, and $18 million (the amount of Grasso compensation that Spitzer alleges was hidden from other directors) from Langone, who was the former head of the compensation committee. The fight has been nasty and very public, with Grasso threatening to counter sue for $50 million. Others are taking cover. Mercer Human Resources Consulting, the firm that advised the board on Grasso's compensation, has agreed to return the $1.3 million it was paid for their work hoping to put the issue behind them.[d] Whether Grasso wins or loses in court will be important to his overall wealth, but what is clear is that he has already lost in the court of public opinion and given up his position as an American icon.

---

[a]Donaldson, William, "Statement by the Chairperson: Letter to NYSE Regarding NYSE Executive Compensation," U.S. Securities and Exchange Commission, Washington, D.C. (2 September, 2003).
[b]Landon Jr., Thomas, and Jenny Anderson, "Report Details Huge Pay Deal Grasso Set Up," *New York Times*, 3 February 005, A1.
[c]Ibid.
[d]Crawford, Krysten, "Spitzer seeks $100 million from Grasso," *CNNMoney*, 24 May 2004. http://money.cnn.com/2004/05/24/markets/spitzer_grasso (6 April 2005).

UNSPOKEN COST: STOCK OPTIONS

There has been much recent debate regarding accounting for stock options. This esoteric debate is deeply relevant to compensation committees. At this time, the cost of options is not truly reflected in the financial results of most companies. The Financial Accounting Standards Board (FASB) has issued new guidance to better reflect the cost of options; but under political pressure, Congress may prevent the new rules from taking effect. Congress has responded with "The Stock Option Accounting Reform Act," which is anything but option accounting reform. The bill is the result of intense lobbying by those companies that wish to keep the true cost of executive option programs from impacting financial results. The Chairman and President of the FASB, Robert Denham, is on record saying, "Advancing this bill in the legislative process harms the credibility of

America's system for providing transparent and unbiased financial information to investors."[6]

If Congress allows special interests to override objective accounting judgment based on due process, then the continuing improvement of our financial reporting process will cease and may even regress. Congress's approach not only flies in the face of the FASB, but also international accounting standards. Those directors serving on compensation committees need to be aware that the cost of options may not be reflected in the financial results of the company. If not, directors should ensure that the cost of these instruments is continually calculated and reported by independent consultants so that sound judgments can be made on facts rather than wishful results. This analysis will also be useful in understanding the potential impact of options already issued if the FASB's recommendation is eventually implemented.

PIECEWORK: TRANSACTION COMPENSATION

Some companies, particularly serial acquirers, compensate top management for the completion of a deal. If your company is a target, additional compensation may be appropriate to align management (who will be out of a job) and shareholder interests, but it is rarely appropriate for the surviving company's management. Compensating executives on finding a target and closing a deal only guarantees that a target will be found and acquired. There is no incentive to find the best fit, to spend the time and effort to ensure it is properly integrated, and that the return from the acquisition is the best use of stockholder funds.

As an example, a report by Tyco's outside counsel claims that the company reported a profit of $79.4 million on the purchase of a small company called Flag Telecom. Based on this outcome, Tyco paid its top managers $24 million in bonuses, most of which went to its CEO, Dennis Kozlowski. The report reveals that management kept the board in the dark about the bonuses for many months. When the board's compensation committee eventually did give its approval, it had no knowledge of the sharp decline that had since occurred in Flag's stock. The report concludes that the acquisition actually resulted in a $26 million economic loss by the time the deal closed. Less than a year and a half later, Flag was in bankruptcy and its stock worth less than a penny. Nevertheless, Tyco managers kept their million-dollar bonuses.[7]

DANGER OF OVERSIZED PARACHUTES

There are times when executive management interests will be naturally conflicted with shareholders. The most obvious example is when management is confronted with an offer to sell or merge the company. In most cases, several managers will lose their jobs as a result of the proposed transaction. The solution most boards implement is to provide fair parting compensation in the form of a golden parachute, or more simply put, a severance payment. This may not only be the humane thing to do, as it is difficult for some to replace that income, but also the best course of action for shareholders as the transaction can unlock shareholder value.

All too often, however, parachutes are put in place, not to encourage a transaction, but to prevent one or to unjustly enrich management. In effect, they have a similar result to a poison pill. Acquirers may be kept at bay due to the added expense, and even if they move ahead, the cost of the parachute is taken into consideration when negotiating the purchase price. In that case, it comes out of the pockets of the shareholders.

Merck serves as a recent example. The company recently recalled Vioxx, one of its best-selling drugs, after a study indicated that it raised the probability of heart problems in people taking the drug. Many regarded the company's drug pipeline as weak, so the sale of existing drugs was critical to the current value of Merck's stock. Not surprisingly, the stock declined over 40 percent on the news, and over 70 percent since 2000 from concerns regarding the company's research and development prospects. The directors responded by adopting a golden parachute plan covering its top 230 managers that would likely cost hundreds of millions of dollars if executed. The plan would pay a manager up to three times his total annual compensation and would take effect if any suitor buys 20 percent or more of the company stock, even if it does not complete a takeover. This is a feature that resembles a poison pill more than a fair compensation plan.[8] While the million-dollar payday will likely not impact the purchase of a company worth billions, the depth of the plan raises serious concerns. Is it truly in the company's interest to protect 230 managers rather than the best and brightest of this large population? Furthermore, how can a board decide that it is in the shareholder's best interests to adopt a plan that encourages employees to leave even if a transaction is not consummated?

Needless to say, the plan has left corporate governance experts shaking their collective heads. It is understandable that the board would want to protect certain high level managers. There is little doubt that many are nervous given the weakened state of the company and may be looking for more stable ground. But there are more stockholder friendly alternatives, such as long-term equity plans, that provide incentive to perform and would also vest if there was a change in control of the company. Granted, such a plan would take more work to actually identify those select managers in which you want to invest (as opposed to 230 of which you can be sure includes some subperformers). Designing a retention package that provides appropriate performance incentives will always be in shareholder's best interest.

The Merck board should be ashamed of the plan they adopted. All boards have a duty to consider alternatives that can achieve stated objectives while fairly representing the well-being of shareholders. The Merck plan appears to heavily favor several levels of management at the cost of shareholder value and, therefore, fails the sniff test.

Fortunately, executive contracts that guarantee severance payments are on the decline. About 40 percent of executives leading S&P 500 companies are doing so without a contract. This is up from 30 percent five years ago. Some CEOs are even giving up their contracts. The CEO of ConocoPhillips, James J. Mulva, did just that as it was his belief that good governance would dictate pay for performance.[9]

MEASURING PERFORMANCE

In an unusually complete and insightful book, *Responsible Executive Compensation for a New Era of Accountability*, Russell Miller of Mercer Human Resources Consulting tells us that in order for a performance measurement system to be effective, it must "align the interests of employees and shareholders, reflect the economics of the business and match the culture and capabilities of the company." He also instructs us that the components of a performance measurement system include:

- *Performance measure selection:* the measure(s) used as the indicator of success
- *Goal-setting:* the desired level of performance on the selected measures
- *Linkage:* the organizational unit (department, business unit, corporate) to which the measure applies
- *Time horizon:* the time period over which performance is measured
- *Corporate process:* the processes that capture the measure[10]

The first component is to identify the measures to be used as an indicator of success. Some questions to help with this process include:

Where is our stock price now?

How does its valuation compare to competitors?

Why is it worth more than the competition or what is holding it back?

In other words, what are the drivers? Understanding drivers helps a director understand how the business makes money.

Drivers are targeted, actionable, and measurable. They have a considerable influence on business value. Related metrics measure how effective the company is executing its strategy. Drivers should be tied to company strategy that impact serving certain market segments, provide unique products or services, deliver bundled solutions, simply serve a specific geographic area, or rely on a differentiated business process. In essence, any dynamic that is key to the company's value qualifies as a driver that should be monitored.

Differentiated business processes can consist of a singular focus on core processes that yield higher output and cost saving, development of unique organizational competencies, or creation of a streamlined delivery process. Companies differentiate themselves based not only on what they make, but also how they make it. For instance, Hewlett Packard (HP) and Dell both make computers, but the way they make computers could not be more different. HP builds standard systems and sells them through a number of channels. Dell builds to specific customer orders and only sells through the Internet or over the phone. How the deliverable is created and distributed can be a tremendous source of competitive advantage, as evidenced by Dell's phenomenal growth and profitability.

Once the drivers and metrics have been identified, a well-controlled process needs to be implemented to measure, monitor, and communicate results. The compensation committee should receive regular reports that compare operational metrics to the starting baseline, to the business plan objectives, and, as a best practice, to stretch goals. Results to baseline and to budget are a common comparison, but the committee should also define what constitutes outstanding performance and be prepared to reward the achievement of these results.

Companies that get performance measurement wrong usually do so because the measurement is not aligned to shareholder value, or it is not considered when making operating decisions. It is not only critical that enough scenario testing is performed to ensure that the drivers and metrics selected impact shareholder value, but the new paradigm must be imbedded into the organization. Most employees do not know that they can impact cash flow or return on investment in their everyday decision making. Measures need to be simple and built into the performance evaluation system. Management must be willing to (1) spend time and effort to explain the rationale for the metrics selected; (2) provide frequent feedback to middle management and employees; (3) share success stories with the whole organization; and (4) reward those that demonstrably contribute to the company strategy. The timing of compensation payments is also important to a successful program. The timeframe for measurement is different for a turnaround or bankrupt business than for a stable consumer products company. As such, the components of an executive's total compensation should align the performance period with the compensation period.

UNWANTED INCENTIVES

A well-crafted compensation plan will encourage executives to make decisions that leverage the value drivers of the business. Yet even a carefully conceived plan can create temptations to manage the metrics. By way of example, the SEC recently charged four senior executives of

U.S. Foods with a $700 million financial reporting fraud. As is the case with many managers, the executives were compensated in part on their ability to meet earnings targets. The SEC alleges that the company executives "went to extraordinary lengths to perpetuate the illusion of stellar financial performance . . . their fraud created the appearance that they had met their budgets and allowed them to line their own pockets with unearned bonuses." In short, the executives "booked to budget" regardless of how the company actually performed.[11]

The compensation committee needs to carefully consider not only the desired incentives produced by a compensation plan, but also the controls around the metrics that will be used to measure that performance. It would be useful for the compensation committee to work with the audit committee highlighting these issues so that the audit committee can focus on these areas of risk while performing their oversight of financial reporting and internal control. For instance, if senior management is being compensated on sales targets as opposed to stock price, return on investment (ROI), or other metrics, the audit committee should recognize the risk that sales will be manipulated has increased. In such a case, they would want to pay closer attention to revenue and cut off accounting policies and controls.

TELL US ABOUT YOUR SHAREHOLDER EQUITY PLAN

The NYSE and NASD recently moved to tighten rules regarding shareholder approval of stock based compensation plans. Previously, both self regulatory organizations allowed exemptions that permitted companies to adopt such plans without shareholder approval. Under the new rules, an award payable in company stock must be submitted to company shareholders for endorsement. This includes any stock awards granted under an established plan or outside such a plan. It also includes restricted stock, stock options, and awards made from treasury stock. There are still certain exemptions that include:

- Tax qualified plans such as ESOPs
- Pension plans
- Dividend reinvestment plans available to all shareholders
- Stock offered to attract potential new hires
- Awards made due to merger and acquisition activity that converts, adjusts, or replaces existing equity awards

■ Awards from a shareholder-approved plan sponsored by a non-listed company involved in the transaction

These exemptions must be approved by an independent compensation committee or a majority of the independent directors sitting on the board and the NYSE or NASD must be advised that an exemption has been used.

THE FIGHT IS ON!

There is plenty of evidence that shareholders have had enough of ever escalating executive compensation and are fighting back. Under pressure from shareholders, the Hilton hotel and gaming group recently cut the contract of its CEO to a one-year rolling term. One-year contracts are considered a preferred practice by many governance experts and they do not restrict a company from implementing a long-term compensation plan.

In the wake of Enron and calls for accountability, it also appears directors are taking a harder line. The chairperson of E*Trade resigned after being forced to return $80 million in compensation a few months earlier. The chairperson of MBNA ran afoul of directors over management compensation and, according to news reports, resigned after a year-long battle between management and the board. In a more shareholder-friendly move, executives at Nortel will voluntarily repay $8.6 million in bonuses and some stock that were paid on manipulated financial results, even though none of the managers had anything to do with the fraud.

The case everyone is watching, however, is the shareholder lawsuit in Delaware Chancery Court against Disney and its directors for approving a $140 million severance package for Michael Ovitz, the former president of that company. Shareholders contend that the board failed to exercise any business judgment or to make a good-faith effort to fulfill their duties as directors. They not only believe that his contract was too rich but also that Ovitz's performance should have resulted in dismissal for cause which would have prevented the large payout. In fact, the case may turn on the testimony of directors who admittedly deferred to the judgment of the chief executive regarding the termination and related compensation. If the court agrees with the plaintiffs, the boardrooms of the country will be shaken to their very foundations. Absence personal corruption, directors are virtually never held liable for business decisions. Given Delaware's status as the incorporation headquarters of the country, most every company in America will be affected by the outcome of this case.

Massive compensation should only follow massive out-performance. How is it that apparently savvy directors are somehow unable to see the coming compensation storm? It is likely a combination of poor outside advice, a dearth of good monitoring tools to map rewards to performance, and difficulty valuing certain benefits.

KEY CONCEPTS

- Smart boards link pay to performance and ignore the common excuses for missing targets. Goals are set based on the key drivers of the business and objectively measured.
- Require regular reports comparing key metrics to baselines to assess performance.
- Support a well-structured plan that consists of components to address different risks and incentives. This will include salary, bonus, and long-term compensation appropriately mapped to cost of living, meeting objectives, and long-term return to shareholders, respectively.
- Directors can unintentionally reward sub-par performance by linking long-term rewards to the company's current stock price. Insist on a better measure based on the performance of company stock versus an appropriate market or industry index.
- Deferred compensation can be a time bomb. Periodically have the plan revalued.
- Avoid transaction compensation.
- Best practice is for CEOs to serve without a contract. Many companies that do offer contracts limit them to one year.
- Evaluate where the compensation plan creates risk for fraud and make certain that such risks are monitored.
- Insist that directors hold company stock to better align their interests with shareholders.

Smart directors will avoid the storm by challenging the structure of the compensation plan, requiring frequent reporting on the current and projected values of compensation packages, and periodic revaluation of deferred compensation and senior executive pension plans to identify those burgeoning threats.

ENDNOTES

1. Timothy L. O'Brien, "Mayday? Payday! Hit the Silk," *New York Times*, 9 January 2005, C1.
2. David Cay Johnston, "Designers of Executive Salary Plans Fear More Abuses," *New York Times*, 5 October 2002, C2.
3. Gretchen Morgenson. "Pay Package at Risk? Quick, Get Creative," *New York Times*, 23 November 2003, C1.
4. Alfred Rappaport, "New Thinking on How to Link Executive Pay with Performance," *Harvard Business Review* 77 (March–April 1999): 91–101.
5. Timothy L. O'Brien, C1.
6. Financial Accounting Standards Board, "Financial Accounting Standards Board News Release: Financial Accounting Foundation Chairman Responds to House Subcommittee's Action on 'The Stock Option Accounting Reform Act,'" *FASB.org*, 17 May 2004. http://www.fasb.org/news/nr051704.shtml (6 April 2005).
7. Floyd Norris, "Tyco Took Profit on Bad Deal, Then Paid Bonuses to Executives," *New York Times*, 25 September 2002, C1.
8. Alex Berenson, "Merck Offering Top Executives Rich Way Out," *New York Times*, 30 November 2004, A1.
9. Joann S. Lublin, "Many High Executives Are Working Without a Net," *Wall Street Journal*, 26 October 2004, C4.
10. Peter T. Chingos, *Responsible Executive Compensation for a New Era of Accountability*. (Hoboken, NJ: John Wiley & Sons, 2004), 34–35.
11. U.S. Securities and Exchange Commission, "SEC Charges Former Top Executives of U.S. Foodservice with $700 Million Securities Fraud; One Executive Also Charged with Insider Trading," Release No. 2004-100, July 27, 2004, http://www.sec.gov/news/press/2004-100.htm.

CHAPTER 7

Keeping It Clean: The Corporate Governance/Nominating Committee

In the past, directors were normally chosen by the CEO of a company. Without an independent nominating or governance committee to manage the process, the potential existed for the CEO to dominate the identification and selection of candidates. He or she was the sole source for candidates delivered to the independent directors for approval. Even if directors were involved in the nomination process, a beholden board, also appointed by the CEO, would likely rubberstamp a nomination. Likewise, a board that lacks independence would not be in a position to evaluate the CEO or ensure the proper development of management for succession planning. Independent governance and nomination procedures are an important practice best institutionalized by the committee structure populated with strong, independent directors. The goal of this chapter is to introduce new Self-Regulatory Organization (SRO) and SEC requirements as well as certain best practices that make certain the directors' efforts have impact.

The Sarbanes-Oxley Act did not specifically address governance or nomination processes. However, the NYSE listing requirements mandate the creation of a nominating or similar committee, and the SEC has added new nomination disclosure requirements. Listing requirements specify that a nominating committee must consist of independent directors and have a formal charter. The NASD does not require the creation of the committee, but does require the majority of independent directors to approve nominations in executive session. Absent a committee with a formal charter, the NASD rules do require a formal written board resolution addressing the director nomination process.

GOVERNING THE BOARD

An important source for directors and boards wishing to implement best practice are the publications produced by the National Association of Corporate Directors (NACD). The NACD is a national nonprofit membership organization that is dedicated to serving the corporate governance needs of corporate boards and individual board members. The NACD's 15,500 members and customers represent companies that range from Fortune 100 public companies to small businesses as well as over-the-counter, closely held, and private firms. The NACD "promotes high professional board standards, creates forums for peer interaction, enhances director effectiveness, communicates and monitors the policy interests of directors, conducts benchmarking research, and educates boards and directors concerning traditional and cutting-edge issues."[1] It publishes a broad range of helpful tools that are highly recommended for any board of directors.

The NACD categorizes a high-performing board as one that has the right people (a careful blend of people with diversity of strengths), culture, issue focus, information, processes, and follow through. The board's responsibilities are many, but will normally include:

- Determining criteria for board and committee membership (people)
- Identifying, evaluating, and recommending director candidates to the board based on objective needs of the board (people, process)
- The process of evaluating board members (people, process, follow-through)
- Oversight of director training (people, process)
- CEO and senior manager succession planning (people, process)
- Establishing board structure and operational rules (process)
- Developing and publishing corporate governance principles (culture)
- Procedures for public communications (culture, process)
- Maintaining open, anonymous communication channels for fraud or hostile work environment reporting (culture, issues)
- Evaluating metrics for the business drivers and key success factors (information, issues)

- Responding to shareholder concerns, governance trends, legislative and regulatory proposals or judicial decisions affecting corporate governance (issues, follow-through)
- Monitoring the execution and effectiveness of the corporate strategy through a formal evaluation process (follow-through, issues, process)

The governance committee is an ideal place to administer the implementation and evaluation of these functions if it is free to exercise good judgment without influence or relationships that could compromise their independence. Regardless of the chosen mandate, a written charter of committee responsibilities should be made publicly available.

SETTING THE RULES

The environment in which companies compete is fluid and ever changing. Boards need to be adaptable as well. Companies caught flat-footed destroy shareholder value or, at least, miss an opportunity to exploit new markets. Active governance committees provide significant value to shareholders by making certain that the board structure adequately protects the company and by vetting opportunities, risks, and threats. Emerging practices can surface in any number of areas, but proposed legislation, regulatory rules, or listing requirements, even if they fail to be adopted, could signal a trend. Concerns of shareholder activists are also an important source of feedback. The separation of the chairperson and CEO roles within a company is an example of this. While widely debated, but not yet mandated, there has been significant movement on this issue as smart companies take the first step of appointing a lead director.

Engaged committees make sure that procedures are in place to see that the full board receives the information it needs to perform their oversight responsibilities in a timely manner. This will include information obtained from outside the company, both positive and negative, relating to relevant regulatory and legal initiatives, management, the company, and the industry.

Thorough and focused governance committees prepare corporate governance principles that include, at a minimum, board leadership, director qualifications, director responsibilities, the structure and functioning of the board's committees, the board's access to management and independent advisors, director compensation, director education, board evaluations, and management succession. These principles should be approved by the full board. The best committees periodically review these principles against governance trends and best practice.

At a more detailed level, the committee should oversee policies regarding meeting schedules, agendas, and management participation in board meetings to ensure proper functioning of the board. These procedures may seem mundane but they are important. No one really cares about them until there is a problem, and then they either become a board's best defense or its worst nightmare, depending on how well they were carried out. Good governance practices ensure that only discussions and actions taking place at a board meeting are documented within the minutes. Minutes should be short, noting the topic, reflecting the action and the vote and capture the fundamental nature of what was said, but not much more. If concerns are important enough to be raised in the minutes, courts have held that they should also be included in regulatory filings (10-Q and 10-K).[2] Minutes should not describe every comment, nor should the meetings be tape recorded. People say all sorts of things at meetings that might be in jest, but could be taken out of context later. Director's notes and preliminary, unapproved minutes should be destroyed as soon as the formal minutes are approved. The same goes for board materials sent out. Best practice requires that all board materials are brought to the meeting, and stay there after the meeting is over. The general counsel or corporate secretary can then keep one set of official records, and destroy everything else. This can prevent a director's notes from being taken out of context and coming back to hurt the company. One record and one story equal a reduced chance of miscommunication or unintended interpretations.

While working on procedures, engaged boards also make sure they have a process for stockholders to communicate directly with board members and members with stockholders. New rules require that the company disclose whether it has such a process and, if not, why. This process may include providing a mailing address, telephone, or e-mail account for stockholders to communicate to the board or key committee chairs. It will likely include a process for vetting communications to identify those requiring board actions. Another issue for the committee to address is director attendance at the annual meeting. Annual meetings are a great opportunity to gauge investor temperament and directors should ensure they are present.

Corporate board workloads are mounting, and the governance committee can play a crucial role in assessing committee structures to help break up the effort into manageable bits. The audit committee, compensation committee, and governance/nomination committees are the obvious candidates; but there are also industry and company specific issues that may best be handled by committee. Finance, environmental, safety, and special investigatory committees are also common. The governance committee is in the unique position to assess the relevance of the committee universe and recommend an optimal structure to the full board. It should also develop membership criteria for each committee. For instance, some financial or accounting background would be a requirement for the audit committee, with at least one member being qualified as an "audit committee financial expert." Smart structure equals wise government. A properly organized and staffed committee structure can lead to focused, quality results delivered in an efficient manner.

EVALUATING THE BOARD

Once considered a best practice most boards ignored, board and certain committee evaluations are now required by the NYSE listing standards. Board appraisals can improve accountability, transparency of director, CEO and committee responsibilities, progress board operations, and advance communication and board relationships. Providing a formal process of communication helps raise issues that might not otherwise be vetted by the board. Such self-analysis is rarely comfortable, and any excuse not to do it has been effective in past considerations. There is a valid concern about the documentation left behind by these evaluations; specifically materials that could be used by plaintiff attorneys to chip away at a board's competence in a bid to gain access to Directors & Officers (D&Os) insurance proceeds and a director's personal assets. Regardless, it is now a requirement for our largest companies, and boards have to confront and actively manage this risk. There are some practices that may help to mitigate litigation risk including putting controls around the preparation and retention of appraisal documents.

A strong board-evaluation process includes an agreement on a process for annual board appraisal, the establishment of board objectives, an action plan for achieving those objectives, monitoring progress, and a formal year end evaluation. There will likely be some project-oriented objectives such as creating governing principles, an audit committee charter, or completion of a corporate transaction that, once achieved, will not be carried forward to the next year. Other objectives may be long term and perpetual, thereby affording the board the opportunity to compare performance across time. The NACD High Performance Characteristics discussed earlier can be a valuable starting point to vet those areas that the board wishes to assess. Some common areas that a board might consider include:

- Director, CEO, and senior management succession planning
- Effectiveness of CEO evaluation
- Director training
- Director participation targets
- Setting ethical "tone at the top" and related initiatives
- Compliance with governance regulations and best practices
- Efficiency and effectiveness of meetings
- Adequacy and timeliness of risk management information/key performance indicators/metrics received
- Effectiveness of process to monitor strategy execution

To help with this task, directors should consider using the NACD Board Evaluation Tool that is reproduced in Appendix C. While generic, this tool reflects the accumulated experience of the best governance minds. In addition to these generic objectives, the board should choose goals that reflect what is most essential to the company and the board over the coming year. Regardless of the goals selected, the governance committee should ensure that both the process and objectives are confirmed by the entire board annually at the commencement of the fiscal year. Once approved, the governance committee can then perform the hard work of developing measurement criteria and monitoring procedures. For example, assume that a large bakery company has a strategy to move beyond wholesale sales into the retail market by opening its own chain of bread stores. The board might have several measurable criteria to properly monitor the execution of this strategy. It might want to bring on a new director with retail store experience, oversee the recruitment and compensation of an executive to lead that line of business, request the development of risk management reporting models that will provide sensitivity and scenario analysis for different operating environments and strategy outcomes, agree on new sources of financing, and require the development of new store openings, same store sales, and customer satisfaction metrics to monitor the status of the rollout, the profitability of stores already built and retail customer contentment.

The work required to reach these goals will take substantial amounts of time. Unfortunately, the board has a premium on its time due to a limited number of meetings, each crammed with critical business. Therefore, it is important that the governance committee identify the resources needed to properly achieve these objectives and assign responsibility, whether internally to management or externally to independent consultants. The use of an external facilitator to structure the evaluation process and help prepare the presentation to the full board can be particularly useful. The board should then monitor progress throughout the year so that there are no year-end surprises. At year end, based on the information produced and activities accomplished, the board can evaluate where they spent their time and the effectiveness of their performance.

Individual directors should also demand information sourced from outside the company to evaluate the board. Organizations such as Institutional Shareholder Services (ISS), CalPERS, Governance Metrics International (GMI), or Moodys all have or are creating governance rating systems that can provide valuable insight. External feedback can help a board assess the effectiveness of their communications to external parties and benchmark their practices against other companies.

The structure of the evaluation can be important, both to the tone as well as to potential liability. Most consultants and authoritative literature on the subject recommend using a numeric grading system such as that used in the NACD Board Evaluation Tool. However, Bruce Taten and Robert Barker, in their *Directors & Boards* article "Ways to Reduce Risks in Board Evaluations," recommend using a nonnumeric scale. In essence, each director would place an X along a continuum ranging from Less Strong to Strong to More Strong. They argue that directors still get the needed feedback while not providing the mathematical accuracy or terms such as "poor" or "weak" that might have to be defended in court at a later date.[3]

Regardless of the chosen approach, the survey results can then be compiled into a single report for review by the full board. Most experts argue that the results should be presented to the board without attribution to director contributions, and is best delivered by the lead director or other trusted outside director. Rather than be defensive, it is important that the board members see this feedback as objective information that can be leveraged. The results are just that, results. The board can use them as a tool to identify areas for improvement, and develop goals and action plans for the coming year.

The first few times the board experiences the self-evaluation process, it is likely to be highly structured, which is appropriate. But, over time, the board should feel free to take the evaluation process in new directions. After all, it is a feedback mechanism designed to help the board. If the directors decide that they want to do an industry governance practices comparison instead of detailed internal analysis, such creativity should be encouraged. The process should be enabling, not stifling.

In summary, the results of a board assessment should include how the board works as a group and whether any changes to board membership would improve board performance. Any weaknesses identified are reported to the board together with a plan to address limitations. The committee should conduct their own self-evaluation and help other committees to conduct theirs. The independence of board members, in fact and appearance, also needs to be evaluated and monitored to ensure a substantial majority remain independent as determined by standards recommended by the committee, set by the board, and conforming with regulatory guidelines. Director evaluations, questionnaires and attestations, regular background searches on the internet (and other sources), and enforced term limits are all parts of a rigorous monitoring program. Now that we understand the importance of board evaluations, let us examine some other areas that require evaluation in greater detail, beginning with director evaluations.

AND THE DIRECTORS

Individual director evaluations are controversial as they can be painful and possibly create legal exposure. But as David A. Nadler states in his *Harvard Business Review* article "Building Better Boards," "Boards must recognize which directors need help, which should not be nominated for another term, and which should be cut loose."[4] Director opposition to individual appraisals can be overwhelming, effectively killing the process before it starts. Even where tolerated, limited exposure to management and a focus on individual optimization can inhibit an effective evaluation process. However, the need for individual evaluations in such situations is even more compelling. Director participation is critical to a successful board, and just the prospect of being subjected to an evaluation process in itself can induce self-correcting behavior. Furthermore, investors are clamoring for director accountability. Together with a smaller membership and increasing responsibilities, boards can no longer afford to carry underperforming directors. Finally, there are issues relevant to an individual director that the board-level assessment does not address, such as the number of meetings attended, committee participation, the amount of company stock owned, and so on. The fact that the full board and its committees are now required to perform self-evaluations may help ease the way for individual appraisals. Once full board and committee evaluations have been performed and proved their worth, directors may be more open to expanding the process to the individual level.

Evaluation practices can range from confidential self-evaluations to self and peer reviews that are fed to the nominating committee. Best practice is to have directors perform a self-evaluation, have board peers and the CEO also individually review them, and provide a summary comparison to the director. In this way the directors can compare their perceptions of their contributions to the perceptions of others. Typical evaluation criteria might include:

- Adequately prepared for meetings
- Attended every meeting
- Deep understanding of the business
- Understands the company strategy
- Free of conflicts or notifies the board when conflicted

- Independent in mind and spirit, not afraid to take a stand
- Honest and open in dealing with other board members
- Good counsel to the board and management
- Measured, value-added contribution to discussions
- Actively contributes to board committees
- Supports a culture of respect
- Demonstrates accountability by owning company stock

This list is not meant to be exhaustive. The board can add or subtract evaluation criteria based on priorities or initiatives. The process can be performed by an outside consultant, trusted advisor, board chairperson, or governance committee chairperson. The feedback would also be provided to the nominating committee so that they can react, where necessary. The committee might decide it is necessary to pull aside an underperforming director to create and agree upon a correcting action plan. Alternatively, the committee may arrange for specific training, or might simply decide to replace the director. Follow-through is important, as keeping an underperforming director can be a liability to the board.

AND THE CEO

One of the more sensitive governance initiatives conceived is that of the CEO evaluation. Properly embraced, CEO evaluations can continually improve the performance of highly successful managers. More important, it can help a board identify managers who are struggling. A nonreactive, poorly performing CEO can not be removed soon enough. But if objectives and measurable criteria are not established to evaluate the CEO, it is unlikely that action will be taken timely.

Performance evaluation and compensation, in its simplest form, is all about leadership and how to provide incentives to move the company forward. There are informal signs outside of the formal evaluation process that might provide clues regarding a CEO's development needs. In his book *The Five Temptations of a CEO*, Patrick Lencioni distills some of the most common practices that can lead to failure.[5] As he notes, performance and compensation schemes that are designed to overcome some of these practices can also seduce compensation committees. Lencioni describes CEOs who put some-thing other than results as their highest priority, fail to hold subordi-nates accountable, put accuracy over clarity, dampen discord (conflict), and discourage challenges to their ideas, as likely to fail. Understanding these concepts may help a board identify a problem and provide timely counsel to correct behavior.

Those executives whose goals are simply to become CEO are generally unprepared to take over the role. Many of the rock-star CEOs fall into this category. They are great at promoting themselves and the company, but are generally unprepared for the task at hand. If the finish line is ascension to CEO, then there is no plan of what to do once in the chair. Herman Edwards, head coach of the New York Jets, in a 2004 interview after an important loss to a strong Pittsburgh Steelers team, echoed this same concept when he said: "We've got to beat a team like this . . . because if not, what happens to you is if you do get into the playoffs, you're going to lose the first game, you're going to be out. That's not a lot of fun. Why even go? You want to try to win it; you just don't want to get in."[6] The same holds true for successful CEOs; they are not impressed by just being there, they come prepared to play. While they may not yet have a clear picture of the ultimate strategy, they will have a plan of attack on the day they arrive to identify the drivers and issues that will lead to the strategy, and will be able to articulate it. They will be focused and unafraid to tie their own performance to measurable results. Beware the CEO that justifies his own performance while the com-pany is failing. A CEO is hired to lead—and to succeed.

Most people want to be liked. It is simply a human desire. A CEO's job, however, is to ensure that they have the most effective team in place and that they are delivering value for shareholders. CEOs cannot hold subordinates accountable if they let the relative intimacy of these relationships impair judgment. Senior managers deserve honest feedback and need to be held accountable for results. Watch closely the CEO whose management team are close friends.

An anal retentive, yet successful CEO is a rare bird indeed. The reason is that successful CEOs need to prioritize issues and must make decisions with imperfect information. They have a unique capability to quickly assess various risks. Yet some managers will never be comfortable making a decision without input from all pos-sible sources and debating every little point ad nauseum. This can have the effect of bogging down a management team. Your antennae should be tuned for CEOs who seem overly concerned with precision or one who has trouble making decisions despite books full of prepared analytical data.

Lack of candor can lead to severe dysfunction. The emperor may indeed have no clothes, but if conflict is avoided, that lone voice, the one who tells the king he is naked, will never be heard. This outcome can occur at two different behavioral extremes: those executives who dominate discussion and reward conforming views, and those executives who just want everyone to get along. Conflict can be constructive. It is vital that alternative views are heard and debated and that there are no penalties for those who speak up. Those who express their views should be treated with respect. But once a decision is made, the entire team should be expected to do whatever it takes (within ethical and moral boundaries) to successfully implement the decision. Issues may be hotly debated, but once a course of action is agreed upon, these boards move forward rather than stewing over the last vote. United Parcel Service's move from Connecticut to Georgia is held up as an example. The board of the parcel carrier giant vigorously and passionately debated moving their headquarters; but once the decision was made, they were able to unanimously choose a new location and move forward.[7]

Reports generally want to please. Even when the emperor is wearing no clothes, and would like to know about it, his subjects still may remain silent for fear of upsetting him. CEOs must encourage discussion, initially putting aside their own views to hear how others assess an issue. A management team stuffed with yes-men should be a red flag that the executive suite may not be in a healthy place.

In addition to lacking these behavioral attributes, CEOs can also fail due to strategies that move the company away form core competencies or fail to recognize disruptive technologies. Attention to these concepts can be helpful in preparing the formal evaluation. A well-designed, thoughtful feedback program can add tremendous value to an organization: some argue a competitive advantage. It not only helps guide the CEO and the company toward strategic goals, but will also identify areas for improvement so that resources can be marshaled to where they are needed. Finally, a formal process can help a board assess whether they have the right CEO to take the company forward. "Chainsaw" Al Dunlap, the CEO who turned around Scott

Paper by cutting people and expenses, failed with the same approach at Sunbeam. It is not that he had any less skill at Sunbeam; it is because the Sunbeam business model did not lend itself to his same approach. The board eventually realized that they had the wrong skill set for the issues that they faced and fired one of the country's best-known CEOs. The needs of the company should drive who leads the company—not hiring the best-known CEO available.

As noted by Stephen George and Arnold Weimerskirch in *Total Quality Management*, many management experts believe performance appraisals support quality improvement under the following conditions:

- "The performance appraisal must be separate from the compensation system." The focus must be changed to improve performance because it is the right thing to do rather than because it is more profitable for the individual. While performance appraisals should be frequent and separate from the compensation process, this is not to say that chronically poor behavior will not result in reduced incentive compensation or even dismissal. Rather, the processes should be distinct from one another. The idea is to frequently evaluate and redirect undesired behavior and pay based on the achievement of corporate objectives. To underscore this separation, the evaluation is best administered by the governance committee rather than the compensation committee.
- "The performance appraisal must be based on observable, measurable behaviors and results." The identification of key performance indicators should be recognized as important in measuring the health of the corporation as it is in measuring the performance of employees.
- "The performance appraisal must include timely feedback. Annual evaluations are too infrequent to support continuous improvement."
- "The performance appraisal must encourage employee participation." In order for an evaluation to be effective, the CEO must be an active participant in the process.[8]

Goals and actions must be owned by the CEO and encouraged by the board. The SMART acronym has often been used as a guide to developing goals and objectives. They must be Specific, Measurable,

Achievable, Relevant, and Timely to be useful for assessment. By having the CEO work with the board to develop their objectives and perform self-assessments against these goals, the board has an active tool to evaluate and counsel themselves. This continuous feedback loop between the CEO and the board helps ensure that the expectations of the board and management are aligned.

An effective performance evaluation program addresses two broad areas: company results and individual behavior. This program must have clear, measurable attributes that are known to the CEO and are regularly reinforced. Some boards, particularly those who are happy with their CEO, may be reticent to suggest a rigorous evaluation process. But performing CEOs who are secure with themselves welcome the feedback. They appreciate knowing how others perceive them. More important, however, is that the process is implemented for underperforming CEOs. These executives may not even know they are underperforming. The appraisal gives them the opportunity to adjust course. With the exception of illegal behavior, it is likely that there are plenty of opportunities to address performance issues in a positive manner *prior* to dismissing a CEO. If the CEO has to ask why he or she has been fired, then the board has failed in properly counseling and advising the management team. However, if the board has the right indicators, and continuous feedback loops are operating, behavior can be corrected without harm to the company or the CEO. The CEO will know where he or she stands at all times.

The process for evaluating a CEO consists of:

- Agreement on the evaluation process
- Agreement on how to measure performance
- CEO self-evaluation
- Director feedback

Evaluation Process

There is ample evidence that employees take greater ownership and accountability for objectives if they have a hand in developing their own action plan. The CEO and the board should agree the details of evaluation process up front. Issues such as who administers it, will outside facilitators be involved, how often reviews take place, and the format of those reviews should be spelled out. Generally, it is appropriate to set objectives at the beginning of the fiscal year so that corporate objectives agreed by the board can be incorporated. Best practice provides for midyear feedback, even if it is much less formal than the year-end evaluation. If there is transparency between metrics and compensation, and there has been midterm discussions regarding performance, it is likely that the CEO will have a good idea what he or she will receive in the form of variable compensation.

But this view of the performance assessment process is missing an important component of a successful evaluation system, the development of the CEO. Just because CEOs are among the best and brightest, it does not mean that they are perfect managers or leaders without need for good, old-fashioned development. As important as compensation is, forward-thinking boards spend as much, if not more time on development of senior executives as they do on remuneration issues.

Development is much broader than simply evaluating a CEO against performance metrics for compensation purposes and should be performed separately. It speaks to those skills that a CEO needs to better manage and lead, in the process improving stockholder returns and his or her earning power. This is a much softer skill than the compensation process as one has to assess difficult to measure proficiencies such as leadership and strategic thinking.

The creation of a development plan is really no different than those put in place for other important employees. The first step is to identify those competencies that are important to the position. Typical competencies include leadership, vision, execution, integrity, board relations, external communication skills, management development, and economic skills. The committee then must agree on the indicators that evidence competency. For management development, the indicator might be the maintenance of an up to date succession plan for key management positions. The hard work of developing competencies and indicators is vital to bringing credibility to the process. The appraisal must be based on observable behaviors and results, not a gut feel, or after-the-fact identification of examples that support that feeling.

The appraisal must also include timely feedback. It is only fair that the CEO receive a midterm evaluation and, possibly, regular informal feedback. The most successful evaluation processes also include a self appraisal by the CEO. Self-reflection is healthy and assists the director helping the CEO understand the assessment and put it into context. Most CEOs are aware that they are not perfect and have some room for improvement. If the CEO is cognizant and raises a developmental issue, it makes it easier for the board and CEO to agree to a course of action. More important, the identification of a gap between the board's view and the CEO's evaluation can be a goldmine of constructive conflict. Each divergence represents an area where more communication is required to ensure that expectations are clear and fair.

Some experts also believe that direct reports should evaluate the CEO. While there is the potential for better, more detailed feedback, it may be difficult to obtain unbiased and fair criticism. The 360-degree review can be extremely positive, however, it can result in peers and subordinates taking the opportunity to malign managers rather than providing constructive feedback. Clearly, an organization needs to have achieved a certain maturity before embarking on 360-degree reviews. On the flipside, General Electric found that 360-degree evaluations helped them identify and eliminate those managers that "kissed up and kicked down."[9] Over time, however, everyone would say nice things about each other so the 360s lost impact. The relative maturity of the organization may well determine if 360-degree reviews are helpful. The governance committee should select the evaluation team carefully, and may choose to conduct interviews where unconstructive feedback can be challenged.

Performance Measurement

Misdirected executive energy is a disservice to all company shareholders. The engine of corporate growth sputters along without the attention and maintenance it needs to run smoothly. To properly direct energy and influence desired behavior, the CEO's objectives must align with company goals, and metrics must reflect those key performance drivers that lead to successful execution of corporate strategy. It is likely that objectives and evaluation criteria have already been developed from the company's competitive strategy process, a controlled method implemented to report results and benchmarks established. If the company has defined its business drivers, tying them to CEO evaluation is a straight-forward endeavor. But identifying the drivers, as difficult as that may be, is the easy part. The CEO and the board must then agree on the target or benchmark against which progress is measured. For example, say that a mid-cap oil company understands that the major oil companies only want high production fields and so they have developed a strategy to buy properties at a low cost that have already been worked and exploit them cheaply until exhausted. Also assume that management and the board agree that the environment is ripe to increase oil reserves in a cost-effective manner. There are several metrics that can be used to assess effectiveness. Total reserves, cost per barrel of known reserves, and cost to deliver a barrel of oil to market are a few metrics that come to mind. The CEO may indicate that he or she will increase reserves by 25 percent. This is a measurable goal, but one that could be easily accomplished if the company overpays for reserves or simply changes its method for calculating reserves. A better measurement might be a 25 percent increase in reserves from new sources at an acquisition cost at or below today's cost (or other benchmark). The benchmark for these metrics can be set today, and easily measured at the end of next year. The board needs to work with the CEO to flesh out fair performance measurements that create the right behaviors.

But the achievement of immediate corporate objectives is only one category that should be considered in an overall CEO evaluation. Additional categories typically include personal goals, stock performance, leadership qualities, succession planning, management of key constituencies (i.e., regulators, institutional investors, unions, etc.), and the press. Obviously, some of these categories are harder to measure than others because they are more qualitative than quantitative. However, better measurement leads to more effective evaluation, so it is worth discussing and agreeing what is meant by "good leadership" and developing metrics or planning activities that will add to this objective.

CEO Self-Evaluation and Director Feedback

It is interesting to note that some boards conduct an evaluation of their CEO without asking them to conduct a self-evaluation. This just makes the job that much harder. The completion of the CEO's self-evaluation at the end of the fiscal year is the first step in the evaluation process. This is the opportunity for CEOs to tell their story, explain achievements, or even why certain objectives were not achieved. The beauty of self-evaluations is that executives who participate honestly will often raise their shortcomings so that the board will not have to. This creates an opportunity to create a positive and healthy dialog with the CEO that will address deficiencies in a constructive manner.

The next step in an effective CEO evaluation is for the facilitator or director leading the appraisal process to solicit feedback from other members of the board. The board should be evaluating the executive on the same categories and metrics used by CEOs to conduct their self-evaluation. The facilitator and/or director can then compile the results into a summary that compares the CEO's self-evaluation to the combined evaluation of the board. The difficult part is sitting down with the CEO to discuss the results.

The person chosen to lead the evaluation process must be a trusted and respected director. The addition of a facilitator will help bring objectivity and a sense of fairness to the process. The director and the facilitator (if there is one, if not a second trusted director) should sit down with the CEO to discuss the results and develop an action plan for correcting any deficiencies identified. These plans can be rolled into the objectives for the coming year and the process starts over. A summary report should be given to the full board that communicates any follow-up actions or new objectives for the coming year.

The success of this process turns on the board's commitment to the process. The board must take the time to properly outline the process and identify key performance indicators. They must also be willing to act on the results. CEOs should know where they stand, and receive specific counsel on how to improve their performance. A high-performing board will provide frequent feedback and create an atmosphere allowing a CEO to excel. Whether the CEO takes advantage of the opportunity is up to them. Yet the board will have failed in their duties if a CEO is surprised by his termination. Those that accept constructive criticism and guidance have the best prospects for optimizing executive performance and creating sustained corporate operating excellence.

Given the emotion that is associated with CEO evaluations, most organizations are too insecure to make their process public.

Fortunately, Champion Enterprises is not one of these companies. Appendix D features an example of a Champion Enterprises' CEO performance evaluation tool. They have kindly provided us permission to reprint it as an example that we can learn and draw from.

NEXT! SUCCESSION PLANNING

The National Association of Corporate Directors (NACD) reports that over 50 percent of companies with revenues in excess of $500 million do not have a meaningful succession plan. This is a failure of monumental proportions and helps explain ever-escalating CEO compensation. Companies have not bothered to develop the next generation of C-level managers. The reasons for not developing the next generation of C-level managers run the gamut from senior management paranoia to plain lack of focus. This is particularly damaging to a company that has to search externally for a CEO's successor. Those CEOs raised internally are more likely to be successful than those who come from the outside. According to Booz, Allen & Hamilton, only 34 percent of departing North American CEOs sourced internally were forced to resign compared to 55 percent for those recruited from the outside.[10]

The pitfalls of poor succession planning and the benefits of doing it right can be compared and contrasted by the experiences of CBS and the New England Patriots, respectively. Arguably, the nightly news anchors at the three largest television networks create and define their marketplace image. While not the top job at these companies, it is the most visible. Given its importance, you would think much senior management time would be spent planning for the unthinkable—the unavailability of their anchor. While NBC seems to have considered this possibility and has seamlessly transitioned their anchor position from Tom Brokaw to Brian Williams, CBS seems lost at sea, initially tapping Bob Schieffer as "interim anchor" to replace Dan Rather. The planning seems to have paid off for NBC as, according to Nielson Media Research, they continued to have the most watched news cast for three months following Williams taking the anchor chair. This has to be a source of pride for the network. Alternatively, think how internal candidates at CBS must feel while names from other networks to replace Rather are bandied about. The inability of CBS to permanently settle on an anchor weakens its image and could destabilize its bullpen.

On the other end of the succession planning spectrum is New England Patriots coach Bill Belicheck, who believes that football games are won before the game is even played. It has been reported that Belicheck, as early as training camp, was concerned about the shallowness of the defensive secondary on his depth chart, despite having strong players at those positions. He had a wide receiver that had some cornerback experience, so Belicheck provided him defensive backfield exposure during team practices. The move saved the Patriot's season when two defensive backs were lost to injury. The wide receiver stepped into the defensive secondary and not only held his own, but intercepted three passes during the season, which was the second highest on the team.[11] Despite the loss during the season of two highly rated starting defensive backs, the Patriots went on to win the Super Bowl. The performance of the defense was superb and validated the effectiveness of Belicheck's planning.

In the corporate world, the governance committee should assist the board in long-range succession planning to ensure that internal candidates are developed and that the company is prepared for the unthinkable. Potential internal candidates should be discussed with the CEO and a development plan for each candidate prepared. The committee should also work with the CEO to prepare an emergency response to sudden death or disability of the CEO or senior managers.

As presented earlier in Chapter 3, the fast-food giant McDonald's has benefited mightily from having a comprehensive succession plan. The world's largest restaurant chain suddenly lost its CEO to a heart attack in April 2004. The board implemented their succession plan by naming Charles Bell as CEO. But less than five months later, Mr. Bell resigned in a failed effort to fight his colon cancer. The board was again in a position to implement a succession plan and immediately named a successor, James Skinner. For most companies, such turmoil in the executive suite would, at best, cause corporate paralysis. But McDonald's had a focused strategy that was well known by the entire organization, thereby enabling the company to not only continually execute, but thrive. McDonald's has added more health-conscious and light items to its menu that resulted in a sustained rise in sales. Succession planning at McDonald's was not the result of a board meeting at which names were simply filled in a depth chart. The company spent decades developing its management team and, even with the losses recently experienced, has tremendous bench strength. McDonald's investors have been rewarded by the diligent planning and development of management talent by the board and farsighted executives of the past.[12] A year after losing their first CEO, the company reported a 42 percent increase in net income.

Arguably, General Electric has one of the most well-developed human resource programs found anywhere. Its historic focus on identifying, developing, and rewarding the top 20 percent of its people—and counseling the bottom 10 percent out of the company—has resulted in tremendous managerial bench strength. This was made abundantly clear when Jack Welch turned over the reigns of General Electric to Jeffery Immelt. At the time, there were two other candidates who could have also easily taken over the company: Bob Nardelli and Jim McNerney. The two "runners-up" became CEOs at Home Depot and 3M, respectively. There are very few other companies that have this much talent and have no difficulty choosing an heir from their internal pool. And these individuals were not the only CEO careers launched from General Electric: Larry Bossidy of Allied Signal and John Blystone of SPX also come to mind.

Importantly, six months before naming Immelt to succeed him, Welch had each candidate identify and develop their replacement. It was clear to Welch that the two that did not get the top job would leave, so succession planning for all three candidates was priority one.[13] By naming the new CEOs of each business before the CEO of the company, Welch helped stabilize the company by transitioning the leadership of key business units to make them impervious to fallout from the final selection.

As experienced at General Electric, thoughtful succession planning is all about management development. A robust development program allows CEO candidates to be identified and observed over long periods of time. The board better understands the strengths and weaknesses of CEO candidates and their level of preparedness. A strong development program has a secondary benefit of keeping directors involved and communicating with top managers. This engagement helps to break down some of the structural barriers between the board and the CEO's reports. Therefore, the board is better positioned to learn of issues as they surface.

FINDING THAT PERFECT DIRECTOR

*Trying to figure out who you want on the board of any
company—and how you are going to get those individuals
to fulfill the board mandate more effectively—has probably
been the single most important question facing corporate
governance over the last five years as we've seen breakdown
after breakdown.*[14]

—Eliot Spitzer

There have been few changes in governance as dramatic as how
we populate our boards. In past years, director selection consisted of
CEOs deciding who they would like to serve, and that would be the
person nominated. This guaranteed that a CEO would be able to
work with their board, but it also made constructive dissent unlikely.
Over the last few years, director recruiting has become much more
professional. Some of the larger, more prestigious executive search
firms have built an entire practice around finding quality directors.
This has become more difficult as the pool of qualified candidates
constricts. One of the unanticipated effects of the Sarbanes-Oxley
Act is that the amount of time a director spends on oversight has substantially increased. A typical director will spend four to six weeks on
board duties. CEOs have limited their board participation due to the
increased time commitment. Compounding the problem, some companies are restricting the number of boards, if any, that their CEO
can join. These forces have dramatically reduced the number of outside boards on which a CEO will sit from 1.6 to 0.9 in just five
years.[15] Governance nominating committees are retaining search
firms to help them overcome these obstacles with an objective
process that will yield quality candidates.

Adding to the need for a formalized nomination process is that
the SEC now requires the company disclose in its proxy statement
such information as:

- Whether the company has a standing nominating or similar committee
- If it has a charter and where to find it (if not available on a company website, then the charter itself must be published in the
  proxy once every three years)

- If the members of the committee are independent
- A description of the procedure for shareholders to recommend a director candidate and the material elements of any policy for considering such candidates
- Minimum qualifications candidates must meet and specific qualities and skills necessary for one or more of the directors to possess
- A description of the nominating process for identifying and evaluating candidates
- The source of a nominated candidate
- Disclosure of paid outside advisors and search firms utilized to identify or evaluate potential nominees

If the company lacks a nominating committee, shareholder nomination processes, formal nominating procedures, and so on, then the company must explain why in the proxy statement. There is also a disclosure requirement concerning large shareholders. (This and the other disclosure requirements are discussed in Chapter 14.)

Julie Daum, the Managing Director of the North American Board Services Practice of Spencer Stuart, a worldwide leader in director recruitment, has worked with many of the nation's governance committees to implement a sound search process. She believes that best practices are still developing, but there have been four important transformations of the nomination process thus far. The most significant change is that CEOs are no longer driving the nomination process. By and large, nominating or governance committees have ownership and work with the CEO in a collaborative way. The second noteworthy modification is the process employed. The chair of the governance committee wants a formal, documented process to ensure the best candidates surface. In addition, nomination procedures are now included in the proxy statement. Directors are reaching out for help from internal staff, such as the head of human resources or the general counsel, to administer the search. Because there are so many more people involved in a search, responsibilities and roles must be clearly defined. The third difference is the type of individual recruited. The CEOs' preferred candidate will be another CEO from a bigger company, while boards will consider a more diverse candidate population, says Daum. Finally, there is more inclusion in the interview process. In the past, only one candidate may have been considered with the decision made by the CEO. Now, not only will directors interview a number of candidates, but the candidates themselves will conduct more due diligence by insisting on speaking to a number of people on the board and others associated with the company. For instance, a candidate for the audit committee will, at a minimum, want to interview the external auditor and the company's CFO.

Outside firms can provide helpful, objective advice and aid the nominating committee in settling upon a nomination process. Spencer Stuart's preferred generic director search outline is shown in Exhibit 7.1.

Designing a nomination process normally occurs only once, with possible adjustment over time as duties are refined. To create a process that stands the test of time, much thought regarding who participates at each stage is required. Besides the nominating or governance committee, human resources, the corporate secretary, or general counsel may also support the process. At some point, the CEO is consulted and the nomination approved by the full board. The board must also decide how they will make the decisions to renominate directors. These details need to be established and documented up front.

The next step is to evaluate the board composition in relation to the mix of skills desired by the board. The committee should have authorization to evaluate the independence, contributions, and effectiveness of directors through a formal appraisal process when deciding their renomination. This also includes the director's contribution,

---

1. Design a selection process and communicate it to all involved parties
2. Assess the board's needs
3. Develop a director specification
4. Decide whether to hire an executive search firm
5. Create a long list of board prospects from a wide range of inputs
6. Review the long list for any kind of potential conflicts
7. Narrow the long list to a short list
8. Research the prospects on the short list
9. Design and conduct a thorough interview process
10. Extend an offer

EXHIBIT 7.1 Spencer Stuart Generic Director Search Outline
Source: Data originally published in "The New Steps of Director Search." Copyright 2004 Spencer Stuart. Used by permission.

attendance, preparation, committee and board criteria, management feedback, and the current makeup of the board. Based on the company's needs and other factors such as retirements, term limits, and the outcome of director evaluations, a decision will have to be made whether to conduct a search. Assuming it is decided that a new director is desired, the committee prepares and recommends to the board written criteria for director selection. Candidates should address any skill gaps identified during the evaluation of the board's skills inventory.

The complexity of most businesses makes it difficult for a director to understand all facets of a company and contribute meaningfully to all issues coming to the board. Therefore, it is important that the board select individuals with complementary expertise. Perhaps additional financial, internal control, or marketing knowledge is desired. The functional criteria can be used as a first cut. Obviously, the composition of the board should also contain a blend of experiences. Diversity in gender, age, race, nationality, and so on, from any number of sources can create a board rich in perspective. While most boards focus on experience and the resumé as reflected by functional criteria, Daum suggests that qualities such as judgment, strategic thinking, and consensus building are most important. These qualities are often unrelated to experience and hard to identify. Generally the only way to determine if a candidate has these qualities is by talking with others who have worked with the person in a similar setting. Other important director criteria include integrity, commitment, objectivity, and independence. Without these qualities, even the smartest candidate cannot properly serve shareholders. Once the director criteria has been prepared and approved, the board is then ready to conduct a thorough search.

The question of what search firm to use for director vacancies, if any, should be determined by the board rather than the CEO. Executive recruiters retained by the board not only bring some objectivity and credibility to the search, they are also able to cast a wide net, accessing nontraditional sources for desired skills. This can be critical as the pool of qualified candidates continues to shrink. They can also help the board focus on candidate characteristics that will provide the best cultural fit. Best practice would also dictate that the board publicly disseminate director criteria so that shareholders can nominate candidates under the same standards as board-generated candidates. The receipt of the nomination should be acknowledged and the stockholders kept updated and informed regarding the determination of the candidate.

You do not want to bring on a director only to find out that he or she does not meet the independence criteria. So once a list of candidates has been prepared, conflicts checks must be performed. This includes an analysis of self-reported disclosures made by the candidates as well as searching other sources. Tools such as the Corporate Library's interlock tool might prove helpful for this task. The interlocking tool graphically maps known relationships between directors and organizations. References are then checked for short-list candidates and structured interviews conducted. At this point, most boards involve their CEO in the interview process to make certain they have a voice in the final selection. Ultimate responsibility for selecting the director, however, should rest with the board, in consultation with the CEO, based on the search criteria, personal style, and cultural fit. Together with the search firm, the board can then make an offer that is both competitive and reflects the risk and effort of serving on the board and related committees.

But the process does not end here. Just as the competitive landscape of business is always changing, potentially, so might the status of a director's independence. The governance committee could be called on at any time to reassess a director's fitness to serve. A change in a director's primary job, acceptance to another board, or notification of a possible conflict require an automatic review of the director's suitability to continue serving. These procedures, and what triggers them, should also be prepared and agreed by the board. A predefined, objective process is easier to initiate if it is seen as standard operating procedure. A board does not want to be in a position of creating a process when a director is most vulnerable, otherwise they may feel singled out, the victim of a witch-hunt. If the procedure is clear and known to all, a director will realize that the board is objectively performing their duty.

IS THE STRATEGY STILL VALID?

Over the past two years, boards have been busy contemplating the requirements of the Sarbanes-Oxley Act and complying with new governance initiatives. The importance of the board's oversight responsibilities cannot be understated, however, directors are also advisors. Arguably, the director's role as advisor may be the most important contribution to the company and its shareholders. To not mine the collective business experience and judgment available to the company would be wrong. But meetings are packed with presentations and information, and if the board has been overly focused on the Sarbanes-Oxley Act, these meetings are generally not the place to call the entire corporate strategy into question. In general, board meetings should be a tool for directors to monitor on-going execution of the company's strategy.

Even before the passage of the Sarbanes-Oxley Act, the only times strategy matters would normally be questioned is when there is turnover in the CEO suite, financial objectives are not realized by a wide margin, or there is merger or takeover activity. Directors who ignore this protocol risk being isolated, and cannot be effective advocates for their shareholder constituency. Yet directors are expected to serve with independence, objectivity, and a modicum of skepticism on behalf of shareholders. What was at one time a brilliant strategy may no longer be relevant if the competitive landscape has changed. If an individual board member has concerns about the strategy, it needs to be raised. The ability of directors to openly discuss important issues without raising the ire of management and other board members is a critical cultural value.

One solution put forward by Harvard's Gordon Donaldson is a regular review that evaluates the effectiveness of the current strategy against expected results. A regularly scheduled strategic audit produces the oversight required while still recognizing management's authority and execution responsibilities. As a regular discussion item, strategy is assessed by the entire board rather than just by management or a rogue director. It is a process instead of an attack on management and will bolster credibility.[16]

Developing a strategy is clearly the responsibility of management. They are closer to the business, better understand the competition, and are uniquely positioned to recognize the company's strengths and weaknesses. However, the board can bring their years of experience to bear on the pros and cons of management's strategies and possibly surface issues or alternative approaches not previously considered.

Healthy boards will participate in a collaborative process in forming the strategy, help establish the metrics to monitor execution, and evaluate the effectiveness of the strategy from time to time. A regularly scheduled strategy audit or "clean slate" retreat can bring the entire board and management team together to help to reset or refocus the strategy through a collaborative process. This is much preferable to an isolated director proposing a new strategy that could be perceived as a very threatening action.

The governance/nominating committee is the linchpin in the organizing to lead model. It performs much of the board's "heavy lifting." The structure and smooth operations of the board; director nominations; board, director, and CEO evaluations are impacted by the competency and work ethic of the governance committee. While the audit committee is best staffed by individuals with financial expertise, the governance committee benefits from members possessing strong process and personnel skills. A well-staffed and functioning committee allows the board to function effortlessly and focus more of its time on business issues.

KEY CONCEPTS

- Monitor the governance rating provided by ISS, CalPERS, GMI, and others provided for your company. These metrics, combined with periodic governance audits, can identify areas for board improvement or reinforce that best practices are operational.
- Formalize the process for conducting annual board evaluations. Implement controls to contain litigation risk, allowing for an effective review.
- Agree on board objectives, timing and administration of evaluations, and feedback mechanics with the board at the beginning of the year.
- Conduct director evaluations to redirect or reinforce behaviors and include a self-evaluation.
- Formally evaluate CEOs (include a CEO self-evaluation) and agree on a development plan.

- Agree on the CEO appraisal process, timing, and administrative responsibilities with the CEO and the board in advance.
- CEO objectives should also include a development component.
- Ensure that objective setting and appraisals are SMART (Specific, Measurable, Achievable, Relevant, and Timely).
- CEOs sourced internally are more successful and the board should make certain that a viable succession plan is continually nurtured. A viable succession plan could be implemented today if necessary.
- Link succession planning to a talent retention strategy for the best and brightest. Take the time to meet top managers.
- Make certain that succession planning oversight has an "owner" on the board, either a director, directors, or the governance committee.
- Independent directors control the director nomination process, with input from the CEO.
- Consider director candidates recommended by shareholders under the same criteria as board sourced candidates.
- Develop director candidate criteria from the needs of the board.
- Qualified director candidates willing to serve are becoming scarce. This can be overcome by the retention of a search firm that should be hired by, and report to the board.
- A regularly scheduled review or audit can address strategy concerns in a nonthreatening way.
- To avoid the perception of a witch-hunt, develop predefined events that would trigger a reassessment of a director's fitness to serve.
- Knowledgeable directors can reduce board liability. Make sure that the board has a viable director development program.
- Directors need access to information. Periodic updates between meetings and the receipt of board materials well in advance of a meeting help achieve this objective.
- To prevent misinterpretation of board actions, unofficial drafts, notes, and other board materials are collected and disposed of after the formal minutes are finalized under a routine record retention policy.

ENDNOTES

1. National Association of Corporate Directors, "Learn More about the NACD," *NACD Online.* <http://www.nacdonline .org/nacd/default.asp?user=036C24854999451DAFC28A49D7 28009B (25 March 2005).

2. Securities and Exchange Commission, *In the Matter of Caterpillar Inc.*, Administrative Proceeding File No. 3-7692, Exchange Act Rel. No. 30532, Accounting and Auditing Enforcement Rel. No. 363, March 31, 1992.

3. Bruce M. Taten and Robert Barker, "Ways to Reduce Risk in Board Evaluations," *Directors & Boards* 25 (Spring 2004): 21–25.

4. David A. Nadler, "Building Better Boards," *Harvard Business Review* 82 (May 2004): 102–111.

5. Patrick M. Lencioni, *Five Temptations of a CEO: A Leadership Fable* (San Francisco: Jossey-Bass, 1998).

6. Richard Lezin Jones, "Jets Inspiring Little Faith In Their Fate," *New York Times*, 14 December 2004, D1.

7. Jeffrey A. Sonnenfeld, "What Makes Great Boards Great," *Harvard Business Review* 80 (September 2002): 109.

8. Stephen George and Arnold Weimerskirch, *Total Quality Management*, 2nd ed. (New York: John Wiley & Sons, 1998).

9. Jack Welch, *Jack Straight from the Gut*, (New York: Warner Books, 2001), 157.

10. Ram Charan, "Ending the CEO Succession Crisis," *Harvard Business Review* 83 (February 2005): 74.

11. Damon Hack, "For Patriots' Coach, War Is Won or Lost Before Game Begins," *New York Times*, 3 February 2005, A1.

12. Leslie Wayne and Eric Dash, "Citing Cancer, Chief Resigns at McDonald's," *New York Times*, 23 November 2004, C1.

13. Welch, 415.

14. Louise O'Brien, "The HBR Interview: Eliot Spitzer: How to Restore the Fiduciary Relationship," *Harvard Business Review* 82 (May 2004): 70–77.

15. Spencer Stuart, *Spencer Stuart Board Index 2004*, 7.

16. Gordon Donaldson, *A New Tool for Boards: The Strategic Audit*, (Boston: Harvard Business School Press, 2000), 53–78.

CHAPTER 8

Other Committees to Have and to Avoid

Every company has particular needs that may be industry driven, culturally related, or determined by the economic environment. Where the risk of not meeting these needs significantly endangers the company, the board needs to make certain that they have the information and processes necessary to monitor them. At times, oversight is best performed by a committee of the board. In this chapter, we evaluate committees, other than audit, compensation, and governance that are popular with some boards.

WHERE HAVE ALL OF THE EXECUTIVE COMMITTEES GONE?

Beware of boards with executive committees. Not only are some of the historic duties redundant with the new responsibilities of the governance and compensation committees, but these benign-looking councils can result in two classes of directors. These super directors often meet and make decisions on behalf of the full board. Everyone else is informed of those decisions at the next regularly scheduled board meeting. Indeed, when this is the case, it is not unusual for the executive committee, usually lead by the CEO, to set the board's real agenda to achieve preestablished results. As of the end of 2003, over 47 percent of companies had executive committees, however, most boards are reexamining the need for them.[1]

Walter Salmon, the Stanley Roth Sr. Professor of Retailing, Emeritus at the Harvard Business School (and, in the interest of full disclosure, a former professor of the author) has served on a number of boards, including Neiman Marcus Group, Hannaford Brothers

Company, and Circuit City Stores. In an article truly ahead of its time published over a decade ago in the *Harvard Business Review*, Salmon states, "The reason [for not recommending an augmented role] is that executive committees with too much muscle, by encouraging the emergence of two-tiered boards, are obstacles rather than aids to better corporate governance."[2] Professor Salmon was, and still is, exactly right.

Some governance experts believe that there is a valid role for an executive committee. They argue that such committees can handle routine business between board meetings and serve as an advisory committee to the CEO. Others argue that executive committees are productive when there is emergency business such as a tender offer for shares of the company. In these circumstances, there is much hard work to be done, and the executive committee can perform that work on behalf of the full board. Finally, some believe that executive committees become the recognized body of independent directors because new rules require that independent directors meet in executive session, without management, on a periodic basis.

A potential director should think twice before serving on a board that has an active executive committee. If one exists, understand its charter and what it is empowered to do. A nonoperational committee designed to come to life in emergencies, and then only with limited powers, might be acceptable—as would a committee consisting solely of the outside directors. However, in today's world, with directors understanding their responsibilities and exposure related to board service, one would expect independent directors to reject the creation of an executive committee. It is just plain dangerous to empower others with decisions that put your reputation and wealth on the line. With rare exception, the interconnected world of Blackberrys and cell phones makes it relatively easy to organize a quorum for an emergency or to conduct business between meetings. Additionally, if there is a true emergency that requires the substantial participation of certain directors, an ad hoc committee can be empowered by the board to work on their behalf.

REEMERGENCE OF FINANCE COMMITTEES

Recently I was invited to participate in a corporate governance conference at Hofstra University cosponsored by the schools of law and business. The conference bore the title "The Changed World of

Corporate Governance," and, among many distinguished experts, were luminaries such as Norman Veasey, the retired Chief Justice of the Delaware Supreme Court; Marty Lipton of Wachtell, Lipton Rosen and Katz; John Coffee of the Columbia University School of Law, with the keynote address offered by SEC Commissioner Harvey Goldschmid. After all of the interesting subjects were assigned, I was asked to speak on the subject of finance committees. Not exactly a headliner, but a role I immediately embraced. Finance committees have been ignored in recent discussions and it was a good time to consider their place in the governance framework.

My research revealed what I suspected, that finance committees were in decline. The need for active audit, compensation, and governance committees had overshadowed the need for finance committees. While a June 2003 study by the National Association of Corporate Directors found that 36 percent of the 5,000 companies polled had a finance committee, many had combined these duties with other working groups such as the audit committee. But audit committees are now becoming overburdened as a result of the many governance reforms stemming from the Sarbanes-Oxley Act. As I dug into my subject, I learned that many companies still rely heavily on their finance committees and, at one time, they were the critical glue that kept public companies together. In fact, the stagflation and high interest rates of the late 1970s and early 1980s tested the ability of these boards to manage company liquidity.

Many companies still benefit from the expertise a finance committee can bring. Companies with complex financial structures (like many large insurance companies), significant market exposure (such as investment banks), high growth rates requiring outside financing (such as Dell), continuing capital intensive investments (like the glass plant investments experience by Corning, Inc.) or companies that maintain minority investments in a number of independent companies with emerging technologies (such as Cisco), all reap benefits from the functional process and oversight their finance committees provide. Some of the financially intensive work that these committees perform include:

- Approving and monitoring the return on material capital investments
- Oversight of stress testing and securing sources of liquidity
- Evaluating dividend and share repurchase policy
- Assessing long-term versus short-term debt offerings

- Interest rate and currency exposure
- Dealing with problems such as exaggerated business cycle volatility

The work surrounding these issues can be intensive and should not be tasked to an already over-burdened audit committee. These issues either require the focus of a separate committee, or the entire board.

Some companies and boards are too small to benefit from finance committees. These boards can easily handle the financial require- ments of the organization. What is important for these companies is that they have adequate financial expertise on their board. Finance committees should not be created just to check a governance box. The need must be assessed and, where required, the committee created.

Not long after the conference, I received calls from journalists to expound on the role finance committees play—and from participants asking for copies of my presentation. One headline in the *Dow Jones Corporate Newsletter* read: "Finance Committees Re-Emerging As Best Practice." It seems that forward-thinking directors recognize that as things change, the more they stay the same. These committees were originally set up for a reason, and smart directors evaluate whether it makes sense for their company to have one. Not all com- panies benefit, but for others, it can be a vital function.

WHEN PUBLIC POLICY, SAFETY, AND RESEARCH ARE DRIVERS

A number of companies recognize the complexity of doing business in countries around the world, each with their own rules and regula- tions requiring special oversight. General Motors, for example, maintains a public policy committee in addition to their governance, compensation, audit, and investment committees. The purpose of the public policy committee is to bring to the attention of the board "cur- rent and emerging political, social, and public policy issues that may affect the business operations, performance, or public image of the company." This includes topics such as "automotive safety, environ- mental matters, government relations, diversity, corporate social responsibility, education, communications, employee health and safety, trade, and philanthropic activities."[3]

It seems that a company doing business in every corner of the world—and making a product targeted by environmentalists as a source of global warming—would be wise to have an ongoing dialog with policy makers and environmentalists. Such a dialog would better position the company to respond to concerns as they arise. The board would also want to make sure that policies are in place to prevent the poisoning of the environment, which could result in a massive future liability. As Ben Franklin said, "An ounce of prevention is worth a pound of cure." General Motors's board is protecting shareholders by emphasizing oversight of these risk areas.

As discussed in Chapter 3, Rinker Group Limited, one of the world's largest heavy building materials companies, has established, in addition to their audit, remuneration, and nominating committees, a safety, health, and environment committee. Focusing oversight in this critical area is only logical for a company exposing employees to greater than normal health risks. Management perceived as uncaring of employees can be a target for labor unrest that results in materially higher labor costs, fines, and penalties.

Pfizer Inc., the pharmaceutical giant, has a Science and Technology Committee to oversee the company's investments in research and development, as well as technology initiatives. The existence of this committee represents corporate recognition of research as a driver of future profitability in this industry.

A company's operating environment is forever changing. As such, boards need to periodically assess important stakeholders and make a determination if they are receiving appropriate attention. Areas that are deemed to contain material risk to the company must be monitored by the board. If such an area is identified, but not monitored, the board may wish to set up a committee to address this gap. It may be an environmental committee for a forestry company, or a safety committee for a steel mill. Regardless, the formation of the committee sends a signal to stakeholders regarding the importance placed on the subject by the board.

ADDRESSING SPECIAL OCCASIONS

From time to time, certain issues may be raised that cannot be adequately resolved at a regular board meeting. Rather than truncating discussion, or allowing the board to be tangled in never-ending debate, the board may want to appoint a special committee to evaluate the issue. The benefit of the special committee is that it does not rush an important decision, rather allows the board to bring appropriate attention to the issue at hand without making management overly defensive. The committee can bring whatever resources it needs to bear to quickly study and report their findings back to the board.

The use of special committees can also be effective for bet-the-company type decisions, issues requiring special expertise, or in those rare instances where the board might have to investigate its own management as was the case at Enron. The flipside is that committees without a well-defined mandate can encroach on management's responsibilities and create tension. Technology or productivity are areas ripe for crossing the line into management of the company and should be avoided unless there is a specific ad hoc issue that the board would like to address.

CASE STUDY: SHORT-TERM PROFITS ARE FOOL'S GOLD

Newmont Mining Corporation is the world's largest gold producer with significant assets or operations on five continents. The company employs approximately 14,000 people worldwide and markets themselves as being "committed to the highest standards for environmental management, health and safety for its employees and neighboring communities."[a] Newmont is also on the record as claiming that it upholds U.S. environmental standards when doing business abroad. In fact, the company website prominently displays a section on social responsibility policy where they proclaim:

> Newmont's future is dependent on its ability to develop, operate, and close mines consistent with our commitment to sustainable development, protection of human life, health, the environment, and to adding value to the communities in which we operate.[b]

The company, however, is currently undergoing a crisis that will put the veracity of their corporate value statement on the line. It was recently revealed that their operations on the Indonesian island of Sulawesi have dispersed 17 tons of mercury into the air and 16 tons into the Buyat Bay. There are accusations that the facility operated, even though the scrubbers designed to remove mercury from the facility's emissions were not working. This would result in dispensing mercury into the atmosphere in quantities far above established standards. There are also claims that mercury and arsenic from the facility have entered the bay's food chain. The local population is experiencing maladies such as chest pains, dizziness, numbness, and cramps. Exposure to mercury can be particularly hazardous for fetal development and children who may develop learning disabilities from neurological damage.[c]

Previous to these recent claims, Newmont was recognized as working with regulators to reduce emissions at its Nevada operation. There is also evidence that the company punished certain managers monetarily for a roadside mercury spill in Peru, thus enforcing its commitment to the environment. However, the company's reputation is now tainted. According to the *New York Times*, a 2001 internal memo from a senior executive suggests that senior executives should forego bonuses for claiming publicly that they were meeting U.S. standards, when in fact they were not.

Newmont's problems have already impacted business. The company had to forego expanding a mine in Peru due to local protests in the wake of the mercury spill there. Company executives are now facing criminal charges in Indonesia. To compound matters, there are concerns about the company's operations in Turkey and Uzbekistan. What will be the response of governments worldwide if Newmont comes to them with a proposal for a new mine? My guess is that the reception would be chilly.

If not already deeply involved, Newmont's board should be monitoring the company's efforts to address these issues. Every scrubber worldwide should be independently inspected, emissions and effluent mercury levels tested, and procedures for disposing of mercury reviewed. Results should be reported directly to the board and an action plan put in place to address gaps. The board should make it clear that compensation will be impacted by achievement of the plan's objectives. Then the board should independently corroborate the results. The company did take a step in the right direction by providing a doctor for primary care for the people of Buyat Bay. The opportunity to create goodwill seems to have been lost, however, as the doctor is perceived by the community as lacking independence, which only fans local suspicion of the company. If they have not already considered it, funding an independent health clinic for the residents of Buyat Bay would also illustrate the company's concern for their neighbors and help repair their reputation. There is evidence that management has been aware of certain failures for some time now, and they may be rationalizing their response given the cost to address these problems. But in the long term, doing the right thing is good for business and for the shareholders—and may warrant the removal of selected executives to make this important point.

---

[a]Newmont Mining Corporation, "Newmont: The Gold Company," *Newmont.com.* http://www .newmont.com/en/ (8 April 2005).
[b]Newmont Mining Corporation, "Social Responsibility Policy," *Newmont.com.* http://www .newmont.com/en/social/index.asp (8 April 2005).
[c]Perlez, Jane, "Mining Giant Told It Put Toxic Vapors Into Indonesia's Air," *New York Times*, 22 December 2004, A1.

KEY CONCEPTS

- Avoid boards with Executive Committees unless it serves as a vessel for all independent directors.
- Finance committees have been on the decline, but add value to companies with complex financial structures, significant financial market exposure, high-growth rates requiring external funding, continuing capital intensive investment, or a significant number of joint-venture arrangements.
- Specific company or industry issues may best be supervised by creating a committee. Safety, public policy, and environment are drivers that might best be addressed by an oversight committee.
- Special committees can be used to study certain issues so that the board does not get bogged down in the analysis.

ENDNOTES

1. Spencer Stuart, *Spencer Stuart Board Index 2003*, 11.
2. Walter J. Salmon, "Crisis Prevention, How to Gear Up Your Board," *Harvard Business Review* 71 (January–February 1993): 68–83.
3. General Motors Corporation, "General Motors Corporation Public Policy Committee Charter," *GM.com*, 5 May 2003. http://www.gm.com/company/investor_information/docs/corp_gov/ppc_charter.pdf (8 April 2005).

Insist on
High Standards

The greatest gamble a potential director can take is to join the board of a company that does not take culture seriously. You can get everything else right, but if the culture is not sound, trouble is just around the corner. Look at CUC International, which was acquired by Cendant in 1997. The culture was rotten, demonstrated by the 22 people it took to achieve a $500 million financial fraud that even Cendant's due diligence did not discover. The pressure to make the numbers triumphed over all moral and ethical considerations. Do you think CUC's board would have liked to know about these pressures? One guess is that they would have. Had a strong message of what is acceptable been repeatedly communicated and reinforced and numerous whistle-blower notification systems been available, the board might have had a fighting chance. The hard work of achieving high-impact governance must include insisting on

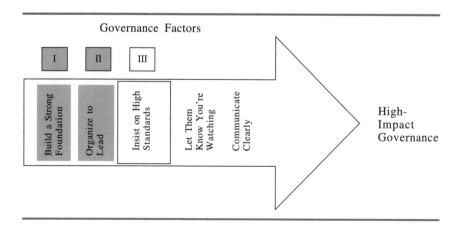

Governance Factors

I II III

Build a Strong Foundation

Organize to Lead

Insist on High Standards

Let Them Know You're Watching

Communicate Clearly

High-Impact Governance

high cultural standards—from the board as well as the company. Culture is the factor most overlooked, often viewed as a soft subject not worthy of rigorous analysis. In reality it is a primary factor that, properly addressed, enables a company to overcome a number of governance sins. Get culture right before anything else, and the director has done the shareholders a service.

For Chapters 9 and 10, we focus on culture, first at the corporate level and then the culture of effective boards.

CHAPTER 9

Hard Work of Building Corporate Values

While no one likes to admit it, organizations completely devoid of ethical behavior can be financially successful for long periods of time. One only has to consider the success of the illicit drug trade. However, where public companies are concerned, creating a culture of positive shared values can lead to profitable competitive advantages. Companies that have "the right stuff" find it easier to adjust to competitive threats and are less likely to be surprised by ethical lapses that threaten their survival. Alternatively, those organizations that tolerate moral and ethical ambiguity spend much of their corporate energy defending their actions. Consider the time and effort Kofi Annan, Secretary General of the United Nations, has had to spend over the past year on the oil-for-food scandal. Healthy organizations accept that mistakes are made, hold individuals accountable for ethical lapses, and correct the systems that enabled the breach to occur undetected, if necessary. In this chapter, we explore how directors can build a strong, lasting culture with the desired attributes necessary for success.

Are corporate values important to business? It can be hard to tell reading most books on the subject of governance. They address the legislative and regulatory need for a statement of ethics, but few really speaks to culture. Incredibly, corporate America is accused of losing its moral compass, and yet often missing from our educational delivery systems is a robust discussion regarding the importance of culture to good governance. Such a dialog eventually reaches the conclusion that culture largely determines how well corporate governance practices are deployed. The absence of strong behavioral boundaries enables a fraudulent environment. Rogues use intimidation, manipulation, protections, and rewards to build a culture of fraud and bend it to their will. They punish those who question them and reward those who do their bidding. In the most recent example, William T. Owen, a witness in the trial of former HealthSouth CEO Richard Scrushy, describes a personally close accounting team that dubbed themselves "the family."[1] According to Mr. Owen, "the family" consisted of those who were in the know and booked phony profits that they called "dirt" at Mr. Scrushy's direction. Mr. Owen also describes how Mr. Scrushy could "sell me on doing things I knew were wrong" and how he could intimidate him saying "over the years, people got to be careful what they said . . . they didn't want to incur Richard's wrath. . . ."[2] Failure to properly develop an ethical culture allows a malignancy to take hold in the company. Those who are willing to commit fraud recruit from the corporate employee pool weak or needy personalities and go to lengths to reward and protect them.

A board does not want to depend on luck to uncover a fraud. One could argue that uncovering the fraud at WorldCom was indeed lucky. The stars seemed perfectly aligned because an accountant—who knew right from wrong—refused to book bogus transactions and was brave enough to tip off the internal auditor despite the participation in the fraud by those around him. The tip, combined with a smart auditor's knowledge of how to build and escalate the case, resulted in the board having everything they needed to immediately remove the CFO. While shareholder value was destroyed, quick action likely saved a number of jobs due to the continued viability of the business. That might not have been the case if the fraud continued unabated much longer. A strong ethical culture, which sets clear behavioral boundaries, effectively provides channels for reporting abuse to those who can act on the information; and strong whistle-blower protections are needed to prevent or unravel the destructive culture. This is not a program that can be set up in a weekend. A strong culture, in which everybody participates to protect the company, can take years to build.

Culture is one of those soft and ill-defined subjects that is hard to grasp, let alone manage. To an executive, it can feel like trying to eat Jell-O with a knife—with more of a chance you will wear it before you ever experience the success of tasting it. But developing a strong ethical culture can be rewarding. To improve the chance of tasting triumph, a board and its executive team need to set the table with the appropriate tools. With a proper structure, continually reinforced and monitored, conditions are in place to define the company culture.

Johnson & Johnson has developed and lived by its corporate credo. The employees of Goldman Sachs are expected to conform to its business principles. Each of these value statements has been in place for a number of years, and these companies have spent time and money defining behavioral boundaries that employees are expected to observe. But then again, there are companies such as Enron. They had a set of nice-sounding corporate values, but did not perform the hard work of embedding them into their organization. Enron's set of corporate values listed communication, respect, integrity, and excellence as important to their company culture. These ideals sound like something to which all organizations should aspire. But words will not result in an effective policy if it is not clear how to apply their meaning to our daily work lives. Even more important, it must be clear that the company leaders actually believe in their stated values. Not too many people would use the word "integrity" to describe Enron's management. It is clear to all that Enron's managers either could not, or did not, care to enforce this value. A fuzzy or vacant set of values is not just neutral, but destructive. Employees can spot insincerity in the executive ranks all the way from the mailroom, and will inevitably make a company pay for it. In order for governance systems to work, employees, vendors, stockholders, and other stakeholders have to believe that management wants to "do the right thing." Otherwise, the hotlines will remain silent, employees will not challenge unusual behavior, and information critical to the organization's survival will not reach the board.

It takes years to implement a program that result in an open, honest, and collegial culture and to maintain it requires a never-ending dedicated effort by management. Such a culture does not occur by accident, but rather by design (although certain strong, ethical leaders have created such a culture by sheer force of personality and example rather than formal process). Common components of effective cultures include:

- Statement of ethical principles or corporate values
- Methodical processes to encourage desired behaviors and to identify and correct activities that breach accepted boundaries

- Numerous delivery systems for reporting ethical or criminal behavior, both directly and anonymously, from within the company and without, with every report dutifully investigated and cleared
- Open and transparent reliance on principles and values in decision making

WHAT WE STAND FOR: STATEMENT OF CORPORATE VALUES

The Sarbanes-Oxley Act requires each public company to disclose whether it has adopted a code of ethics for senior financial officers—and if not, why not. The NYSE raises the bar by requiring listed companies to go beyond financial officers by making publicly available a code of business conduct and ethics for the company's directors. The NASD has similar requirements. The NYSE requires a code of business conduct and ethics that includes sections concerning conflicts of interest, corporate opportunities, confidentiality, fair dealing, protection and use of company assets, compliance with laws, rules and regulations, and encourages the reporting of illegal or unethical behavior.

Conflicts of Interest

Conflicts of interest can arise when an employee or relative receives personal benefit as a result of his or her position in the company. The most famous conflict of interest in recent times was the management of off-balance sheet entities by Enron's CFO. The amazing thing is the board waived its conflict of interest policies to allow Andy Fastow's management company to administer the legal entities. Conflicts can also occur innocently. For example, a director who sits on the board of a company that plans to tender for another company, where she as a director, would now have a conflict of interest preventing her from objectively deliberating the merits of the acquisition. The company must have procedures for employees, officers, and directors to report potential conflicts of interest. Once notified, the potential conflict must be actively managed by separating or otherwise preventing the individual from participating in decisions affecting the conflicted matter. Generally, the conflicted director would recuse him- or herself from related debate and refrain from voting on those matters.

Opportunities that Arise from Corporate Employment

The NYSE guidelines state that a code of conduct should include a discussion prohibiting employees, officers, and directors from taking for themselves personally opportunities that are discovered through the use of corporate property, information, or position; using corporate property, information, or position for personal gain; and competing with the company. An example might be the recent scandal at the Pentagon where Darleen Druyan, the former number two acquisition executive for the Air Force, negotiated for a job at Boeing at the same time she was involved negotiating contracts with the company. Druyan admitted that she did favor Boeing as a result of her pending employment and altered her personal journal to make it appear that she had no conflicts with the company. Clearly, she used the leverage of her position for personal gain. As a result, she was sentenced to nine months in prison and several more months at a detention facility.

Confidentiality

Most companies now have their employees sign annual confidentiality agreements to protect against disclosing any nonpublic information that might be useful to competitors or harmful to the company or its customers. However, best practice is to not limit confidentiality agreements to directors, officers, and employees, but also include contract and temporary workers as well as vendors with access to confidential information. Not long ago, the law firm of Jones Day experienced what many in the investment banking and legal world fear, the leaking of confidential and material information. In this case, Jones was representing a provider of media content via satellite in a patent dispute. An individual affiliated with one of their reprographics vendors downloaded technical information and put it up for sale on the Internet. The buyer would obtain the information needed to intercept and decode the satellite signals. The result would be similar to buying a box to get cable television for free. The lesson learned is that it is not only important that the company maintain a robust control structure, but that its vendors do as well.

Fair Dealing

It can be tempting for companies to feed business to a particular vendor for the promise of returned business down the line. Several years ago, while owning ultimate oversight of procurement for an investment bank, I was asked by one of the business units to change office supply vendors to a client for whom the bank was underwriting an issue. We were in the process of converting to just-in-time delivery and it seemed a good opportunity to put our contract out to bid. Given the political pressure to sign our client, we had to err on the side of caution when preparing the bidding packages to ensure that we were fair and making the best decision for shareholders of the company. Fortunately, the client in question bid aggressively for the business and was awarded the deal. However, shortly thereafter, their prices started to rise as they claimed to be losing money on the contract. My procurement manager stood firm and enforced the contracted pricing. She was able to keep her objectivity and ensure fair dealing through a politically charged bidding process and subsequent vendor difficulties. It would be unfair to the other competitors and our shareholders to allow our client to raise prices above what the competition was willing to provide. However, not everyone in the organization saw it the same way. As senior management, we supported her through this process as she was staying true to the values we embraced.

Protection and Use of Company Assets

All company assets should be safeguarded and used for legitimate business purposes. Using corporate assets for personal gain has been a common theme in many of the recent prosecutions. While not as interesting as a toga party in Sardinia, the disclosure that Adelphia's CFO, Timothy Rigas, used the company jet to ferry the actress Peta

Wilson around the country—and with him on a Jamaica vacation—provided great fodder for the nation's newspapers. The jet was also used to transport a Christmas tree 300 miles to John Rigas daughter's house in New York City. Evidently, the tree was not the right size, so another was fetched at a cost of between $10,000 and $20,000, all to the detriment of shareholders.

Compliance with Laws, Rules, and Regulations

You would think that obeying the law would be the no-brainer component of any code of conduct. But consider federal regulators who reported recently that they are looking to file civil charges against a former CEO of Lucent Technologies and his head of Saudi Arabian operations. The SEC alleges that the two violated the Foreign Corrupt Practices Act through bribery. The company has been separately accused of providing cash and gifts in excess of $15 million to the Saudi Arabian telecommunications minister as a way to gain business. Likewise, Monsanto recently agreed to pay a $1.5 million fine to settle accusations that it directed an outside consultant to pay a $50,000 bribe to an Indonesian government official in 2002. The company also admitted to previously paying over $700,000 in illegal or questionable payments to government officials.[3] So while it may be a no-brainer, as long as individuals are willing to embrace this practice as a cost of doing business, this component still needs to figure prominently in any code of conduct.

Reporting of Illegal or Unethical Behavior

One would also think that this is an obvious value, but many people witness unethical or improper behavior but say and do nothing out fear of retaliation or because they believe it is "snitching." The company policy must not only speak to reporting unacceptable behavior, but require it. The policy should clearly protect the whistleblower, and penalize those that know of illegal or unethical behavior, but choose to ignore it.

The NYSE also requires that any waiver to a company's code of ethics be promptly disclosed. A strong code of ethics, statement of corporate values, credo, business principles, or whatever else you want to call them, will also speak to how a company conducts its business, its interaction with clients, expectations of employee behaviors, how employees treat each other, expansion through fair competition, and other key competitive drivers specific to the company. Goldman Sachs' business principles value creativity and imagination, which is important in investment banking, while AutoZone's code of conduct values cost control, which is a competitive advantage in delivering standardized auto parts. Both are appropriate values given the drivers of their respective businesses, but neither at the expense of business and personal ethics.

Most experts explain how the establishment of a code will put management and employees on notice and discourage unwanted behaviors by restricting their actions. On the contrary, such documents free employees to further the objectives of the company in new and creative ways, secure in the fact that their actions are aligned with the culture of the company and within established behavioral boundaries. It empowers employees to actively improve the way things get done. This creates "ownership" and an employee class that identifies itself as a part of the company. How value statements are presented and enforced determines how they are received. Opportunities can be lost if pent-up ideas and energy are never released due to fear.

The most complete and eloquent code means nothing if a company does not live by it. Johnson & Johnson (J&J) exemplifies what it means to communicate and live by good corporate values. J&J is a company synonymous with compassionate health care. When people think of Tylenol, they think of safe and effective pain relief. This view remains despite the fact that, in 1982, several people were poisoned when a murderer introduced cyanide into Tylenol bottles in the Chicago area. J&J's response was true to its values. It did not want its consumers feeling that it was playing Russian roulette with their lives by using its products, so it immediately withdrew all Tylenol products. Some estimate this cost the company over $500 million, which illustrates the priority of J&J's corporate values. Money was not the primary concern, and one only has to refer to their credo, which has guided the company since 1943, to understand.

The credo begins by announcing the responsibility of the company: "The first responsibility is to the doctors, nurses, and patients, to mothers and fathers and to all others who use our products and services." Note that it does not start with management, employees, shareholders, profits, or corporate accounts that buy the product. Rather, the focus is on the people who use its products. If this is the first priority, that frees a manager from having to consider short-term profits when faced with a moral dilemma. The type of question a manager asks shifts from "How can I address this problem at the lowest cost?" to "What steps must I take to protect our consumers?" CEO James Burke did not have to think twice about quickly removing all Tylenol products from all shelves, regardless of cost. It was in the best interests of those who used its products; and, in the long run, it was also the best decision for the long-term reputation and financial health of the company. Johnson & Johnson's credo can be found in Appendix E.

ESTABLISHING BEHAVIORAL BOUNDARIES

The J&J example puts into sharp relief how senior management's decisions can be driven by a code of conduct. As one moves down the hierarchy, it is not hard to imagine that the message could be diffused and may not even reach certain far-flung operations. But if decision rights and procedures are properly defined and assigned, if corporate objectives are communicated and understood and cultural values are known and respected, then employees should not inadvertently bump into control boundaries on a regular basis, no matter how innovative their response to an objective. Employees know what is expected of them; and operational key performance indicators will alert management if their efforts need to be redirected toward a company objective. For a heavy industrial company, safety metrics are one example of a behavioral key performance indicator that might alert management or the board to a budding cultural problem. If the number of accidents or incidents per hours worked begins to rise, the cause needs to be studied. Have procedures changed? Has awareness of known dangers atrophied, indicating a possible cultural problem? Or could it be the result of one unpreventable accident? The answer will determine the response as well as the increased threat level faced by the board. A cultural problem would require new initiatives to review and improve process design, increase safety awareness, and make adjustments to evaluation and compensation schemes to incorporate safety objectives. Regulators and workers' unions tend to be concerned when safety issues are not addressed. By proactively identifying and addressing the issue, larger problems such as further injuries, militant worker dissatisfaction, or regulatory enforcement can be avoided. (Techniques for monitoring key performance indicators are discussed further in Chapter 11.)

To ensure that everyone in the organization is aware of corporate values and policies, every employee should attest annually to having read and complied with them. To set the proper tone, the organization's values should be cited whenever making decisions that materially impact employees as well as other stakeholders; as was the case with J&J. To reinforce these values, compliance with the code of conduct should also be taken into account when making compensation and promotion related decisions. American International Group (AIG), one of the largest insurance companies in the world, recently did just that. The CEO required that a $126 million fine paid to settle allegations made by federal regulators come from the bonus pool of the business that was the focus of the investigation. The fine was a result of products and services sold to some companies from 1999 through 2001 that used them to manipulate their financial statements. By requiring the fine to be paid out of the bonus pool, a strong message was sent to the organization that personal compensation would be severely cut for improper conduct. In some cases, normal bonus payments were cut to zero. Importantly, shareholders did not have to bear the burden of the fines for unacceptable behavior, rather, those who behaved badly had to bear the cost. While AIG's interaction with regulators is often clumsy, short sighted, and self-defeating, the CEO's handling of this federal fine was appropriate and exemplifies best practice.[4]

Finally, certain companies will determine the effectiveness of their efforts by conducting confidential employee surveys. Conducted appropriately, these surveys can tell management and the board whether employees are getting the appropriate messages and, if not, where the company needs to focus their efforts.

REPORTING BAD BEHAVIORS

Too many companies put the burden of identifying fraud or damaging behavior on a few individuals or small groups such as internal audit, security, or human resources. But as an enterprise grows, more people, assets, and control points intersect creating an even greater number of opportunities for that one aberrant to disrupt or corrupt the organization. Would it not be better if the entire organization were empowered to identify those who would put our workplace at risk? This behavioral nirvana can be the most effective and cost-efficient control system in which a company can invest. It is possible to achieve if employees are encouraged to speak openly without retribution and it is widely recognized that management wants to do the right thing by rewarding those who come forward.

One of the first things that come to mind when discussing reporting systems is the hotline: the proverbial red-colored phone that should be used only in emergencies. In fact, a hotline is an essential component of a well-structured compliance system. It is imperative that the board sponsors the hotline so that employees who may have information regarding the most senior managers of the company will feel that they have an avenue to report poor behavior without retribution. Normally, outside counsel will also have responsibility for vetting and clearing calls received and report back to the board.

A strong compliance system also exhibits an active complaint reporting mechanism. Complaints from customers, vendors, regulators, stockholders, and other stakeholders should be captured, vetted, cleared, and reported. As discussed in some detail in Chapter 14, the SEC now requires a company to disclose whether there is a mechanism for shareholders to communicate with the board. The board need not be made aware of every complaint, but the number and types of complaints received should be tallied and reported together with any action taken by management. Such systems can provide critical information regarding the health of the business, whether employees throughout the organization are living the company values, and whether management is reinforcing those values through corrective action.

Key performance indicators are not always thought of as a compliance reporting tool, but in fact they can be insightful components to an overall culture development program. If customer waiting time or number of manufactured units needing to be reworked is an important driver of the business, then these factors should be measured, reported, and reinforced as central to company values through the employee performance evaluation and compensation systems.

Exception reports can also be effective. An exception report can tell management if a boundary has been tested or breached. For instance, has an employee repeatedly attempted to access unauthorized human resource systems? Such information on boundary "outliers" provides management the opportunity to reinforce their values through warning and termination tools.

REWARDING THE GOOD

It is often easier to identify problem behaviors rather than those exceptional behaviors that a board will want to reward. To the extent possible, management and the board needs to highlight and reward behaviors that represent the values of the organization. It can be an employee who saved a life, volunteered their personal time to community or pro bono work, found a new and creative way to do their job that benefited many other employees, had perfect attendance, was elected by peers as the mentor of the year, found and reported an unintentional material error, or reported improper behavior in the management ranks. Regardless of the valued behavior performed, it is vital that executive management not allow these actions to go unrecognized. The board should ensure that this happens. Whether the reward consists of a ceremony, mention in the company newsletter, monetary reward, or promotion is less important than the fact that such employees are recognized and that the organization as a whole is aware of their contribution.

Counseling management to maintain an active program for identifying good deeds is an underappreciated but effective method to instill values into an organization. Good deeds often go unnoticed because they are not visible to those in a position to communicate them to the rest of the organization. Management must actively seek this information. If it waits passively for these behaviors to surface, they may never be identified or rewarded. Management can sponsor awards for attendance, mentoring, community activity, and so forth. Regular employee surveys can also uncover activities, awards, and achievements that the company might want to make public. Monitoring press reports can yield additional information about the company and employees, both positive and negative, leading to senior management responses. While this may seem to be too detailed for board involvement, a board that takes company culture seriously will champion these efforts. It only takes five minutes for a board to make inquiries regarding these programs or decide to sponsor an employee award plan. The message, however, is heard throughout the organization.

LEARNING TO COMMUNICATE OPENLY

Much board business requires candid debate, advice, and feedback that appropriately occurs behind closed doors. However, important conclusions reached by the board, the reasons for them, and how they relate to company strategy and values need to be clearly articulated to many audiences on a regular basis. Stakeholders have a right to current, material information and the board serves itself by tying these communications into company strategy and values. Reinforcing values and getting information out in a timely manner builds trust, which in turn creates goodwill that the board can call on when it has more difficult decisions to face. The Sarbanes-Oxley Act now requires that material information be disseminated real time that the SEC has defined in most instances to be within four days of discovery. Despite the obvious need to understand the issue and related facts, it is equally important how the message is communicated. If the message is not good news, a communication of only naked facts may unnecessarily destroy shareholder value. The issue needs to be put into context with a reminder of other factual strengths that help the audience properly frame and assess the issue. Most important, explain how the actions taken, or those that will occur, are aligned with corporate strategy and values. Reassure the markets that the board is interested in doing the right thing. This can be difficult if the announcement concerns layoffs, plant closings, outsourcing, product recall, discovery of illegal activity, regulatory investigations, and the like. But if the overall message is that the action taken will be in the best long term interest of remaining employees, shareholders, and customers, and it truly is, the bad news will be digested with the knowledge that medicine is being taken to make certain that there are better times ahead. Recalling Tylenol was certainly costly, but it was the only decision J&J's credo would allow. Their customers understood this and remained loyal.

CASE STUDY: CULTURE AT THE UNITED NATIONS

To be fair, Kofi Annan inherited a mess, and he was seen as someone who could restore confidence in the United Nations (U.N.). From his upbringing in Ghana, Kofi seemed to be preparing to lead the U.N. He was schooled in Ghana, the United States, and Switzerland, and then joined the U.N. in 1962, where he steadily rose through the ranks to become the seventh Secretary General on January 1, 1997. While he has achieved much success, he now faces a crisis that threatens his legacy and the credibility that the U.N. needs to accomplish its mission.

There can be no single organization on the face of the earth that is home to greater diversity than the U.N. Headquartered in New York City, the U.N. was established in 1945 to preserve the "peace through international cooperation and collective security." Today, over 191 nations are members. In contrast to the many beautiful cultures that its member nations represent is another kind of culture that is not so desirable: the culture of fraud, mismanagement, and poor oversight. This is not just the billion dollar oil-for-food program. The U.N. has a long history of fraudulent practices enabled by slack management controls and supervision. This was raised by Dick Thornburgh in a 1993 U.N.-sponsored report that charged widespread mismanagement. Another internal investigation, conducted in just seven short months in 1994, led to an interim report that found nearly $17 million in fraud and waste. This included fuel distribution services that were never provided, diversion of money to personal accounts, and loans authorized by U.N. personnel to companies in which they held an interest. More recently, nearly $4 million was reported stolen from U.N. offices in Somalia[a] and $3 million embezzled from World Meteorological Organization, an affiliated U.N. agency.[b]

Rather than embracing these investigations, the U.N. seems to drag its feet or bury its head in the sand. Is it any wonder then that others would see this response and adopt similar practices? Given the U.N.'s history, no one should be surprised by the revelation that the oil-for-food program became among the largest frauds in history. It is believed that as much as $11 billion were siphoned off from the $64 billion program. The amounts involved are simply stunning. It is alleged that the U.N. allowed the Iraqi government to decide who it would do business with under the program, and they favored those entities that would kick back money to the regime. In return, the Iraqi government would sell favored individuals and companies oil at prices well below the market price. In a program designed to get food and medicine to those in need, everyone but the Iraqi people got rich on the deal. According to an interim report issued by the independent investigator Paul Volker, the former head of the Federal Reserve, the actions of Benon Savon, the head of the oil for food program "seriously undermined the integrity of the United Nations." Mr. Savon is accused of helping a friend to obtain below-market contracts to sell Iraqi oil. Investigators also claim that Mr. Savon was able to block an internal audit of his office during the critical period when he was suspected of soliciting oil deals from Iraq.[c] In a separate investigation, a U.S. Senate subcommittee says documents show that Mr. Savon may have personally made up to $1.2 million from illegal Iraqi oil shipments. There are other examples of preferential treatment, mismanagement, and poor judgment from the hiring of contactors to questionable payments received by Mr. Savon. Even more telling, the former Secretary General, Boutros Boutros-Ghali, was criticized in the Volker report for his role in selecting the primary banker for the program. According to the *New York Times*, Mr. Boutros-Ghali called "Mr. Volker's investigators ignorant of the United Nations system."[d] On the contrary, it appears that Mr. Volker fully understands that the U.N. system is infested with conflicts of interest and is not impressed by it. If there was a question regarding how the U.N. culture became so damaged, one only has to consider the former Secretary General's response.

On the peacekeeping front, it is being reported that U.N. peacekeepers are actually the enemy of the people they are sent to protect. The U.N. reports that they have uncovered over 150 allegations of peacekeepers sexually abusing women and teenage girls and of running prostitution rings in the Congo. And the allegations are not limited to soldiers from one or two countries. They include Nepal, Pakistan, Morocco, Tunisia, South Africa, and Uruguay.[e] These soldiers are simply turned over to their home countries for punishment.

A recent book, *Emergency Sex and Other Desperate Measures: A True Story from Hell on Earth,*[f] also discloses revelations about this other U.N. culture. The author, Dr. Andrew Thompson, who has worked as a U.N. doctor in Cambodia, Haiti, Somalia, Bosnia, Rwanda, and Liberia, tells about his loss of idealism with the organization. He tells stories of digging up graves in Rwanda and Bosnia after mass killings in areas protected by the U.N.—and of wild parties with drug use and sex.

After almost a decade of contract renewals with the U.N., the organization severed their relationship with Dr. Thompson after his book was published. Dr. Thompson has since filed a whistle-blower suit against the U.N.[g] Likewise, Kathryn Bolkovac was fired for "time-sheet irregularities" after she reported dozens of alleged sex crimes involving U.N. employees in the Balkans.[h] The threat of being fired for speaking up is very real as it seems that retaliation is the norm. A survey of U.N. staff revealed that four out of five were afraid to challenge corruption and 65 percent were witness to it.

The mission of the U.N. is indeed important, but the culture of the institution threatens to be its undoing. The people of the United States, which provides over one-fifth of the U.N.'s funding, will not continue to support an institution that behaves in this fashion. The problems encountered by the U.N. are not surprising given its structural inadequacies. Public corporations have more checks and balances and enforcement tools than those available to the U.N. To begin with, the oversight of the U.N. is politically diverse, so doing the right thing usually takes a back seat to national interests. The concept of fiduciary responsibility is totally lacking from the members of the Security Council. The U.N. also lacks the ability to enforce a code of conduct on its troops. They are simply sent home rather than to the Hague for trial, a process also opposed by the U.S. government due to fears of abusing this power against American soldiers (not such a farfetched concern, given the history of the U.N.). Finally, where the U.N. does have the ability to correct poor behavior within its own staff, there is a lack of controls that would alert management to abuse. When abuse is discovered it has not been aggressively dealt with, and whistle-blowers are summarily dismissed.

On the other hand, corporate boards have a fiduciary responsibility to their shareholders, ethical boundaries are required by legislation and listing standards, assessment of internal controls are also mandated, and whistle-blower protections are in place. These measures do not guarantee good behavior, but the structure and process is in place to provide the board and management a chance to implement a positive culture.

While saddled with a disgraceful history, the U.N. has an opportunity to fully investigate the oil-for-food program and to do the right thing—and early indications suggest that Mr. Annan is prepared to address what is found. He has already made a series of top management changes at the U.N. and he suspended Mr. Savon. We are still waiting for Paul Volker's final report on the oil-for-food program. When issued, it will be up to Kofi Annan to hold staffers accountable and bring respect back to the U.N. Changing the culture of fraud at the U.N. is a big job, but no one else is in a position to get it accomplished. The Secretary General has no choice but to succeed if the U.N. is going to survive as a credible world resource . . . and if he is to leave a lasting legacy of which he can be proud.

---

[a]Cato Institute, "Section 51. The United Nations," in *Cato Handbook for Congress: 105th Congress.* http://www.cato.org/pubs/handbook/hb105-51.html (18 December 2004).

[b]Miller, Judith, "Theft and Mismanagement Charged at U.N. Weather Agency," *New York Times*, 9 February 2005, A12.

[c]Associated Press, "Oil-for-Food Director Blocked Audit, Investigators Say," *New York Times*, 13 February 2005, A8.

[d]Miller, Judith, and Warren Hoge, "Inquiry on Iraqi Oil-for-Food Plan Cites U.N. Diplomat for Conflict," *New York Times,* 4 February 2005, A1.

[e]Lacey, Marc, "In Congo War, Even Peacekeepers Add to Horror," *New York Times,* 18 December 2004, accessed at www.nytimes.com/2004/12/18/international/africa/18congo.html?oref=longin.

[f]Cain, Kenneth, Heidi Postlewait, and Andrew Thomson, *Emergency Sex and Other Desperate Measures: A True Story from Hell on Earth* (New York: Miramax Books, 2004).

[g]Associated Press, "U.N. Doesn't Renew Whistleblower's Contract," *FoxNews.com,* December 16, 2004. http://www.foxnews.com/story/0,2933,141681,00.html (16 December 2004).

[h]Malkin, Michelle. "The U.N. Rape Club," *New York Post*, 16 February, 2005, 29.

KEY CONCEPTS

- Adopt strong shared values. Strong values, properly enforced, will establish behavioral boundaries and aid decision-making.
- Benchmark and monitor employee surveys. The board can then assess how effectively management communicates and lives by these values.
- Continually communicate the company's shared values and enforce them through compensation and evaluation schemes. Ensure that there is a personal cost to those that do not conform and rewards to those whose actions support the company's shared values.
- Make certain that numerous whistle-blower delivery systems exist to improve the opportunity for people of conscience to report code of conduct violations.
- Support an active program that recognizes and rewards good deeds throughout the organization.

ENDNOTES

1. Glynn Wilson, "Ex-HealthSouth Officer Says He Faked Numbers for Chief," *New York Times*, 2 February 2005, C5.
2. Glynn Wilson, "Witness Tells of Maneuvers With Numbers at HealthSouth," *New York Times*, 3 February 2005, C7.
3. New York Times Staff, "Monsanto to pay $1.5 million in Penalties," *New York Times*, 7 January 7, 2005, C4.
4. Joseph B. Treaster, "A.I.G. Hits Bonus Pool To Pay Bulk of Penalty," *New York Times*, 10 February 2005, C1.

CHAPTER 10

Healthy Board Dynamics

Just like the people they lead, every board is unique. Each has a distinct personality and behavioral norms. The way directors interact with each other, management, and other stakeholders helps determine their success. Simply checking off the corporate governance boxes on the latest best practices checklist is not enough. A board's social system must also work well for it to be effective. Board activity can range from a passive or limited role to managing or interfering involvement. The best boards are engaged, but understand their boundaries. There may be times when directors need to intervene, but boards are in place to provide oversight and guidance, not to manage the company. That is what the high-priced executive team has been hired to do. The board must let them do their jobs. In this chapter, we study the attributes of effective board culture and techniques directors can use to improve their interaction with each other and company management.

Most directors understand their responsibilities, both their primary duty to shareholders and their broader role with stakeholder groups. They recognize that they are ultimately accountable for oversight of the company. Shareholders, creditors, employees, customers, vendors, and those in the local communities where they do business count on the company to not only better their economic lives, but to serve as a good corporate citizen as well. Boards that understand this spend time defining their roles and responsibilities for each of their stakeholders and take steps to meet these expectations. Good corporate governance is one way to make certain that the company is perceived as a good citizen of the community.

Quality directors are honest yet constructive. They work hard to understand issues facing the corporation and do not hesitate to ask questions and challenge leadership when appropriate. They respect the views of other board members, actively seek out their opinions, and continue to support management and the board, even after difficult debate. A board might consist of good people and good directors, but still have mediocre corporate governance due to "groupthink." This weakness is hard to recognize, but supporting candor and respecting differing opinions can keep groupthink at bay.

The most effective directors have an internal code of conduct regarding their board service. They understand that they have a responsibility to come to board meetings fully prepared to actively participate. They take pride in the work performed by the board. Most directors do not recognize that they are living by a code because it is hardwired into them. They know what is right in their gut; and if they are unsure, they trust their instincts and will spend more time examining the issue. These directors recognize that if they have become too busy to perform their duties, they need to take appropriate measures to correct their behavior or resign. Likewise, they will resign from board service if they do not agree with the overall direction a board has taken and can no longer add value. Resignation should be a last resort, as a director gives up the opportunity to change the company from the inside. However, it does send a message to investors that all may not be well at the company and that they should start asking some questions.

Finally, effective boards are led by chairpersons who ensure meeting agendas limit presentation time and plan for ample discussion. There will be social events and breaks that allow for informal interaction. These unstructured moments are recognized by enlightened directors as valuable rather than a waste of time. It is an opportunity for them to communicate informally without the confines of an official meeting.

DECIDING WHO WE ARE AND HOW WE WILL OPERATE

My grandfather liked to say that service is the debt you pay for occupying the earth. Implied in that comment is the concept that we all have a duty to serve, and that it never comes without a cost. We all want to serve, but an unprepared director entering their first board meeting will likely succumb to its velocity. He or she will quickly find themselves disoriented by the issues, pace, and politics of the board. This is no time to evaluate why you are here, what your role should be and where you can potentially fit in. Caught off guard, the director may sit back and let deliberations continue until he or she is comfortably oriented. Or worse yet, make comments that lack understanding of the issue at hand. In either case, directors are not adequately doing their job. Homework should be done before the first gathering to understand both the people and working components of the board and, importantly, how this compares to the most effective boards.

Effective boards have similar characteristics in that they:

- Exhibit a healthy culture (lack arrogance)
- Are engaged
- Are informed
- Are largely independent
- Regularly meet in executive session
- Are well balanced functionally and technically
- Have their own quality experts and consultants

The following discussion explores these characteristics in more detail.

COVETED CULTURE

Healthy boards exemplify what Jeffrey Sonnenfeld, Yale School of Management's Associate Dean for Executive Programs, calls "a virtuous cycle of respect, trust and candor."[1] Where directors trust each other to openly discuss difficult issues, the results are informed counseling and decision making and effective oversight. However, board dynamics often mimic many other settings where bright, Type-A individuals are brought together, whether it be on the field of battle in an athletic contest, competing at a top business school (faculty or class), participating in competitive tournaments, joining executive roundtables, admittance to selective clubs, and the list goes on. At times, there is healthy discourse among members, but often there is an unspoken competition to show others one's true worth. Comments designed to lift one above the crowd (rather than to add value to the meeting) can be as infectious as the flu, quickly spreading to other directors who also want to show that they too are not slouches. By the time everyone has proven their brilliance, the meeting is over, having accomplished little. It goes without saying that directors are already highly successful men and women with far-reaching responsibility for the institutions they lead. Why there is an inclination by some to have to reassert this value is best explored in another field of study altogether. But once unleashed, it can negatively affect the outcome of a board meeting.

Another dysfunctional board behavior is the defensive CEO. A defensive CEO may not be open with the board, which breeds distrust and retards knowledge transfer. The underlying tension may be performance related or simply just an outsized ego that is not used to being challenged. Regardless, the lack of information can make it impossible for directors to perform their supervisory role. In response, a director may try to obtain information from other executives and managers, which can fuel the CEO's defensiveness. The firing of Carly Fiorina, Hewlett Packard's (HP) highly visible CEO provides an example. Since the summer 2004, HP's board had pressed Fiorina to open up the office of the CEO, to make it more inclusive and spread operational responsibility and decision making to other senior executives. The board did not take issue with the strategy to buy Compaq, as reported by some media, but rather its execution. In fact, certain directors wanted to see more transactions that would bolster HP's formidable businesses. Fiorina's forceful, but closed management style and detachment from the daily operations were viewed as an impediment to the successful implementation of that strategy. In January 2005, three of HP's directors met with Fiorina and bluntly told her she needed to make changes, but she stood firm. Time was of the essence, and the board sensed that Fiorina's resistance to opening up the office of the CEO and speeding the consummation of transactions was impeding execution. So the board convened a special meeting over a weekend in February that excluded the CEO that culminated in their requesting Fiorina's resignation.[2]

Another worrisome behavior is a CEO who is not necessarily defensive, but spends the entire board meeting making presentations. The talking-head meeting may embrace the passing of information, but it is only one-way communication often with key decisions having already been made. There is not time for discussion or debate, only affirmation. This problem occurs more frequently where the CEO is also the chairperson and controls the agenda.

Without guidance as to what constitutes favored behaviors, the board cannot hope to accomplish much in the short time that they have together. Harvard professors Colin Carter and Jay Lorsch in *Back to the Drawing Board* identify minimum requisite and expected behaviors that should be agreed by all directors and executive managers:

1. "Directors can ask tough questions without management becoming defensive.
2. Dissent among directors is encouraged, and pressures for conformity to the majority opinion are acknowledged and guarded against.
3. Directors are not intent on scoring points by putting managers or other directors down. Instead, they engage in discussions of relevant issues, with respect for each other's opinions and expertise, and with the goal of reaching understanding and consensus.
4. Directors understand when to listen and learn from management and each other, and when to stimulate discussions.
5. Any discussion between executives and directors is two-way. Executives can disagree with directors if they believe the latter are misinformed or wrong, and directors really listen to management's ideas.
6. Directors respect the agenda. They are mindful of the schedule and understand the importance of staying focused on the important issues. Discussion is encouraged, but everyone recognizes the limits imposed by time."[3]

While maybe not a minimum requirement, another can be added: "Directors can learn much about the company from employees of the company and will be expected, from time to time, to tour facilities and enter into dialog with managers and employees." Such a statement can help prevent the CEO from perceiving what is a good faith effort by a director to educate themselves as snooping, but more importantly, engage directors. For example, Home Depot board members are required to visit stores between board meetings so that they can knowledgeably discuss issues.

The most effective way to combat poor behavior is to define it and then shine a light on it. That is not to say that the first director to toot his or her own horn should be held up to ridicule, or that the CEO should be confronted at the board meeting. Instead, the chairperson, lead director, or other trusted director needs to play the role of mentor and periodically reinforce those behaviors that are acceptable and address those that are not through regular individual, informal, and private feedback. Combined with new director training (where the desired board culture can be discussed) and director evaluations (discussed in Chapter 7), mentoring can be a potent activity that really brings a board's culture together in a positive way. Some will clearly be more receptive to mentoring than others. But, to further imbed preferred behaviors into the culture, the board needs to rate each director on their boardroom performance as a part of the annual appraisal process. Passive or grandstanding behaviors will likely surface from the peer review as a performance issue, at which time the director can be counseled and nudged back toward an engaged but constructive posture.

Changing the behavior of a defensive CEO is actually a much greater challenge. Some, like Ms. Fiorina, resist board-directed development at all costs, and the board must be prepared to deal with that possibility. Directors can only execute their duties successfully if they are able to receive information from management and, where necessary, have it corroborated.

Alternatively, if the board culture is one of superiority over management, then a defensive CEO would not be a surprising outcome. All CEOs want advisors and counselors—not a judge and jury. Although boards hold the power to execute, it should not be held over managers' heads. They only come to resent it. Handled properly, a receptive CEO recognizes that he or she could do the job even better and, with board assistance, take the appropriate measures to improve without placing blame or alienating members of the board. The discussion to replace a CEO only comes after frequent feedback and counseling has failed to achieve results.

The board should act as advisors, counseling when appropriate, posing tough but fair questions, challenging assumptions, and conducting rigorous diligence where necessary. While the oversight is of no less a caliber than that sought by boards flush with superiority, the tone is different. Because of the free and honest exchange of information, the chance of success is greater. In a healthy relationship, both the board and CEO recognize that each serves the interest of shareholders and it is their job to work together toward that end.

WANTING TO BE ENGAGED

Effective boards are engaged in that they contribute valuable insight and advice for the CEO and management team to leverage. They recognize their job is to provide oversight of the CEO and company performance on behalf of shareholders and it is management's responsibility to run the company. These roles are clearly defined and behaviors outside of recognized guidelines are quickly redirected, with directors still obliged to change management when in the best interests of the company. There is an ongoing, open dialog about key issues facing the company, and directors do not hesitate to bring in outside resources they need to do the job.

Many think of engaged boards as hands-on and immersed in the details, but that is not an engaged board; that is a description of an interfering or managing board. With certain exceptions, managing should be left to the managers and oversight to the directors. Directors may have to become more imbedded in the operating environment when there is a crisis and the company needs them to bring their leadership and skills to bear on the problem at hand. The board may temporarily make key decisions that management then implements. But once the crisis has subsided, it is generally expected that the board moves back to an engaged posture. A basic model of board activity for passive, engaged, and managing boards is illustrated in Exhibit 10.1.[4]

While this model generally holds true, a board can be highly active in a company, but in all the wrong places to be effective. That is, the activity may not result in healthy engagement. But it is safe to say that for most boards activity is positively correlated to engagement. An example of a board that temporarily became a managing board can be seen in the response to the collapse of the telecom market by Lucent directors. Unrestrained demand up to 2000 was followed by a collapse in demand for equipment supporting telecom and Internet infrastructure. This resulted in Lucent going from $33 billion in revenues to under $9 billion over a period of months. To

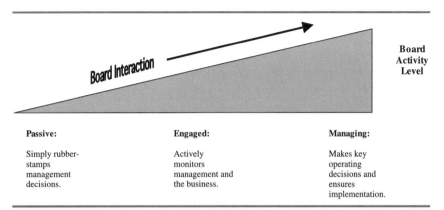

EXHIBIT 10.1   Board Activity Continuum

make matters worse, there were concerns about the aggressiveness of the company's accounting and an SEC investigation regarding possible violations of the Foreign Corrupt Practices Act involving its CEO. The board had to take radical and decisive action to save the company. The entire board met frequently (over 58 times in one year) and worked overtime to keep Lucent liquid and viable.[5] In October 2000, the board, recognizing that the situation required a different executive skill set, replaced their chief executive with the former chairman and CEO, Henry B. Schacht. Schacht eventually brought on Patricia Russo as President and CEO in January 2002. After disclosing that the company previously overstated revenue by $679 million for 2000, the company realized net losses of $16.2 billion and $11.8 billion for the fiscal years 2001 and 2002, respectively. Massive losses of these proportions would be a survival challenge for most of the world's largest companies. This is not a situation where a director could afford to sit back to see what happens.

To return to profitability, the company rapidly sold noncore assets, spun off two major subsidiaries, Avaya and Agere, eliminated money-losing products, and actively pared down its workforce from 126,000 employees to less than 35,000. By fiscal year-end 2003, the company had returned to profitability, reported a full-year profit for 2004 of $2 billion, and generated operating cash flow of over $600 million.[6] While the stock is still depressed at under $4 a share, many expect Lucent to do well with even a modest recovery in telecom spending. At this early stage, it appears that the board did a remarkable job of accepting and quickly reacting to the many threats that the company faced. Without such urgency and aggressive action, the company might not have survived and the remaining jobs would have been lost as well.

In contrast to the managing board, is the passive board. Passive boards are staffed with sycophants and function at the discretion of the CEO, generally an imperial CEO. The activities of board members are restricted and directors exist primarily to ratify management's decisions. The board can also consist of a number of inside managers—or relatives of a founder as was the case with Adelphia Communications. The founder and his three sons sat on the board, and continued to run the public company as if it were private. The company collapsed once the public learned of Adelphia's debt obligations resulting from the family's activities. John Rigas, who is 79, was found guilty and faces decades in jail, as does his son Timothy.

A passive board can be destructive, not only to the company that they are tasked to oversee, but to the market as a whole. As companies collapse, the loss of confidence can cause capital to dry up overnight. This can and has occurred as the market ascertained there were plenty of red flags, but the system of oversight failed calling into question the safety of investments. The failure itself radically shifts the paradigm of risk, and the aftershocks make it difficult for investors to regain their balance and confidence. Paranoia sets in that all boards might by lax and no investment is "safe enough for our money."

Engaged boards are somewhere in the middle of these extremes. The board is in control of their agenda, exercises oversight in the areas of importance, but also lets management do what they were hired to do. Engaged boards prod, poke, advise, challenge, corroborate—but avoid managing. If the board begins making operational decisions without a crisis at hand, it has moved beyond engaged to interfering.

INFORMED AND PROUD OF IT

As we learned earlier, informed decision making is one of the key criteria used by the courts in evaluating a director's commitment to their duties. Uniformed boards cannot be effective, and a director who does not actively seek feedback from various independent sources can not expect to be informed. There are many sources of information, the most obvious being the CEO and other levels of management. There are, however, other important sources such as consultants, customers, regulators, industry publications, and the all-important whistle-blower.

Management: The Impeachable Source

Many frauds in 2001 and 2002 had the common characteristic of involving deceitful management that kept important material information from their board of directors or, when such information was disclosed, the potential impact to the company was understated. The fact remains that if a board does not trust their management, they should replace them. But every director, even if he or she trusts management, needs to have a bit of healthy skepticism when evaluating information sourced from them. In the famous words of Ronald Regan, "trust but verify." In other words, directors need to corroborate key representations.

While not completely independent, a good source of information can be managers below the C-level who are closer to the pulse of the company. Often these managers have not been included in preparatory meetings and are not "coached" in the party line, that is, what to say and not say for board ears. Building relationships with managers in key business lines or functions can lead to a source of unvarnished information that may reveal unknown problems, corroborate management's representations, or even call into question the veracity of management's statements.

Consultants: Let Me Tell You What Time It Is

Consultants are an obvious source of information. The old adage that consultants only "take your watch to tell you what time it is" may be true. However, even if they corroborate what you already think you know, consultants bring an objective view to important decisions and provide credibility to those processes that are ripe for conflicts of interest. Consultants may be independent legal counsel, accounting and control experts, compensation and recruiting professionals, or those with specific knowledge such as former regulators, security experts, diversity specialists, or environmental activists. Whatever the issue at hand, if it could have a profound impact on the company, the board needs to have its own quality counsel.

Congress recognized the value independent consultants can add to key board duties. Section 301 of the Sarbanes-Oxley Act expressly provides that the audit committee shall have the right to "engage independent counsel and other advisors, as it determines necessary to carry out its duties." This section also requires the company to pay for advisors retained by the audit committee.

Do We Know What Our Customers Think of This?

Customers are a terrific source of information, but boards spend little time on this critical stakeholder. One survey of 30 large-company boards of directors found that more than a third spent less than 10 percent of their time on customer matters and few receive presentations from major customers.[7] The board should be regularly involved in assessing customer satisfaction on many different levels. For industrial companies with a limited client base, direct conversations with the decision makers can provide valuable insight. For example, the General Electric board has dined with large suppliers and distributors before their annual meetings.[8]

For companies selling to the general public, information is harder to glean as you cannot simply invite people off of the street to discuss your product and surveys can often overlook important data. For instance, a consumer might respond that your coffee is the best in town and they are willing to pay more for it. But in reality, that customer is unlikely to do so due to the lack of a nearby coffee shop or, worse yet, long lines at the store. To be effective, the key success factors and drivers of the business need to be understood and then surveys need to be carefully worded to map to these drivers. The effort is well worth it. Reported before every meeting, the board will be armed with the latest data about customer satisfaction and trends for key business drivers. By way of example, as healthcare becomes increasingly competitive, hospitals are becoming more creative in providing services other than primary care to attract patients. A hospital network on Long Island, New York, obtains and aggregates patient surveys from each hospital. Results are presented to the board and strategies for improving the patient experience shaped.

Let the Regulators Know That Your Hair Is on Fire

The case against Abbott Labs discussed in Chapter 4 serves as an example of directors who are aware of a regulatory notice, but do not take the requisite action to proactively correct the problem. In such a case, a director may lose his or her business judgment rule protections. All regulatory agency communications need to be taken seriously, and the board should have a process to monitor and track such correspondence. This cannot be stressed more: When dealing with regulators or government officials, each problem should be addressed *as if the board's collective hair is on fire.* The government has unlimited resources it can bring to bear if it believes a company is unresponsive. Furthermore, the first notice may be only a hint of bigger problems.

For example, take the recent flu vaccine shortage. The shortage was caused by the British authorities yanking Chiron Corporation's license due to contamination problems. According to the U.S. Federal Food and Drug Administration (FDA), however, the company knew about these problems a year earlier. During a limited inspection, the FDA found batches of contaminated vaccine that had been reprocessed, which was not allowed by the license. Chiron told the FDA it was addressing the problem. But one year later, the problem had not been fixed, causing British regulators to take action. The financial implications and damage to Chiron's reputation were substantial and will cause regulators to view the company with a jaundiced eye in the future. The board should have been monitoring the corrective actions at the factory once they learned of the FDA's concerns. It would have been appropriate for them to require local management to provide updates, and once they represented the problem as corrected, to independently verify their claims. The damage to Chiron's reputation is now done, and it will be difficult to regain the trust of the public, regulators, and investors.

I Read It Somewhere

Much can be learned about your company by simply reading the newspapers. Negative stories, while unpleasant, can be terrific sources of information. The company has an opportunity to respond quickly and show their commitment to doing what is right before the media moves on to their next victim.

While it is unlikely that you will read a negative article about your company in a trade publication, they can alert you to competitive threats. Most CEOs cannot help bragging about the next best thing their companies are preparing to deploy. If your CEO is one of these, have a "sit-down" with him and rein him in. If it is a competitor's CEO, use the information to evaluate the relevance of your strategy, and a corporate response, if any, to the new threat.

Publications by Wall Street analysts are useful, too. One must recognize that in the past—and potentially in the future despite reforms—conflicts might color the analyst's view. However, their analysis of the company and its competitors can help provide an outsiders' view of the strengths and weaknesses vis-à-vis the competition.

Attraction of Whistle-blowers

The newspapers seem filled with examples of corporate wrongdoing and, as in most recent cases, the pattern emerges of an individual with integrity who comes forward and reports the fraudulent activity. At Fannie Mae a midlevel accountant emerged as a central figure in uncovering that company's financial irregularities. Roger L. Barnes repeatedly voiced concerns about accounting irregularities and became a key informant—and in this he was articulate, stating that the "culture in the controller's division was such that many employees knew or suspected that the company was regularly engaging in improper income management, and it became a joke that the controller's division could produce any income statement that the company wanted."[9]

Barnes claimed that he faced recriminations for his criticisms, including being passed over for promotion. Those who willingly flout the law reward the ones who cover for them—and they punish those they perceive as a threat. In order for corporate governance systems to identify such behavior, there must be a strong culture that rewards doing the right thing and provides an effective means for reporting bad behavior. While the audit committee of the board of directors must establish employee procedures for confidential and anonymous submission of concerns regarding questionable accounting or auditing matters, direct communications with managers and employees can also yield important information. Effectively fighting fraud in the management suite requires more than just having a hotline. Although the fraud hotline is important, the board must go further by actively engaging management at levels below the most senior level, vigorously questioning the internal and external auditors, and cogently enforcing the company's code of conduct by rewarding compliance and properly admonishing those behaviors that do not conform. Fannie Mae's board should have been looking for Barnes and investigating his concerns rather than letting the company's problem rise to the level of a Congressional investigation.

IN THE SPIRIT OF INDEPENDENCE

To be truly independent in mind, spirit, and fact, a director must always represent the best interests of the company. If a director finds herself (or himself) in a position where, either perceived or in fact, she is potentially conflicted with the best interests of the shareholders she represents, it is her duty to notify other board members and recuse herself from any deliberations. As an example, while serving on the board of Tyco, Frank E. Walsh was not always positioned to represent its shareholders. Walsh helped negotiate Tyco's purchase of CIT Group with the understanding that he would receive a fee for his services. How can a director represent the best interests of shareholders when he stands to earn $20 million for himself and his charity on successful completion of the purchase? The obvious answer is that he can not. Walsh was arrested and pleaded guilty to fraud, admitting his failure to disclose to the rest of the board that he stood to make millions from the transaction. He pledged restitution and paid a $2.5 million fine in a settlement with the Manhattan district attorney's office.[10]

Another nefarious example is provided by Roland Fahlin. As a member of the audit committee for the Dutch-based Royal Ahold, he was a party to a side agreement that inflated sales by improperly allowing the full consolidation of a joint venture. He participated in the scheme when he worked for a joint venture partner of Royal Ahold, ICI Forbundet. There he executed a control letter (stating that Royal Ahold controlled the joint venture), which the auditors relied on to allow the consolidation. Fahlin later signed a rescission of the control letter and soon left ICI and became a member of Royal Ahold's supervisory board. As an audit committee member, he was aware that the auditors relied on a control letter to accept the consolidation of ICI, yet he made no effort to determine if it was the same letter that he signed and rescinded (of course, it was). The SEC charged Fahlin with causing violations of reporting, books and records, and internal controls provisions of the securities laws. Dutch prosecutors have taken the lead in pursuing justice on behalf of shareholders.[11]

Given the new independence requirements of the Sarbanes-Oxley Act and the listing requirements of the NYSE and NASD, it is not surprising that independence on public boards of directors is increasing. Directors are more active, and independent audit committees have been strengthened. They now have real oversight authority, including the ability to retain their own independent counsel. These are all positive steps that will benefit shareholders for years to come.

TALKING FRANKLY: EXECUTIVE SESSIONS

Every board meeting should include a routine, regularly scheduled executive session with an agenda prepared by the independent chairperson or lead director. The board has a fiduciary responsibility for selecting new directors, setting executive compensation, and evaluating executive performance on behalf of shareholders. These issues should not be deliberated at a full board meeting with the CEO present because the CEO often is, or should be, the subject of these board discussions and will be directly affected by decisions on matters such as who joins the board, management team performance, and compensation. The solution is to call an executive session so that directors can deliberate these matters candidly without fear of offending the CEO. Such frank discussion can be important for raising issues, bringing focus to problems, and uniting the board toward a common course of action. But if executive sessions are not part of regular board meetings, then even discussion of such a gathering can be threatening to a sitting CEO. The NYSE has made this task somewhat easier by requiring that independent directors of listed companies periodically meet in executive session.

Nevertheless, little can make a CEO more insecure that an unstructured meeting of the outside directors that takes more than 15 minutes. As the clock ticks, the CEO begins to pace and imagine what the directors are talking about and if he is in any trouble. If the board then breaks without any feedback, he breaks out in a sweat— and the experience will remain with him long after everyone has gone home.

Healthy boards hold regularly scheduled executive sessions with a formal agenda that is shared with their CEOs. Comfortable that each session is not a subversive plot to oust them due to the formal agenda and feedback mechanism, the meetings have the blessing of their CEOs. They know what will be discussed in advance and that they will be debriefed later.

A successful executive session should have enough time in its agenda to address the issues at hand. The board may also bring in compensation, recruiting, or performance evaluation specialists if it needs these resources to accomplish their objectives. The key is process. To keep speculation at bay, not only is a formal agenda required, conclusions from meetings also need to be openly communicated to the full board, and the CEO in particular. If nonagenda items are discussed, the chairperson or lead director needs to communicate the message that the independent directors want delivered to the CEO. It is unfair to keep informal evaluations secret when there is a formal evaluation process available that all sides understand. To be effective, executive sessions need as much attention and care of due process as the board meeting itself.

BALANCE THE BOARD

The Sarbanes-Oxley Act's Section 407 first introduced the concept of requiring certain skills on a board, in this case, an "audit committee financial expert," in response to the many financial reporting frauds that surfaced during 2001 and 2002. In practice, however, the best boards have functional and technical diversity. Underappreciated by many is the importance of a balanced board to a company's oversight capability. Accounting is the language of business, and the financial statements represent the stories told by each company. As such, it is imperative that there are financial experts on every board of directors. But financial literacy is not the only competency that a board requires. Highly specialized and complex fields such as drug development, military procurement, nanotechnology, and so on, will need experts who possess the specific knowledge necessary to provide effective oversight of these businesses. A competent board exhibits both functional and technical expertise relevant to the company that they supervise. A director must recognize where they fit in the board competency matrix and where they are expected to add value to board deliberations. If the board is missing a critical function or technical expertise, then the nominating committee should set out to correct it. In the interim, the board should have access to experts who can bring the needed knowledge to the board.

INSIST ON THE BEST AND THE BRIGHTEST

We have already discussed the importance of a board obtaining the services of independent experts when confronted with the possibility that the management team may have a conflict of interest. We have examined the use of advisors for developing compensation plans, recruiting directors, and auditing the company's books, records, and controls. Nevertheless, there are many more scenarios in which specialists might be needed. The evaluation of a targeted external tender or management buyout offer for the company is one obvious example. Others might include buying, leasing, or selling real estate to or from executives, hiring relatives, and investing in companies owned by an executive or a relative.

For example, a publicly held real estate investment trust (REIT) that owns commercial properties in the Southwest entered into cross-ownership investments and loans between the company and insiders, a structure it claimed was tax-driven. The company also used shareholders' capital to buy a house from its Chief Investment Officer for $2.7 million. Later, the company took a charge of $900,000 on the loss from that deal. In general, the Sarbanes-Oxley Act's Section 402 now prevents companies from making loans to its executives on terms not available to the public. However, existing loans made by the REIT to its management were grandfathered under the legislation. But not to leave well enough alone, the board lengthened the term for over $30 million of existing loans for its executives.[12]

You can be sure that this company's management hired the best advisors to counsel them, and for this reason this company's board needs to do the same to protect its shareholder interests. Nevertheless, it is unclear how a savvy board of this REIT, with oversight responsibility, could have believed the practices there would be good for shareholders. Perhaps they received good independent advice before investing in the house, extending the terms of executive loans, and investing in business relationships that appear to conflict management. One would also trust that each conflict was evaluated and is being monitored. One would also expect that if any terms disadvantage the company, the difference would be considered compensation and included in management's overall performance evaluation and compensation calculations. Shareholders have the right to be skeptical and this REIT's board needs to take steps to provide some transparency regarding their dealings with management.

FINAL DECISION

The most effective boards are in that zone of respect, trust, and candor. Dissent is not considered disloyalty. They discuss difficult issues, make decisions, and get on with the business of the company without looking back. Issues may be hotly debated, but once a course of action is agreed on, these boards move forward rather than stewing over the last vote. As discussed earlier in Chapter 7, UPS's move from Connecticut to Georgia is held up as an example of constructive board behavior. Despite strong debate over an emotional issue, once the decision to move was made, the board put the issue behind them and turned their focus to selecting the best location.[13] The ability to stay focused on business is an important quality of effective boards. Only in the rare situation where an ethical issue or overall strategy/direction of the company is at stake should a director continue to insist on additional debate after the decision is made. In these circumstances, the director is properly doing their job representing shareholders and will either come to terms with the decision made, effect change, or resign to send an important signal to the investment community. This is a judgment personally made by each director based on what is in their gut. The gut check is the bottom line for most directors: are you comfortable with the outcome. If not, keep at it.

KEY CONCEPTS

- Schedule unstructured time to build relationships with other directors and senior managers.
- Actively manage board behavior by using mentoring, training, and evaluation tools.
- Schedule executive sessions, prepare a formal agenda, and allow enough time to properly address issues. Debrief the CEO on any conclusions reached.
- Effective directors are engaged but do not normally manage the company.
- Corroborate important information obtained from a single source.
- Hire the best. Management hires the finest consultants, so should the board.
- Keep current on company and industry happenings. Sources for staying informed include management, consultants, customers, regulators, publications, and whistle-blowers.

ENDNOTES

1. Jeffrey A. Sonnenfeld, "What Makes Great Boards Great," *Harvard Business Review* 80 (September 2002): 109.
2. John Markoff, "When + Adds up to Minus," *New York Times,* 10 February 2005, C1.
3. Colin B. Carter and Jay W. Lorsch, *Back to the Drawing Board* (Boston: Harvard Business School Publishing, 2004), 169.
4. Activity continuum adapted from David A. Nadler, "Building Better Boards," *Harvard Business Review* 82 (May 2004): 102–111.

5. National Association of Corporate Directors, *Report of the NACD Blue Ribbon Commission on Risk Oversight* (2002), 77.

6. Lucent Technologies, *2004 Annual Report: Letter to Our Shareholders*, 2.

7. Gail J. McGovern, David Court, John A. Qulech, and Blair Crawford, "Bringing the Customers into the Boardroom," *Harvard Business Review* 82 (November 2004): 72.

8. Sonnenfeld, 113.

9. Eric Dash, "A Whistle-Blower Is Kept in the Wings at the Hearing," *New York Times,* 7 October 2004, C12.

10. Associated Press, "Tyco Dealmaker Admits Fraud," *CBSNews .com,* 17 December 2002. http://www.CBSNews.com/stories/2002/12/18/national/printable533415.shtml (9April 2005).

11. U.S. Securities and Exchange Commission, "SEC Charges Royal Ahold and Three Former Top Executives with Fraud. Release 2004-144," *SEC.gov,* 13 October 2004. http://www.sec.gov/news/press/2004-144.htm (9April 2005).

12. Elizabeth McDonald, "Crony Capitalism," *Forbes*, 21 June 2004, 140–146.

13. Sonnenfeld, 109.

Let Them Know You Are Watching

A former mentor of mine said that people behave differently when they think you are watching. To a certain extent, he was speaking about deterring wrongdoing; but well-intentioned employees also work harder on those areas where they know management is focusing their attention. Likewise, the board needs to signal management that they are monitoring the operations of the business and will diligently review any transactions presented from internal or external sources.

Governance Factor IV concerns the art of oversight and the actions a board should take if the barbarians—investment bankers and their acquiring clients—show up at the gates of the company. We discuss how directors can most efficiently and effectively monitor the company and properly represent shareholders when confronted with an offer to buy or sell a business.

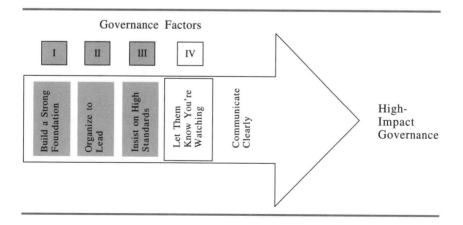

Governance Factors

I II III IV

Build a Strong Foundation | Organize to Lead | Insist on High Standards | Let Them Know You're Watching | Communicate Clearly

High-Impact Governance

CHAPTER 11

Art of Oversight*

When considering board service—after the pomp, circumstance, and corporate rituals are stripped away—what is left is oversight, the heavy lifting hidden in a beautifully wrapped honor and recognition package called the *public company director*. Oversight is art rather than applied science. Because every company is different, there is no single approach that works for everyone. To do the job correctly requires time, effort, skill, integrity, and judgment. To complicate matters, there are different types of oversight functions performed by directors. They have a responsibility to monitor the business, make certain that risks are properly assessed and managed, and ensure that management is adhering to company policies and code of ethics. Each of these perspectives (operational, risk, and compliance) require different but interconnected oversight skills. The goal of this chapter is to prepare supervisory black-belts—masters capable of monitoring the company from all three perspectives.

BUSINESS PERSPECTIVE: MONITORING OPERATIONS

Although monitoring progress and redirecting corporate activities toward strategic objectives is not a new concept, it is where many organizations fail. In these cases, feedback loops are not functioning, may be functioning but ignored, or do not exist at all. One of the more popular frameworks for monitoring and redirecting business activities and behavior is the balanced scorecard presented in 1996 by Robert S. Kaplan and David P. Norton in their book of the same name. Their framework focuses on four perspectives: (1) financial,

---

*Portions of this chapter are taken or adapted from Scott Green, *Manager's Guide to the Sarbanes-Oxley Act* (Hoboken, NJ: John Wiley & Sons, 2004).

(2) customer, (3) internal business processes, and (4) learning and growth. Monitoring tools are needed at all levels of the organization, and what is required in the bowels of the finance department or in the supplies area of the shop floor may not be particularly relevant to the board of directors. Nevertheless, they are important, and the board needs to obtain comfort that experts are regularly reviewing the effectiveness of processes at these detailed levels. However, there are processes that a company must excel at to succeed, and the board not only needs to know what these are, but also have the ability to monitor them.

Kaplan and Norton identified certain core measures that apply to most companies, regardless of strategy. These include core:

- *Financial measures* such as return on investment (or economic value added), profitability, revenue growth/mix, and cost reduction productivity
- *Customer measures* such as market share, customer acquisition, retention, profitability, and satisfaction
- *Learning and growth measures* including employee satisfaction, retention, and productivity[1]

Add to these company/industry-specific internal processes such as production cycle time, quality metrics for a manufacturer, or pick-up time for a call center and you have a useful report that both management and the board can utilize to monitor the health of the business.

Information can overwhelm the board, so the key is to keep it focused and relevant. Even the number of metrics discussed above can be difficult to digest and follow. The board should select those perceived as most important, and periodically revisit the menu of available metrics to determine if they are, in fact, focusing on those that are vital. Strategies, the operating environment, and corporate leaders all transform over time. The information needed to run the business may also change.

Developing Key Performance Indicators

Good *key performance indicators* (KPIs) succinctly communicate the health of the business. They tell the rest of the story that the financial numbers alone cannot. These indicators can also be used to educate investors, outside analysts, and employees about the drivers of success. Apparel retailers who quickly identify and react to customer buying trends can create a competitive advantage. Wal-Mart, for one, has identified buying trends as a key indicator. The retailer uses an active data warehousing system to immediately adjust inventory to buyer habits, thereby enabling it to respond to changes in consumer behavior in real time. These trends do not tell Wal-Mart how successful they have been, but the company's ability to spot and react quickly to them is widely recognized as one of their competitive advantages.

The New York City Police Department tracks the number of complaints to determine the effectiveness of crime fighting under the theory that a strong but targeted presence results in a reduction of crime. The New York City Crime Index has, in fact, decreased from approximately 700,000 complaints in 1990 to under 250,000 in 2003. The department has also identified response time as a key indicator. It is used as a measure of efficiency in reaching a crime scene. Obviously, a quick response improves the chances that a criminal will be apprehended and can help limit the severity of injuries to victims. According to the Mayor's office, as of June 2002 the police response time improved 29 percent over the same period from the year before. This occurred even though the number of police declined. This indicator is relevant feedback to patrol officers, city management, and the community. It is clear that the police force has been able to do better with fewer resources and all stakeholders can find good news in this metric. Police can be proud that their efforts resulted in this improvement, the community will perceive the police as more responsive and the streets safer, and the city government can report productivity gains to the taxpayers. There are other benefits not anticipated with these improved metrics. The murder rate in New York has fallen from 2,245 in 1990 to 566 in 2004, which works out to 6.9 murders per 100,000 people. This compares favorably to most other large cities such as Los Angeles (12.8), Chicago (14.8), and Philadelphia (20.6). New York's success has freed up police resource for developing new databases to understand violence in their city. No longer are drug-related murders New York's largest problem, although they still account for a significant number of killings. The largest number of murders fall into the dispute category, which can be initiated by road rage, an exchange of angry words, or just a dirty look. This category accounted for 28 percent of murders, followed by drug related (24 percent), domestic violence (12 percent), robbery (11 percent), revenge (7 percent), gang related (6 percent), and other (12 percent).[2] Interestingly, of all the murders committed in 1997, half of the victims were drunk or had an intoxicant in their blood. Fully 39 percent of the victims tested positive for alcohol. This information requires new antiviolence strategies to address dispute resolution and domestic violence in addition to drug related crime. Without this information, the New York City police would be fighting crime the same way they were in 1970, with the same results. The fact is that their key performance indicators have helped them form strategies that save lives.

Certain indicators are self-evident and will tell the whole story. For instance, an exception report will tell you that a boundary has been tested or breached. Other indicators are more meaningful if put into context. Just as the New York Police Department is able to track its results against other cities, the establishment of goals or comparisons in the form of benchmarks can help directors to understand the full meaning of the information available.

Outside Point of View

Benchmarking is a terrific management tool that helps provide perspective to raw data. There are many sources from which management can draw, both internal and external to the organization. Traditional external sources would include industry association statistics, statistics compiled and reported regularly by accounting, consulting, and service firms such as the Gartner Group, and now Internet participation groups from which management can glean data.

The advantages of going the extra mile to develop external benchmarks are significant. External benchmarks help identify best practice, highlight performance gaps, and can help management identify sources of competitive advantage. Data that is developed independent of the company can provide a litmus test to the success of the organization. During a start-up in 2000 at ING Barings, the company compared the effectiveness of its new brokerage clearing activities to industry data published by the National Securities

Clearing Corporation and the Depository Trust Company. The company knew it had an effective operation when its operating statistics beat the industry averages by a wide margin.

Internally developed benchmarks may be all that is available or relevant for certain KPIs. The strengths of internal data are that they are relatively easy to access and tend to come from common systems. By adding trend analysis and comparative data, additional perspectives can be gained regarding the health of the operation. For instance, a report may tell management that they have the same dollar amount of aged receivables outstanding as they had over the last three months. This is helpful as it makes clear that the company's maximum dollar risk is not increasing. But if management combines that data with sales and understands that revenues have fallen significantly, then the risk of loss has actually increased. The company has more aged receivables per sales dollar than in prior months.

Benchmarking can also be used as a continuous tool for improvement. Periodically, revisit and brainstorm certain benchmarks to determine if they need to be revised to reflect best practice. If results are falling well short of best practice, then management time and resources need to be spent studying this process with an eye toward re-engineering.

RISK PERSPECTIVE: MONITORING THREATS AND DANGERS

When discussing a board's risk oversight obligation, there is no better description than that provided in the *Enterprise Risk Management Framework* published by the Committee of Sponsoring Organizations of the Treadway Commission (COSO). They summarize the board's responsibility as follows:

> *Management is accountable to the board of directors, which provides governance, guidance and oversight. By selecting management, the board has a major role in defining what it expects in integrity and ethical values and can confirm its expectations through oversight activities. Similarly, by reserving authority in certain key decisions, the board lays a role in setting strategy, formulating high-level objectives and broad-based resource allocation.*[3]

The COSO Enterprise Risk Management (ERM) Framework further details a director's oversight responsibilities as:

- Knowing the extent to which management has established effective enterprise risk management in the organization
- Being aware of and concurring with the entity's risk appetite
- Reviewing the entity's portfolio view of risks and considering it against the entity's risk appetite
- Being apprised of the most significant risk and whether management is responding appropriately[4]

Given this mandate, the board has to be active participants in the development and oversight of risk management processes as well as the company's response to organizational threats. This includes oversight of the organization's performance against key indicators, benchmarking against the competition, and even monitoring management's compliance with policies—and, importantly, it includes oversight of risk identification and assessment.

Developing Risk Assessment Capability

How can you mitigate threats if you cannot see them coming? The obvious answer is that you cannot. Management must build an early warning system to alert them of trouble before it arrives. The board must make certain this happens. The development of integrated risk identification systems is difficult as threats can be both internal and external to the company. Internally, risks can migrate from deep within the organization. Externally, competitor moves or regulatory changes can threaten the business. Some risks require event reporting; others need to be constantly monitored. Certain risks must be closely watched at the board level. Financial reporting, executive compensation, and director nomination are processes that exhibit significant inherent risk to the enterprise. As such, boards monitor these processes closely through designated committees. Other processes will be monitored by the board on an exception basis as key indicators merit. Successful risk management programs identify problems early, clearly assign responsibility for each type of event, and document well-defined thresholds or trigger points where escalation to the top echelons of the enterprise is required. It is less important that every manager perfectly analyze every threat. It is more important to understand that there is an owner for every risk and how that owner identifies and communicates essential changes in the danger assessment.

Another important concept often overlooked by management is that risks migrate. For instance, a liquidity crisis may impact the COO's ability to source enough raw materials to maintain consistent production levels. While the COO is not expected to manage the company's liquidity—that is generally the province of the CFO and his or her reports—the COO's ability to perform his or her job is directly impacted by this key factor. Thus directors need to ensure that adequate attention is paid to communicating evolving threats to all impacted stakeholders in the enterprise. In this case, the COO would need to make certain to be informed of a pending cash crunch so that he or she could do everything possible to ensure the supply of raw materials and production continues unimpeded and with as little impact as feasible on the cash position of the company.

There are many types of threats to a company, and new subcategories seem to appear daily. The in-depth exploration of all risk types is not relevant to most directors, and so is beyond the scope of this book. However, a director must be able to determine if the company has established effective enterprise risk management and can use these topics as a checklist to determine if management is covering all of the relevant areas. Specialists can handle most of these threats; nevertheless, it is important that all directors understand the impact they can have on the company, as well as the methods employed to control them. Where the board is not satisfied with the answers received, they can focus their energies and investigate further. Different organizations group and view risks in diverse ways. While there is no one right method, most risks can be grouped into seven generic categories and assigned to specific executives for monitoring and resolution:

- *Market.* This risk emanates from sales practices, brand/trademark impairment, publicity, new delivery vehicles (such as e-commerce), and adverse effects of consumer/customer sentiment or tastes. An example of the last item includes the preference of travelers to book their flights and hotels online. Market share for this delivery method is growing exponentially and already accounts for 23 percent of all domestic travel.

■ *Concentration.* This risk can take several forms such as over reliance on a single or limited number of customers, investments, or products. The type of concentration determines the owner. If one customer accounts for 80 percent of the business, one can argue that the CEO should take responsibility for this critical relationship as well as helping identify new customers or markets. If it is reliance on one bank or market as the supply of financing, it would be the CFO's responsibility to identify other sources.

■ *Credit.* This risk includes counterpart default, where value has been delivered but not yet fully received in return. A recent example of credit risk is the massive write-off taken by Sichuan Changhong, a Chinese-based manufacturer of televisions sets. Changhong had allowed a receivable to one of their largest customers, Apex Digital, to exceed $450 million. This occurred despite some well-publicized problems at Apex. One example is that the U.S. government had moved to slap 25 percent tariffs on Changhong's sets as an antidumping measure. Apex's major customers tended to be retailers such as Wal-Mart, which have a knack of squeezing suppliers and are only interested in sourcing from the lowest cost vendor. Tariffs mean higher prices, which mean fewer sales. Apex also had been ignoring significant royalty payments for DVD technology it apparently had difficulty paying. Apex's inability to pay Changhong resulted in a write-off of over $300 million (representing half of company sales for 2003) as the company moves to stem further losses. In a move reminiscent of the old debtors prisons, China took Apex's president into custody for financial fraud.[5]

■ *Financial and liquidity.* Examples of this risk type include an amount of leverage used by a company that is unsustainable, or access to credit and funding sources that has been compromised. Enron is an interesting example. Its energy trading business needed liquidity to fund its positions. Once word of trouble hit the Street, no one wanted to chance having Enron as a counterpart because it might not be able to honor its trading commitments. Funding sources quickly dried up, revenue could not be produced because counterparts stopped trading with the company, and its expensive trading platform became a white elephant that it could not sell. Within a matter of weeks, Enron could no longer pay its bills.

- *Operational.* This risk relates primarily to the internal breakdown of controls relating to initiation, pricing, delivering and booking a transaction, and making good delivery of product or service, including systems controls and errors. Operational risk can be differentiated from other risks in that it exists in every step of the business process or value chain. The examples here are numerous and varied. They include fraud, embezzlement, and unintentional losses due to a lack of functioning controls such as the manufacturing of a defective product that is widely distributed before the defect is discovered. The health and safety of the workforce is another important operational risk that must be actively managed.

- *Technology.* Technology dangers can take the form of system malfunctions, hacker incursions, or even new technology-driven disruptive forces that give a competitor an advantage. Technology is pervasive throughout every organization as a productivity tool and enabler. The risk that a given technology may not work, or be compromised, is an operational risk, hence obsolescence and availability must be assessed as a part of the company's business continuity planning. It may be that for some businesses technology differentiates a product. For instance, the new third-generation cell phones allow users to snap photos, retrieve e-mail, browse the Internet, and buy products online—capabilities that did not exist just a few years ago. In this and similar cases, new or disruptive technologies raise the possibility that customers will choose a new product or delivery system over your current offering. If technology plays an important role in product design and differentiation or impacts the ability of the enterprise to compete as a low-cost producer, then technology should be considered in the development of the organization's competitive strategy and market placement.

- *Event.* This risk refers to a specific action or occurrence that affects the company's ability to do business, such as changes in the political, legal, or regulatory environment, a natural or man-made disaster, disruption of the supply chain due to war, the unavailability of a key executive, or other events that have the potential to negatively impact the reputation of the company. An example might be a notice of investigation by a government regulator such as the SEC.

Now there are other ways to categorize risk, such as the important risks managed by human resource departments. These risks can be independently categorized if it is useful for the board. Employee turnover, too, is viewed as an operational risk that every manager should be cognizant of and prepared to manage. At the executive level, the unavailability of an executive should be categorized as event risk as well. In either case, it has to be managed with support of the human resources department. But the responsibility to guarantee depth in a department and replacement of departing staff lies with a line manager or an executive. Regardless of how threats are categorized, once they are identified, they need to be assigned.

Assigning Sentries

During most successful military battles, there are a number of discrete units executing their duties to ensure the overall success of the mission. There may be troops on the ground, ships bringing heavy equipment ashore, others firing missiles at inland targets, aircraft providing cover, and supply lines replenishing fighting resources. In short, the complexity of supporting a military campaign requires the delineation of responsibilities and coordination of resources. The ability to fight depends on everyone knowing their responsibilities and when and where they need to be delivered. Miscalculation can result in lost lives. These managers must work together to ensure all risks are accounted for and monitored.

Just like the military, corporate managers need to define duties, understand the risks that they are expected to manage, and know how their efforts contribute to the overall plan of attack. As mentioned earlier, credit, financial, concentration, market, and event risks can generally be assigned to a specialist, department head, or committee for study, monitoring, and management. This person or committee becomes the "owner." It is relatively easy to understand the impact these threats have on a company and the steps required to address them. In contrast, operational risk is diffused across the entire enterprise, and for this reason can be difficult to identify, let alone assign to an owner. Therefore, network access, system errors, turnover of key personnel, purchasing controls, proper classification of revenues and expenses, and so on, must be supervised at the managerial level and problems escalated to the appropriate level of management as they surface.

In a large corporation, the COO, CFO, or assigned committees cannot effectively micromanage every executive in every business line—a COO at headquarters in Peoria cannot, for example, determine whether system access rights for programmers in India are appropriate. Yet poor access controls can lead to stunning losses. This is not to say that executive management should not establish organizational strategies and policies and evaluate each manager on how well he or she conforms to the established protocol. The point is that each manager must own and control threats to his or her people and processes and executive management and the board of directors must communicate and enforce this fact. Exhibit 11.1 illustrates the various generic risks and the senior managers typically responsible for monitoring these threats.

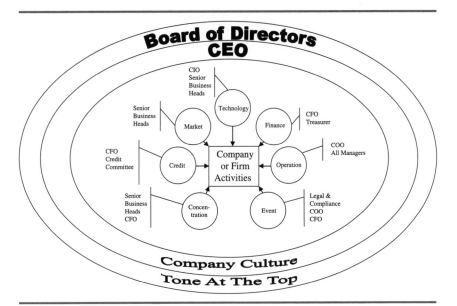

EXHIBIT 11.1 Generic Risk Owners

The CEO and the board of directors are responsible for setting the overall tone of the control culture and assigning risk owners. Good CEOs formally assign market and product/customer concentration risks to business heads and/or strategy and planning groups, credit risk to credit committees, financial and liquidity risks to the CFO, legal event risk to the legal department, and *disaster recovery planning* (DRP) to a DRP specialist. They then monitor the outputs from each of these risk owners. They review and actively participate in business plans and strategies produced, as well as evaluate their progress, and manage the capital allocation process in line with these strategies. They review reported credit exposure and expect to see periodic stress-testing of the company's financial structure and resources. They expect frequent legal updates, complete with an analysis of the impact that pending legislation in the field will have on the company. They also want to know the results of periodic testing of the firm's offsite recovery center, to ensure that the company is prepared to remain operational in case of a disruptive event. Finally, CEOs link company managers' ability to control risk objectives to their performance review process. And the board wants to ensure that their CEO understands this responsibility and that a process is in place to manage these risks.

But what about operational risk? Just as a doctor uses an EKG to monitor the heartbeat of a patient, every manager—including the CEO—needs a way to monitor the health of his or her business processes. This can be accomplished by establishing key indicators that alert management to a problem. Furthermore, it is the responsibility of senior executives and the board to establish a culture that enables communication of increased threats. This entails creating an environment that rewards candor and honesty, even if the news brought forward is bad. The more eyes that search for a potential threat, the greater the likelihood that the menace is spotted early. Without a strong control culture and an effective monitoring program, there is a much greater chance that the company will experience a severe loss.

No Surprises: Escalate!

There are times when there is no question that a problem deserves both escalation and widespread communication. A train running a signal is such a situation. Once a train has missed a signal, the risk of a disaster becomes a clear and present danger. Only good detection alarms, properly routed in a timely fashion, enable a well-disciplined dispatcher to regain control. The difficult events are those where the decision to escalate is not clear. This is why it is important for each responsible manager or executive to prepare a risk assessment that identifies thresholds and triggers for escalation. If the risk has been considered, and the escalation benchmark established, it becomes easier to identify reportable events at differing levels within the organization. The overriding message to those down the chain of command is "err on the side of reporting." To initiate discussion of an issue deemed nonreportable should not be penalized, rather encouraged. What you want to avoid is someone recognizing a problem, but not its significance and, therefore, allowing it to grow.

What should be penalized is surprise. No manager, executive, or director wants to learn from the media that they have a problem. Enforcement of control boundaries and corporate policy is the responsibility of every manager. As such, it should be a component of their annual evaluation. Raising potential issues should be reinforced through positive performance reviews. Likewise, surprises due to lack of appropriate oversight also merit mention. Tying good management control practices to the appraisal process is one of the most effective ways to build a culture of doing what is right for the company. By including this category in the appraisal process, management is saying that they not only talk about good internal controls, adherence to corporate policy, and observing the highest ethical standards, they act on them.

Once a material event is escalated, however, the company needs to be prepared to manage the problem. The breakdown in communicating the coming tsunamis in the Indian Ocean in December 2004 is a case in point. Scientists at the Pacific Tsunami Warning Center in Hawaii knew of the underwater earthquake immediately after it happened. An hour later, as they analyzed their data, they were aware that the threat of a devastating tsunami was possible. They sent out a formal warning, but they were unable to get word to those who needed it most. Because their work primarily deals with Pacific countries, they did not have contact information for those in countries ringing the Indian Ocean who would have been capable of warning their public. They worked continuously to get the word out, but with little effect. While the waves would not hit Africa for several hours, they were unable to escalate their information to the right people and prevent the loss of life eventually realized in Somalia.[6] Events and crises happen, so we need to prepare for them. The Sarbanes-Oxley Act requires that many events be reported within four business days, so the time to organize a response team is not after the event has already occurred. (In Chapter 13, we will further discuss the need for a rapid response team.)

COMPLIANCE PERSPECTIVE: MONITORING MANAGEMENT[†]

It is a sad truth that today's boards must become savvy overseers of management. As I often tell disbelievers, "trust is not a control." We want to believe our managers will do the right thing, and nearly all will. However, if we are lax, it creates opportunity. As the frauds perpetuated by management have become more sophisticated, they become harder to detect. In addition to financial reporting fraud, which we discussed earlier, some other behaviors that have damaged our public companies include insider trading, misuse of corporate assets, and conflicts of interest that disadvantage shareholders.

Insider Trades

Stockholders in general want the management team of a company in which they own stock to hold significant shares in that company. This comes on the belief that it aligns the management's interests with theirs. Unfortunately, some managers use their position to trade based on their intimate knowledge of the company. One of the most egregious examples of trading abuse was embodied by Enron management who sold their stock while freezing employee shares held in company plans. The freeze was accomplished by creating a blackout,

---

[†]Portions of the following sections have been excerpted by permission of Hofstra University Frank G. Zarb School of Business from Scott Green, "A Look at the Causes, Impact and Future of the Sarbanes-Oxley Act," *Journal of International Business and Law* (Spring 2004): 33–51.

a normal procedure used when switching plan administrators or making other adjustments. Many employees and retirees saw their life's savings evaporate while executives cashed out their company shares. As a consequence, Congress inserted language into the Sarbanes-Oxley Act that prohibits insider trades during pension blackout periods. Section 306 of the Act spells out that it shall be "unlawful for any director or executive officer . . . to purchase, sell, or otherwise acquire or transfer any equity security of the issuer during any black-out period." The Act further authorizes the company to recapture any profits made on such trades. It also puts in place notification procedures regarding blackouts.

The Act did not stop with the pension blackout period. Congress also amended the reporting requirements for directors, officers, and principal stockholders. Changes in holdings of company stock must now be reported much more rapidly (within two days of the transaction) on SEC Form 4 with certain exceptions. As required by the Sarbanes-Oxley Act Section 403, these communications will be posted on the SEC's website, and if the issuer maintains a website, it must be posted there as well no later than the business day following the filing.

It is truly in a board's best interests to monitor all trading of senior executives and directors in company stock. Not only are there SEC reporting requirements, but improper trading can severely damage the organization. Insiders are privy to information that produces unfair advantage. For instance, the management of ChoicePoint, an identity and credential verification service, is being investigated by the SEC for allegedly dumping their stock after they became aware of a security breach. The executives in question made $16 million on their sales before the information was made public. There is little question that the security of personal information is paramount to the public and that this news could severely hurt business. Best practice would have the board restrict executive and director trading to certain predefined periods, say the first week of each fiscal quarter after release of the financial results, and investigate any trades made less than 30 days of releasing material information, good or bad.

There are many examples of management abusing their position to improperly enrich or protect themselves by trading stock. One high-profile insider trading case is the ImClone scandal in which the CEO, Sam Waksal, dumped his stock and tipped off family members of an unfavorable FDA ruling allowing them to trade ahead of the market. The loss of confidence in management kept the stock depressed despite evidence that the drug under consideration still had promising potential. Martha Stewart was also caught up in the scandal, which did not involve her company, but nevertheless caused the sell-off of her company's stock, Martha Stewart Living, from around $20 to below $10. While an executive compliance program generally is limited to company stock and does not specifically contemplate a Martha Stewart-type fraud, it does show the impact bad executive behavior can have on a company's stock price.

Corporate Assets

Among WorldCom, Enron, Adelphia Communications, and the other great frauds of 2001 and 2002, was the conglomerate Tyco International. Unlike these other companies, Tyco did not go bankrupt, and the alleged fraud did not result in a cataclysmic loss of jobs, or render worthless the pensions of company retirees. So what is all the drama about? While there were significant accounting irregularities at Tyco that were similar to these other cases, this was not purely an accounting scandal. Rather, Tyco is a case study of corporate largess, abuse of power, and absence of executive fiduciary duty to shareholders. In Dennis Kozlowski, prosecutors believe they have found the perfect poster child for executive greed and unethical practices. They may be right.

Prosecutors originally indicted Kozlowski and his management team for bilking the conglomerate out of some $600 million. Excesses the State of New York and the SEC accused him of included:

- Forgiving tens of millions of dollars in loans to executives and directors, including himself
- Deciding what bonuses would be paid to whom, and when, without regard to restrictions that the board placed on executive compensation
- Accelerating the vesting of Tyco stock for himself and others
- Using the company treasury to pay his personal bills
- Selling corporate residences to the CEO at far less than fair value

- Using $7 million of Tyco's funds to purchase a Park Avenue apartment for his first wife, from whom he had been separated
- Using corporate money to buy his New Hampshire house for three times its apparent fair market value

The State of New York believed the illegal activity of the Tyco management team to be so sophisticated and pervasive that they dubbed it the "Top Executives Criminal Enterprise," a title they used to describe Kozlowski's team throughout the indictment.[7]

Congress addressed some of the abuses in the Sarbanes-Oxley Act by restricting the ability of a company to make loans to executives. Section 402 of the Act specifically prohibits companies from extending credit to executives other than those with terms made available to the general public in the ordinary course of business. But as the Tyco example makes clear, loans are only one way management can abuse corporate assets.

The board needs to ensure they have the ability to monitor other benefit programs. These include employee pension, relocation, and stock programs. Regular discussion with the chief human resource officer regarding executive participation in these programs, combined with regular internal audits, help provide directors with the comfort that these programs are not being abused.

Dennis Kozlowski must be feeling like he dodged a bullet with his name on it. In his recent trial with codefendant, former CFO Mark Swartz, the jury became deadlocked. All that stood between him and a New York State prison cell was Juror Number 4. Eleven jurors were prepared to find Kozlowski guilty on several counts and see him off to the big house. Juror Number 4, it seems, stood on principle (although what principle that would be is not clear to everyone), and would not be moved by forces of heaven or earth. The drama played out on the front covers of our nation's newspapers, with the inevitable mistrial an anticlimactic result for all that followed the story. Determined prosecutors, however, have brought a new, more focused trial with fewer counts that will once again put Kozlowski's freedom on the line.

Regardless of the verdict eventually rendered, directors, corporate executives, and gatekeepers should take to heart the lessons from the Tyco fallout. Now is a good time to revisit board composition, governance processes, and corporate culture initiatives. Not only is it the right thing to do for the company, these actions also send an important signal to employees, shareholders, and regulators. It signifies that the board and senior management understand the risks of poor governance and that unscrupulous practices like those at Tyco will simply not be tolerated.

Conflicts

As defined in the Sarbanes-Oxley Act, a "conflict of interest occurs when an individual's private interest interferes in any way—or even appears to interfere—with the interests of the corporation as a whole."[8] Not all conflicts are detrimental as some arrangements might benefit the company. Because of this, related-party transactions are numerous and widespread. In fact, a recent *Wall Street Journal* survey evaluated over 400 of the nation's largest public companies and it revealed that "some 300 of those companies reported one or more related party transactions . . . many of these transactions involved millions of dollars."[9] Where conflicts do arise, they must be well communicated, managed, and subjected to detailed and unimpeachable oversight. Only strong, active, and ongoing supervision will ensure that stockholders benefit from doing business with a related party. This difficult and risk-laden task is best avoided altogether, but that can only happen if the company is devoid of conflicts. Otherwise, directors must recognize this risk and actively manage it.

As mentioned earlier, Andrew Fastow, Enron's CFO, managed the creation of off-balance sheet entities resulting in an unrealistic picture of financial health for the company. He was also responsible for managing certain off-balance sheet vehicles in which he had a financial interest. An investigation by Enron's Board of Directors found:

> *These partnerships . . . were used by Enron management to enter into transactions that it could not, or would not, do with unrelated commercial entities. Many of the most significant transactions apparently were designed to accomplish favorable financial statement results, not to achieve bona fide economic objectives or to transfer risk.*[10]

Special Purpose Entities (SPEs) can be effective financing and risk management vehicles if used properly. A parent company's debt level or other risk factors can hinder the capability of a strong business segment in obtaining favorable interest rates to finance its operations. In such a situation, the parent can create an SPE and transfer the asset to it with the goal of receiving more favorable lending rates. As long as there is another independent third-party investor that has contributed at least three percent of the assets, the SPE does not have to be consolidated into the parent for financial reporting purposes.[11] Furthermore, if the assets in the SPE are of high quality, banks will lend to the entity at lower lending rates than could be received by the originating company. The SPE will then use this money to pay the parent for the asset received. The bottom line is that the company obtains the money it requires, but pays less to obtain it than would otherwise be the case.

In 1997, Enron's CFO began creating SPEs to hold assets and provide the appearance of creating legitimate financing transactions. However, Enron ran out of quality assets to transfer, so inferior assets were reassigned and Enron stock pledged as a guarantee of payment to the banks. And who did Enron find to be that three-percent investor in the SPEs? The CFO, through a partnership called LJM, among others.[12] But why would he want to invest in poor quality assets? Because the fees Enron paid LJM for managing the transaction eliminated his risk in these vehicles. He effectively cashed out; so while he was an investor on paper, he really had no downside risk.[13]

Enron's Board contained a former accounting professor, the former executives of an insurance company and a bank, the former head of the Commodity Futures Trading Commission, and a hedge fund manager.[14] Enron's financial transactions were confusing even to these highly knowledgeable individuals. What was clear is that the Board did waive their conflict of interest rules to allow these transactions to take place. The Board's responsibility to understand these transactions is paramount where related parties are involved. They must make sure the transactions are in the best interests of the company and continue to monitor the conflict to ascertain that it continues to benefit shareholders.

In conclusion, a strong oversight program helps focus the board's time. With such a program in place, the board can bore in on any risk gaps identified, metrics flashing red, or exception reports, as they arise. Risk mitigation activities deemed critical by the board, such as those covering financial reporting, can be subjected to more intense oversight by standing committees. Strong director oversight includes monitoring the organization from many different perspectives. A mix of risk analysis and event reporting, monitoring of business drivers, and ensuring management's compliance with ethical standards enable a director to demonstrate strong oversight processes and help protect the company. Effective compliance programs should also help lessen the likelihood that a criminal proceeding or a SEC civil enforcement action is initiated against the company.

KEY CONCEPTS

- Add key performance indicators to your arsenal. KPIs are an important supervisory tool that directors can use to identify those areas that will benefit most from their time.
- Establish benchmarks for KPIs. Benchmarking using sources external to the company is a best practice that can provide perspective and depth to metric reporting.
- Ensure that individuals or groups are assigned specific risks and have responsibility to monitor and report on threat levels.
- Restrict executive and director trading in company stock to predefined periods, such as the first week after the release of quarterly and annual financial statements.
- Regularly discuss executive use of benefit programs with the Head of Human Resources and have this information corroborated through periodic internal audits.
- Avoid related-party agreements. If there are such agreements, make certain that they are closely monitored and information is corroborated by someone independent of the agreement.

ENDNOTES

1. Robert S. Kaplan and David P. Norton, *The Balanced Scorecard* (Boston: Harvard Business School Press, 1996), 306.

2. Shaila K. Dewan, "As Murders Fall, New Tactics Are Tried Against Remainder," *New York Times*, 31 December 2004, B1.
3. Committee of Sponsoring Organizations of the Treadway Commission, *Enterprise Risk Management* (September 2004), 19.
4. Ibid.
5. Chris Buckley, "Leading Chinese Exporter Has Huge Loss," *New York Times*, 28 December 2004, C1.
6. Andrew C. Revkin, "How Scientists and Victims Watched Helplessly," *New York Times*, 31 December 2004, A1.
7. Supreme Court of the State of New York, County of New York, Criminal Term. *The People of the State of New York against L. Dennis Kozlowski and Mark H. Swartz, Defendants*. Indictment No. 5259/02.
8. New York Stock Exchange, *Final Corporate Governance Rules* (4 November 2003), 16. This Section 303A compliance document can be viewed at http://www.nyse.com/pdfs/finalcorpgovrules.pdf.
9. John R. Emshwiller, "Business Ties: Many Companies Report Transactions with Top Officers," *Wall Street Journal*, 29 December 2003, A1.
10. William C. Powers, Jr., Raymond S. Troubh, Herbert S. Winokur, Jr., *Report of Investigation by the Special Investigative Committee of the Board of Directors of Enron Corp.* (1 February 2002), 4. This document, known as the "Powers Report," can be viewed at http://news.findlaw.com/hdocs/enron/sincreport/. *See also* Arthur L. Berkowitz, *Enron: A Professional's Guide to the Events, Ethical Issues, and Proposed Reforms*, (New York: CCH Inc. 2002). This book, in Appendix A, provides an excerpt from the Powers Report.
11. Arthur L. Berkowitz, *Enron: A Professional's Guide to the Events, Ethical Issues, and Proposed Reforms*, (New York: CCH Inc. 2002), 148.
12. Ibid., 151–152, 156.
13. United States District Court, Southern District of Texas, Houston Division, *United States Securities and Exchange Commission v. Arthur S. Fastow*, *SEC.gov* (2002). http://www.sec.gov/litigation/complaints/comp17762.htm.
14. Ibid.

CHAPTER 12

Hostile Activities

J ohn C. Malone, the chairman of Liberty Media Corporation, is working with Merrill Lynch International to exchange his non-voting shares in the media giant News Corporation for voting ones. Malone has been doing large block trades without previously notifying News Corporation's CEO, Rupert Murdoch, with whom he has had a long-term friendship and mutually profitable business dealings. Understandably, this has created some hard feelings between the two. Why is Malone doing this? Some speculate it is to take over the company, others believe it is to make money on the spread between the voting and nonvoting shares. Still others believe a type of greenmail may be in the offing with Malone wanting the News Corporation to buy his stock in a tax-preferred transaction. Regardless of the motivation, it has Murdoch's attention. It is a poorly held secret that he plans to turn over the company to his sons sometime in the future, so there are some serious conflicts between what management wants, and what might be best for shareholders. In response to Malone's accumulation, the News Corporation adopted a poison pill designed to keep his stake below 18 percent.[1] This is but one example of a corporate defense. In this chapter, we will briefly review the more common corporate defenses available, the conflicts that can surface, and their impact on a public company.

REPELLING SHARKS

One of the most important issues a director can face is the prospect of selling or merging the company. Just like the News Corporation scenario previously described, these transactions are often a public, high-stakes game of chess. A director has a duty to represent shareholders' interests and, as such, must carefully weigh solicitations with the understanding that management is deeply conflicted. What may be in the best interests of shareholders might result in management losing their jobs and dissolution of the board. Courts also understand this conflict and take them into consideration in a takeover-related challenge. Regardless of the potential outcome for directors personally, they must remain objective and give due consideration to valid offers for the company. Directors have a burden of proof that they have shown good faith and properly investigated and reviewed an offer to buy the company before making an informed decision. Some say a director has a duty to reject all first bids, as the second is bound to be higher. In reality there is no simple template. The decision to sell is not easy. Using shareholder defenses might be a rational response to protect shareholder interests, but only up to a point. If you reject a fair price, you have failed your shareholders, but you also fail them if you sell too cheaply. By way of example, a court held that Revlon's board, in adopting a poison pill, acted reasonably to an offer at $45 a share; however, the defense was no longer reasonable when the offer was increased to $53 a share.[2]

On the other hand, boards need to be careful buyers when considering large transactions brought by management. An acquisition should make financial sense. The track record of most large acquisitions is not good; and if management is selling the notion of synergy or strategic fit, it may be that it cannot justify the purchase based on valuation. If the business case is not persuasive and will not add meaningfully to earnings, then the board should be skeptical. The Baxter Healthcare purchase of American Hospital Supply (AHS) in 1985 is a good example of this. Baxter wanted to keep AHS from merging with another competitor, Hospital Corporation of America. The deal was sold on its potential synergies, and Baxter purchased AHS for $3.8 billion. The synergies were never realized and resulted in Baxter taking hefty charges.[3]

There are a number of shareholder defenses that are available to the board. Some are more shareholder-friendly than others. Tactical measures include staggered boards, poison pills, fair price provisions, confidential voting, and some decidedly more punitive maneuvers such as green mail, strategic asset sales, and pac-man or new stock issuance defenses.

STAGGERING BOARDS

Prior to the 1980s, all directors were almost always elected each year at the annual meeting. Terms were for a single year and a director would be reelected annually until retired or replaced. To protect themselves against raiders nominating their own slate of directors, companies lengthened director terms to three years and staggered their election so that only one-third of the board would be replaced in any given year. In theory, it would take a majority investor two years to gain control of the board. Studies conducted by the SEC suggest that staggered boards can destroy shareholder value.[4] Shareholder activists have been calling for boards to return to annual elections. Goldman Sachs, the investment banking powerhouse, is one of the latest to adopt annual director elections for one-year terms. Qualcomm, the owner of 3G mobile phone technologies, has a proposal detailed in their proxy statement to phase out staggered board terms. As each class of directors comes up for election, they will only be elected to one term. At the 2007 annual meeting, all directors will be elected for only one year.[5]

Despite voluntary movement toward better nomination practices, there have also been some recent setbacks. Most notably, the SEC has backed away from a proposal that would change proxy rules in such a way as to promote better shareholder access and participation in the nomination process. Vocal opposition from business and political pressure seems to have effectively scuttled this initiative. There are some valid concerns regarding unfettered proxy access. Many believe that large shareholders, such as union pension funds, could buy large stakes in companies simply for the purpose of installing employee-friendly directors that would advance causes important to workers, such as increased wages and benefits. The agenda of such special interests would be inconsistent with the interests of all shareholders and could hurt competitiveness. However, the status quo protects underperforming management and boards of directors. Other available remedies are either expensive or leave management entrenched. A hostile takeover is expensive and beyond the financial capability of most shareholders, particularly for large companies. Simply selling the stock may take care of the individual shareholder's problem, but still leaves entrenched, underperforming, and overpaid management.

Determining the right process to both advance and protect shareholder interests is not easy, but the difficulty of finding a workable solution should not result in no solution. Perhaps SEC Commissioner Harvey J. Goldschmid, said it best. He was quoted by *The New York Times* as saying "By this change in position, the staff has taken a half step backwards at a time when the commission should be taking two steps forward. The commission's failure to finalize a proxy access proposal has protected a small number of weak, inefficient and grossly overpaid CEOs. Leaving such CEOs invulnerable to shareholder challenge hurts the American economy. Unfortunately, the worst instincts of the CEO community have continued to triumph."[6]

INGESTING POISON PILLS

Since 1985 Delaware courts have upheld a company's right to adopt a shareholder rights plan. These plans can take many forms, but commonly consist of distributing rights or warrants that have no value unless activated by a hostile takeover. If activated, existing shareholders can buy stock cheap, or sell their stock back to the company at dear prices. Whether poison pills create or destroy shareholder value is inconclusive. A number of studies have supported both sides of the question. Boards do not have to obtain shareholder approval when adopting or maintaining a shareholder rights plan. Shareholders, however, have sponsored resolutions to redeem poison pills, and there is some evidence that companies removing poison pills experience some short-term gains. There are also derivatives of the poison pill that are shareholder friendly. One form consists of a pill that is not triggered if a bid is for all outstanding shares and fully financed. Shareholder rights plans can be useful if they are used to increase shareholder value, that is, make the suitor deal with the board to ensure a fair price is received. All too often, however, these defenses are used to prevent the sale of a company, no matter the offer.

VOTING CONFIDENTIALLY

Another tool used by management to their advantage is the voting process. Management, or their agents, receive proxies and tally votes, so they know an entity has voted. Since proxies can be changed up until the time they are officially counted, management can then use this knowledge to put pressure on those voting against them. As an example, Hewlett Packard (HP) publicly pressed Deutsche Asset Management to approve its 2002 merger with Compaq Computer. The battle to approve the merger was pitched with the sons of HP's founders (and their family foundations) opposing the merger. They spent (as did HP) tens of millions of dollars supporting their position.

The spectacle began when a Deutsche Bank subsidiary agreed to work with HP to promote a favorable shareholder vote. In return, Deutsche would make $2 million if the vote was successful. Interestingly, Deutsche Asset Management, which only had 1.3 percent of the stock, was planning to vote no. HP management counted on their business partner to fully support the merger, and under pressure, they eventually did. It turns out that HP needed to press for every vote as shareholders approved the merger by a thin 3 percent margin.[7] Confidential voting would relieve these pressures.

But the issue is more complex than just protecting institutional investors from undue corporate pressure. Confidential voting does reduce transparency. Investment companies that vote their proxies for entrenched, ineffective boards deserve to be exposed so that their shareholders can effect change. In my view, transparency trumps management pressure. In large part, companies are not embracing confidential voting for proxy contests in a meaningful way.

ANTISHAREHOLDER PROVISIONS

Some actions taken by boards are so damaging to shareholders, it is nearly impossible to see how they are justified. One of the most egregious acts is to pay greenmail to a corporate raider. If an investor (raider) buys enough stock and threatens to boot management, the board could authorize the company to buy back the raider's stock at a premium. In effect, existing shareholders are paying the raider to go away. Now why would a shareholder want that to happen? Cash leaves the company, the stock goes down once the pressure from the raider is relieved, and the competitive position of the company is not improved and may even be degraded by the ransom paid. Under a greenmail scenario, shareholders bear the cost of management entrenchment. It is one thing to adopt a shareholder rights plan to defend the company against a sale on the cheap; it is another thing to sell out existing shareholders.

Another trick only marginally better for shareholders is the strategic asset sale. In this scenario, the board sells the company's crown jewels to another company, leaving only sub par assets. Unless the assets are sold at a premium price and the proceeds distributed to existing shareholders, the move only entrenches management and makes holding the stock less desirable.

Under a "Pac Man" defense, the target turns the table and bids on the hostile company. This unusual approach results in both company's managements spending time and effort trying to acquire the other's stock at higher and higher prices until one side cries uncle.

Another method is to create a new class of stock with super voting rights (see case study Battle of the Generations) that are issued to management-friendly investors. This defense prevents a hostile force from replacing management, no matter how much of the company they own. This action dilutes the voting rights of existing shareholders and will make boards less responsive to shareholder concerns.

In summary, a director can expect more scrutiny by the courts where offers to buy a company and related defenses are involved. A smart board will recognize that management is conflicted, retain their own counsel, and repeatedly ask themselves what is the best decision for their stockholders. These issues are not easy, and the results are highly visible. This is when the shareholders need your good judgment the most.

CASE STUDY: BATTLE OF THE GENERATIONS

Not all threats come from outside the company. At the end of the day, those that hold the most voting rights are deeply empowered to create change or maintain the status quo. The recent rift between James Dolan, the CEO of Cablevision, and his father, Charles Dolan, the chairman, serves as a cautionary example. James convinced the board of directors, above his father's objections, that a satellite subsidiary, Voom, should be shut down as it was losing over $600 million a year. The board voted to suspend operations and authorized the sale of Voom's only satellite to Echostar. They also gave the chairman a few weeks to find a buyer for the remaining assets. Shareholders were elated; however, this was deeply embarrassing to the father who has spent the better part of a decade pushing the company into the satellite business that he considers the future of programming delivery to the home.

As the deadline to find a buyer approached, Charles Dolan made his move. He used his majority position in a special class of stock with super-voting rights to oust three directors, who voted against funding Voom, and replaced them with executives with whom he had close personal ties. He also replaced a vacant director's seat and disclosed that he planned to award a seat to his son-in-law. The company then told the SEC it was suspending efforts to shut down Voom.

Charles Dolan's actions, without the approval of the full board, left corporate governance advocates howling. Despite owning only 26 percent of the company, the Class B super-voting shares allows the Dolans to elect 75 percent of the board's directors. Charles Dolan has warned that Class B shareholders will exercise its right to elect 75 percent of the board at its next annual meeting although he has backed off on that threat recently.[a] Furthermore, Cablevision's board previously voted to become a family "controlled company" under NYSE rules, which exempts the company from some independence standards required of other public companies.

The remaining independent directors, in a letter to Charles Dolan filed with the SEC, expressed concern about Voom continuing to take on subscribers given its status as a discontinued operation. They have a right to be worried, not only because of the perception of Voom as a going concern, but also the potential of the board to move in a new direction. The new directors can overturn previous board decisions as long as they are in the best interests of all shareholders, but this could be hard to prove and will certainly open the directors up to shareholder litigation. Ironically, Charles may have done the ousted directors a favor as they may be the best positioned to avoid personal liability.

The fireworks may be just beginning, and this case promises to be one worthy of watching as the bitter family battle escalates. The father and son own homes next to each other that overlook Long Island Sound and two of James' older brothers also sit on the board of directors. With the son-in-law joining the board, family get-togethers will undoubtedly be a bit uncomfortable.

---

[a] Grant, Peter. "Chairman's Board Purge Alters Cablevision Picture," *Wall Street Journal*, 4 March 2005, A1.

ENDNOTES

1. Geraldine Fabrikant, "Liberty Media Accelerates Swap of News Corp. Shares," *New York Times*, 21 December 2004, C4.
2. *Revlon v. MacAndrews & Forbes Holdings*, 506 A.2d 173, 181 (Del. 1986).

KEY CONCEPTS

- Pay close attention to offers to buy or sell the company. Given possible conflicts of interests, directors have a burden of proof that they have shown good faith and made an informed decision.
- Choose annual elections. Staggered boards destroy shareholder value. Best practice is to elect an entire board of directors annually for a one year term.
- Remember your shareholders. Poison pills should be designed to be shareholder friendly so that they are not triggered if a bona fide and fully financed offer for a company is tendered.
- Greenmail, selling the company crown jewels, issuance of new classes of stock, and other antishareholder provisions should not be authorized by the board under pressure from a hostile offer.
- Be aware that an existing class of stock with super-voting rights can unfairly protect privileged shareholders and bring greater risk of conflicted decisions to the board. Be prepared to work in the best interest of all stockholders.

---

3. Tiffany Kary, "Board Needs to Be Synergy Skeptic in M&A," *Dow Jones Corporate Governance,* 27 October 2004, 3–4.
4. G. Jarrell and A. Poulsen, "Shark Repellents and Stock Prices: The Effects of Anti-Takeover Amendments Since 1980," *Journal of Financial Economics,* Vol. 19, 1987, 128–167.
5. Qualcomm Incorporated, "Appendix 2, Proposed Amendments to the Restated Certificate of Incorporation of Qualcomm Incorporated," *Proxy Statement for Annual Meeting of Shareholders* (8 March 2005), 2.
6. Stephen Labaton, "S.E.C. Rebuffs Investors on Board Votes," *New York Times,* 8 February 2005, C2.
7. Robert G. Monks and Nell Minow, *Corporate Governance,* 3rd ed. (Malden, MA: Blackwell, 2004), 171–172.

Communicating Clearly

The final governance factor is to communicate clearly. While always important, communication becomes critical during a crisis. This final part of the framework provides tips regarding how to communicate to various stakeholders during times of corporate stress. Additionally, Congress and the SEC have placed new disclosure requirements on public companies and accelerated the reporting period for existing disclosures. The more informed eyes are that remain alert for a disclosure-yielding event, the better the chances of remaining in compliance with a company's obligation to the public. In this part we will examine these requirements in some detail, not only because it is essential to recognize important triggers, but also to demonstrate why they are vital for healthy governance.

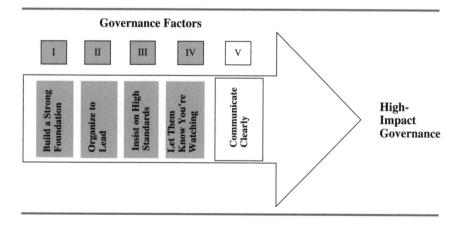

CHAPTER 13

Speaking to the Crowd

Many assume that a failed company results from a derelict board. This is rarely the case. Most directors are experienced, savvy, committed, and want to do the right thing for their shareholders. Even with the most diligent stewardship of a public company, if things do not go as planned, there is an inevitable assessment challenging the board's oversight and whether losses occurred as a result of its failure to act quickly or in a manner that protected the interests of shareholders. The difficulty is identifying the problem and acting on it before the proverbial train wreck destroys the company. Directors need to be sensitive to the signs of distress and take action to save shareholder value. These signs are distress markers. The goal of this chapter is to identify the big distress markers so that immediate action can be taken and to be prepared to manage a crisis if, despite best efforts, the board is faced with one.

There are many distress markers (some of which are detailed in Exhibit 13.1 later in this chapter). Here are the Big Three:

1. Management integrity
2. Operating weakness in the core business
3. Unusual regulatory scrutiny

IMPORTANCE OF MANAGING INTEGRITY

As discussed in Chapter 4, the board should have a zero-tolerance standard regarding management's ethical behavior. Having a code of conduct that is not enforced is worse than having no code at all. Employees watch management's response to violations and draw their conclusions about how serious the company takes its rhetoric. The best response is: one infraction and you're gone. No excuses.

The board of PeopleSoft and Computer Associates seemed to have learned this lesson. When the veracity of Craig Conway's statements came to light, the PeopleSoft board moved quickly to remove the CEO. Likewise, the board of Computer Associates cut ties with their CEO, Sanjay Kumar, when they learned that he pressed customers to falsify the timing of sales.

Compare this to Bausch & Lomb's handling of its CEO, Ronald L. Zarrella. The eye-care giant's CEO enhanced his resumé by improperly claiming he graduated from NYU's Stern School of Business. Rather than terminating the company's relationship with Mr. Zarrella, the board withheld $1.1 million in bonus. Seems like a steep price to be paid, for sure, but the larger question of integrity remains. How can shareholders trust their leader when he admits to misrepresenting himself? What message has been sent to Bausch's employees?

Executive management needs to be held the same or even a higher standard than the rank-and-file employee. Too often, so much importance is placed on an executive that a board is uncomfortable taking aggressive action. But executives without integrity cannot gain the respect of an organization and, therefore, can not be effective no matter the other qualities they may bring. Even worse, they may attract like-minded sycophants. Save your company future pain. Ensure you have a workable succession plan in place and cut bait as soon as a real ethical violation has occurred.

DISCLOSING OPERATING WEAKNESS

If we have learned one thing from the implosions resulting from the corporate frauds of 2001 and 2002, it is that it is better for a company to take its medicine up front rather than covering up weak operations in the hopes that it can later rectify them. While the stock may initially be punished, at least investors and the board are aware of the real challenges the company must address. The board then has the opportunity to help management attend to any structural problems. Covering up weak performance and hoping for a future turnaround is a bit like whistling past the graveyard. Yet this is exactly what happened at WorldCom. The company's CFO, Scott Sullivan, continued to manufacture profits in the hopes that the business would turn around, at which time he could correct the accounting. The business, however, continued to slide and was effectively committed to bankruptcy by the time Cynthia Cooper completed her investigation.

Other than short-term or seasonal swings, signs that the main operating business is weak should be a cause for concern. If the operations are using cash instead of generating it, this is an unworkable model that eventually bankrupts the company. Management can delay the day of reckoning initially by borrowing and then selling assets; but eventually the business model implodes. Directors also need to be aware that these pressures also increase the risk that those in a position to do so may game the numbers.

Management and the board need to work quickly to reassess corporate strategy, evaluate execution, and prepare a plan to correct course. This only happens if management is open about operating performance and there is trust and candor in the boardroom. WorldCom's management was not honest, yet the board listened to the internal auditor when she brought bad news. They set out to determine the true financial condition of the business.

Directors who make certain that they understand the true profitability of the business, which hopefully will match what management is reporting, are supremely positioned to protect shareholders and their own personal liability. They can act with urgency and confidence regarding what needs to be done regarding the operations or strategy of the company. Tardy detection of deteriorating performance results in even more disruptive and difficult decisions down the road. This usually includes personnel and financial reorganization rather than strategy or operational reviews. Regardless, representing shareholders must be the paramount concern and company communications to the investor community must be clear and accurate if the organization wants to maintain credibility with its public.

RESPONDING TO REGULATORY SCRUTINY

We have already appreciated how the lack of response to regulatory concerns resulted in the suspension of operations at Abbott Laboratories (Chapter 4) and Chiron (Chapter 10)—and that a company should react to a regulatory concern the same way it would if its hair were on fire. You want to put it out as soon as possible, not later today, tomorrow, or next week—but now. If management does not have this sense of urgency regarding regulatory concerns, then you have just diagnosed a disease spreading in the heart of the company. Management is either hiding the seriousness of the problem, or its judgment is so compromised that you have to wonder about other aspects of the company's operations.

Management must aggressively address regulatory concerns—even when there is disagreement about the seriousness of the problem. The recent manufacturing concerns at another pharmaceutical drug manufacturer, GlaxoSmithKline are a good example of underestimating the seriousness of a problem. For over two years, the FDA attempted to get the company to fix quality control problems at two of its plants. At first glance, the problem does not seem to be significant: bilayered tablets kept splitting apart. But the problem can be serious if each half contains different medications—or one side has no medication at all. Despite taking a pill, patients could end up taking only a buffer or no medication. Rather than aggressively determining why the pills would split, the company responded casually, first recalling some of the pills, and then inspecting and removing damaged pills before shipment. Obviously, this process would do little to remove pills that were damaged during shipment.

In response, the FDA seized millions of Paxil CR and Avandamet pills from the affected facilities, an event which was reported by the nation's media. So what had been viewed as a minor problem became a public relations nightmare as GlaxoSmithKline must now convince the public that their products are safe in the face of media exposure. An FDA official, quoted in the *Wall Street Journal*, said, "We felt that we had been working with the company for a couple of years now, and although they have made some progress in correcting the problems, we felt that without our intervention, we couldn't get them to where they needed to be."[1] Clearly, the company failed to convince this regulator that they were addressing the problem. Rather, GlaxoSmithKline behaved more like a teenager half-heartedly picking up some clothes after his parents told him to clean his room. Finally, the teenager GlaxoSmithKline got grounded by their FDA parent.

Directors need to encourage management to work positively with regulators and become knowledgeable about proposed rule changes that could impact the company. A policy of openness with regulators, be they FDA, OSHA, SEC, NYSE, or other regulatory bodies, is the best way to address a regulatory business problem. This is not always easy and certainly not second nature. Basically, there is not much upside to interaction with regulators, but the downside can be the complete cessation of business. The government has unlimited resources, and, absent judicial relief, will likely get what it wants.

This is not to suggest that an unwarranted government action should not be contested, only that it be recognized as serious; and if a challenge is the chosen route, that the cost and time commitment are also recognized. The company should also be honest about why it is contesting the action, bring the best resources it can muster to resolve the issue, and keep the lines of communication open. Where possible, recruit other companies to join in diffusing risks and costs. The automakers' challenge of California's tough new emission requirements is one example where companies band together as they believe the legislature has overstepped legal boundaries. Automakers need to tread this route with care and with eyes wide open. They have to overcome the public's disapproval for taking on a popular law. Right now their arguments are largely based on cost and the arcane argument that only the federal government can legislate fuel economy. By banding together, they may be able to keep the public from painting any one company as the villain. When an entire industry takes on legislation, it levels the playing field with regulators and legislators and reduces the risk for each individual company.

AIG stands apart as a company that has long had a reputation of challenging regulators. Their bullying tactics may have finally backfired. The company recently agreed to pay an $80 million fine and accept the imposition of a monitor to oversee its business due to the sale of products it sold from 1999 through 2001. These products received the attention of the New York Attorney General because they were designed to help companies manipulate their earnings. This is on top of a $10 million fine paid a year earlier to settle similar claims. Now, these fines are not all that material when one considers the size of AIG, and perhaps the board contemplated this in their decision making. However, the monitor has to be an unpleasant and unexpected addition. Monitors are basically attorneys hired by a company to investigate it, and the results of the their investigations are normally published. Their work can be very disruptive as internal staff respond to document requests and try to explain away whatever dirty laundry is found. AIG initially balked at accepting a monitor; but the company finally acquiesced to the government's demands in order to put the issue behind it. AIG still faces other hurdles, as the New York Attorney General has implicated the company in bid-rigging schemes. The company has also received regulatory scrutiny of its public announcements. And more recently, federal prosecutors are investigating Hank Greenberg himself, the irascible former chairman of AIG, for his personal role in selling a nontraditional insurance product to General Re that allegedly helped it manipulate its financial statements. Regulators are also digging into suspicions that AIG may have improved its own operating results by doing business with captive offshore subsidiaries. In AIG's case, it seems that standing up to regulators has invited even more scrutiny.

Directors and managers should also be aware that regulators can come across as defensive or uneducated regarding your business. It is obvious to any intelligent manager that an outsider can never know his business as well as he does. Also, many government jobs are a training ground for the industries they regulate. In that regard, they do not pay as well as the private sector and experience high turnover. Inexperience does not make regulators unintelligent, and it would be a mistake to treat them as such. At the end of the day, you will be asking them to give you a clean bill of health available for investor inspection. The board must make sure senior management is involved in any response to regulatory concerns raised and that they are addressed to everyone's satisfaction.

SHAREHOLDER ACTIVISTS: THE EMERGING MARKER

There is a fourth emerging distress marker. It is identified by a shareholder activist no longer politely knocking on your door, but threatening to kick it open. The collapse of Enron and WorldCom have emboldened shareholder activists, such as the pension fund giant CalPERS, to become aggressive advocates for governance reform. TIAA-CREF, another fund behemoth, has targeted 50 companies identified as having independence issues. The only reason this marker is not already one of the Big Distress Markers is that the activists may be picking too many battles and waging war against the wrong targets. For instance, CalPERS recently opposed the election of Warren Buffett to the board of Coca-Cola. Most view this action as absurd. Buffett created substantial wealth for his shareholders, not just for a five- or 10-year period, but over decades. Any rational shareholder would want his presence on and counsel to the board of their company. It is hard to elevate the importance of shareholder activists if their actions are not targeted, truly threatening, and on the right side of the issue. I suspect that eventually the institutional shareholders will get their act together, at which time this will become the distress marker to watch. Other distress markers are provided in Exhibit 13.1.

- There is evidence of an ethical lapse with one or more senior managers.
- Operations are using cash instead of generating it.
- Regulators are concerned with any aspect of the business.
- Shareholder activists are organizing against management.
- Earnings are restated or large write-offs proposed.
- Militancy exists among the labor force.
- Negative surprises to earnings are a regular occurrence.
- The company is forced to sell assets to raise cash.
- The company has a consecutive string of quarterly losses.
- Management is unwilling to recognize signs that its strategy is flawed.
- Management devises a bet-the-company strategy/moves into risky markets or countries.
- Execution of strategy or operational plans is constantly substandard.
- Acquisitions are presented as "strategic" rather than on the price and expected return.
- It is not clear who is responsible for failures.
- Management wishes to decouple compensation from company performance.
- Key managers leave the company for a lateral position or abruptly resign.
- Management pushes for board approval of major transactions on short notice.
- Management appears defensive, opaque, and speaks with one voice.
- The company's operating metrics do not stack up well against competitors.
- Company stock and debt trade at a significant discount to peers.
- Management is selling significant amounts of company stock.
- Pattern of rating agency downgrades.
- Disagreements exist with auditors.

EXHIBIT 13.1 Distress Markers

WHAT NOT TO DO

Even when adequate precautions are taken, incidents still occur. Some incidents are mishandled to the point that the bungling leads to a lack of confidence in the source, which in turn leads to a full-blown crisis. A natural reaction when an incident becomes public is to clam up or cover up. It is one thing to tell the press that you are meeting and will have an announcement later; it is another to just say nothing, which is exactly what the lawyers will tell you to say. You might as well put a note on your back that says "kick me." The press will smell blood and so much light will shine on the company that the board will become a one-issue body. The idea is to truthfully disclose as much as possible, but within the bounds of good sense. More important, communicate the process by which you will address the problem.

You also do not want to minimize what is perceived as an important issue. If you do, you lose credibility, and then you are no longer "The Source." The media will go elsewhere for their information and you lose any chance to form the message. If this occurs, do not compound the problem by blaming them. Attacking the media, unless you are a politician, will generally work against you. As the old saying goes, "Don't pick a fight with someone who buys ink by the barrel." Also do not justify your actions based on cost—think about those studies that sometimes pop up showing that the cost of settlements for lives lost will be less than creating a safe product. A lives-for-dollars analysis is to the plaintiff's bar what the bell was to Pavlov's dog. You win points with the public and investors by showing intelligent compassion. You investigate and do what is right because, in the long term, that is best for business.

And speaking of politicians, it is not wise to pick a fight with them or the regulators, or worse yet, motivate them by blaming a victim. Coming to the rescue of the little guy is gold to public servants. Who does not want to be the hero? Finally, do not take your time preparing a response. Act with a sense of urgency. Otherwise, your lack of response becomes the story and people are convinced you are covering up.

DAMAGE CONTROL

What if prevention measures have failed and there is a material event on the horizon? Great leaders rise to the challenge. Those with strong character stand up to the problem with integrity, objectivity, and great energy. You know what not to do; here are steps every director can take to protect shareholders and themselves:

- Independently determine the scope of the problem.
- Determine a corporate response to remedy the problem.
- Communicate transparently to the public.
- Commit the time and effort to oversee the chosen solution to completion.
- Reevaluate risk management procedures and adjust them, if appropriate, in light of new information learned from the crisis.

Independently Determine Scope

Once an issue is raised, it is in someone's interest to convince others that it is a problem of minimal proportions, regardless of its severity. They are fearful that disclosure could derail their career, affect their compensation, or worse yet, expose their unethical activity. You are likely to hear from that party: "Don't worry, it's under control." It may be an employee trying to convince his or her supervisor or a senior manager trying to influence the board. Just know that there are countervailing forces working against transparency somewhere in the organization that must be overcome. As a director, it is imperative that you take steps to actively obtain independent corroboration of the problem's scope.

Section 404 certifications can be used as an example of how to approach bad news. Assume the management of an imaginary company, Fair Disclosure Corp., has determined it can not demonstrate that its controls over financial reporting are operational. A number of questions come to mind. Specifically, what areas are at risk; how long have they been at risk; what is the financial impact, if any; what will it take to correct the exposure; when will the fix be in place; what will be communicated to the public and when?

The answers to each of these questions must be received with some good old-fashioned skepticism. Remember that somewhere in the organization, someone may believe that they are fighting for their job and may go to extremes to cover or minimize the evaluation of exposure. A director needs to hear directly from more than one trustworthy source the true scope of the problem. External and internal auditors are good sources, but a director would be well within their rights to retain their own advisors to independently confirm what management and the auditors are representing. Once you know the full scope of the problem, the board can begin to form a response for correcting the weaknesses identified.

Prepare a Response

Assume that we have received from Fair Disclosure's management and corroborated by independent means the following responses to the questions we introduced above:

- The financial reporting control weakness relates to a program used to calculate loan reserves and was discovered during management's testing of the control environment.
- Further assume that a lack of change control (a specific process to control changes to a computer's programs) resulted in a corruption of the program calculating the reserve during the first quarter of this year.
- The calculation resulted in an understatement of reserves in the first, second, and third quarters.
- The range of the error is between $1 and $1.5 million on revenues of approximately $26 million.
- To eliminate the weakness, the program will have to be fixed, tested, and change control procedures implemented to prevent a repeat occurrence.
- The solutions are relatively easy to implement and can be performed and tested over the next two weeks and corrections included in the year-end financial statements prior to their release.

The board will now want to oversee the corrective actions by requiring a project plan or other document detailing the action steps to be taken, the person responsible for the action, and the target date for completion. The board should plan frequent meetings, even if by telephone, with those responsible for implementing the fix to ensure that they remain on schedule and that any unanticipated issues are quickly made known to senior management and the board. The board should also plan to have its independent consultant review the changes and agree they were made properly.

Communicate to the Public

One of the event triggers the SEC developed in response to the "real-time issuer disclosure" mandate in Section 409 of the Sarbanes-Oxley Act is the instance where interim period financial statements are no longer reliable. The issuer has four days to file Form 8-K after event triggers such as this, and the SEC's final rules require the issuer disclose:

- The date of the conclusion regarding the nonreliance and an identification of the financial statements and years or periods covered that should no longer be relied upon
- A brief description of the facts underlying the conclusion to the extent known to the company at the time of filing
- A statement of whether the audit committee, or the board of directors in the absence of an audit committee, or authorized officer or officers, discussed with the company's independent accountant the subject matter giving rise to the conclusion

Therefore, the board should ensure a press release is issued no later than four days after the company becomes aware of the event and addresses the disclosure items. There may be more disclosure requirements if the public accountant is the one that identified the weakness.

Generally lawyers advise a company to disclose as little as possible, but a lack of information may unnecessarily frighten the market. From this perspective, more disclosure is usually better than less. If investors believe that management is doing all it can to remedy the problem and that it has been forthright regarding the extent of the financial impact, the pain will be measured and quick. Conversely, if investors are waiting for another shoe to drop, they may overreact, punishing a stock for a long period of time.

While it is imperative that the company communicate accurately and clearly the potential impact of the triggering event, it is entirely appropriate to put the event in context. For example, a communication regarding the crisis at Fair Disclosure Corp. might read:

For Immediate Release: Fair Disclosure Corporation Discloses Control Weakness.

Fair Disclosure Corp. has identified a control weakness preventing the company from assessing internal controls over financial reporting as reliable. The weakness was discovered two days ago during the company's testing of the system of internal control. The company intends to report its financial results on time, and restate this year's first, second, and third quarter results due to the control weakness. The restatement is expected to reduce net income in a range of $1 to $1.5 million for the year. The loan loss reserve error stems from a change in a loan reserve program made early in the year. Management is correcting the program and instituting new change control procedures that will prevent reoccurrence. The audit committee of the board of directors has notified and discussed the remediation plan, which is expected to take two to four weeks, with the external auditor. The company is still comfortable with its earlier earnings guidance of annual net income of between $25 and $28 million and believes all issues will be resolved prior to the announcement of year-end results.

The strength of this communication is that it answers all of the questions we introduced earlier: the source of the problem, how it occurred, the impact of the error, what needs to be done to fix the problem, and how long it will take. In short, the paragraph provides all the information an investor would need to put this event into appropriate context. It also addresses the regulatory requirement regarding whether the independent accountant was notified.

Monitor to Completion

Finally, a board must monitor the progress made to complete the project. This may require a significant number of special meetings to obtain information and provide guidance. Recall the 58 board meetings Lucent held (also relevant are the 33 meetings called in one year by the University of Idaho Foundation to address its crisis, which is presented in Chapter 15). Once presented as complete, the board will want to independently corroborate this assertion. There are many ways to do this, but it most frequently consists of the board reviewing the action taken to ensure it is operating or hiring an advisor to independently review the fix and report back to the board.

For Fair Disclosure Corp., the board wants to monitor progress against the project plan and, when completed, obtain comfort that the fix was made correctly. The board also has a right to review new change control procedures to assure themselves that the correction is permanent and that the error does not happen again.

The change control weakness has been deliberately chosen for this example because this is the most underrated weakness a company can experience. Companies of all sizes experience such problems—and the headaches that emanate from poor change control can be serious. Any changes to a program should not be made in production; instead, they should be developed and thoroughly tested on a dedicated server. Once the program is readied, it then must go through a number of supervisory and end-user approvals before it is migrated into production. Even after migration, an old copy of the previous program should be kept in case the new program develops an unforeseen hiccup down the road. This process must include control over key spreadsheets that produce material information for inclusion in the financial statements. It is always amazing how fairly large businesses, which spend respectful amounts of money on strong information system controls, can be humbled by a single spreadsheet error.

Post Mortem

Once the crisis has passed, management—with board oversight—should evaluate what it has learned from the crisis. All too often organizations fail to institutionalize knowledge gained from unpleasant incidents. By evaluating how the crisis arrived, and the effectiveness of the company's response, new risk-management practices or crisis procedures can be implemented providing more timely notice of a pending problem or, at least, improve the company's response if a similar issue occurs again.

CASE STUDY: RICHARD SCRUSHY, THE INDICTED CEO-TURNED-TELEVANGELIST

One similarity of the Enron, WorldCom, CUC International (Cendant), and other super-frauds is the use of the "ignorance-defense" by the indicted CEOs who led these companies. The way the defense works is that the CEO, despite making millions of dollars to run the company, claims he (or she) really had no idea what was going on there or that he was accountable for the accuracy of the company's financial statements. In the case of CUC, the defense worked. A jury was unable to reach a verdict on Walter Forbes, the former chief executive. Mr. Forbes denied any involvement in the "day-to-day operations" of the company, so only the CFO was held accountable. Bernard Ebbers of WorldCom was less convincing as a jury found him guilty of conspiracy, securities fraud, and seven counts of filing false statements. Mr. Ebbers faces up to 85 years in prison. Kenneth Lay of Enron will also be evaluated under much the same criteria as Mr. Forbes and Mr. Ebbers: What did they know and when did they know it?

The prosecution of these executives is largely occurring under a number of laws that existed prior to the passage of the Sarbanes-Oxley Act. However, one indicted executive is not so lucky. At this writing, one of the first major cases utilizing the deterrents built into the Sarbanes-Oxley Act is underway. Richard Scrushy, the former Chairman and CEO of HealthSouth Corporation, one of the nation's largest healthcare providers, is on trial for committing a financial fraud. Some see Mr. Scrushy as a churchgoing, value-preaching nice guy being persecuted. Others see a high-living, mean-spirited fraudster. The federal government believes he is the latter. They have thrown the book at him. Among the original 85-count indictment brought by the U.S. Department of Justice, is the prosecution's allegation that Mr. Scrushy personally certified financial statements filed with the SEC while knowing them to be false. This count, made available by the Sarbanes-Oxley Act, together with the other counts, means that, if convicted of all of the original charges, Mr. Scrushy could be sentenced to over 400 years in jail(!), be required to pay $36 million in fines, and have to forfeit over $275 million of real estate, airplanes, yachts, and other property. Interestingly, false certification under the Sarbanes Oxley Act only counts for about 20 of the possible years of jail time. However, it is the effectiveness of the certification requirement that all are watching and just may differentiate Mr. Scrushy's case from those that preceded him.

So what did Mr. Scrushy do to run so afoul of the government? Prosecutors contend Mr. Scrushy devised a scheme to ensure that HealthSouth would make sufficient net income to meet the expectations of Wall Street analysts without regard to true operating performance. Their indictment charges management created $2.7 billion of fictitious income between 1996 and 2003 specifically to "fill the gap" between reality and Wall Street targets. As a part of the fraud, the prosecutors allege that Mr. Scrushy obtained large compensation packages for those helping him manipulate the financial statements. Additionally, he personally accumulated in excess of a quarter billion dollars over the fraud period.

The fraud at HealthSouth began to unravel in August 2002 when accounting staff advised management that they would no longer make false entries. According to the indictment, a senior officer also refused to sign a financial report until Mr. Scrushy agreed to a plan to correct accounting problems and promote the senior officer to CFO of a HealthSouth spin-off. Finally, on or about November 13, 2002, Mr. Scrushy and other coconspirators certified and filed a quarterly financial statement with the SEC. This is the event that allowed prosecutors to indict Mr. Scrushy under provisions of the Sarbanes-Oxley Act.

The ability of HealthSouth to "make its numbers" and the resulting impression of profitability drove HealthSouth's stock price up to $30 a share, and the ensuing disclosure of fraud saw it collapse to pennies. The stock has since recovered to about $6 a share, although this is little solace to those who bought at $30.

In preparation for the trial, Mr. Scrushy has set about to remake his image. He and his wife recently left their church and began attending a predominantly African-American ministry across town in Birmingham. They also started a local morning television show that focuses primarily on Bible-related topics. The show was bought by his new church and broadcast from a television station owned by his son-in-law to approximately 5,000 viewers each morning. His lawyers have also been actively appearing on local radio shows calling the prosecution politically motivated and bringing into question conflicting statements of former HealthSouth employees.[a] Needless to say, the jury will be selected from the local community and their view of Mr. Scrushy could play a role in the trial. Soon, all eyes will be on Mr. Scrushy. Inevitably, the near simultaneous trials of Mr. Ebbers, Mr. Lay, and Mr. Scrushy will be compared and contrasted, and the effectiveness of the certification requirements of the Sarbanes-Oxley Act assessed. As this book goes to press, the jury is struggling to reach a verdict in the case. Like others in their community, they also seem to be wrestling with the question of who Mr. Scrushy really is, sinner or saint.

---

[a]Farrell, Greg. "Former HealthSouth CEO Scrushy Turns Televangelist," *USA Today*, 26 October 2004, B1.

ENDNOTE

1. Gardiner Harris, "F.D.A. Seizes Millions of Pills from Pharmaceutical Plants," *New York Times*, 5 March 2005, A7.

KEY CONCEPTS

- Engage distress markers. They are a threat to shareholder value.
- Proactively respond to regulatory scrutiny.
- Corroborate management assertions.
- Approach negative operating cash flow as a crisis.
- Actively address ethical lapses. Failure to do so will only lead to more risk for the company.
- Keep an eye on the Emerging Marker–shareholder activists.
- When communicating during a crisis:
  - Truthfully disclose as much as possible within the bounds of good sense.
  - Do not try to minimize the problem or displace blame for it.
  - Show intelligent compassion.
  - Disclose when you can provide a more complete response.
  - Act with a sense of urgency.
- In response to a crisis:
  - Obtain independent corroboration regarding the scope of the problem.
  - Evaluate the corporate response to it.
  - Communicate the response to the public.
  - Commit the time to oversee the chosen solution to completion.
  - Reevaluate risk-management procedures in light of what was learned.

CHAPTER 14

Required Communications

As baseball great Yogi Berra says, "The future ain't what it used to be." As much as we like to believe we can execute our strategy and drive straight toward our company objectives, the truth is that uncertainty exists. While the goal might stay the same, it will look different from where we stand next year. We cannot know with certainty whether or when an event will occur, but only that there is potential for it to happen. If it does occur, how the board and management respond will be assessed by investors and other stakeholders. Character and courage cannot be acquired at the point of crisis, only exhibited. The world will be watching, and we need to be ready. In this chapter, we prepare for the difficult task of identifying and responding to a reportable event.

PERFECTING EVENT REPORTING

Congress understands that timeliness and availability of event reporting is as important as its accuracy. As a result, Congress required the SEC to establish rules regarding disclosure on a "rapid and current basis" of material information regarding changes in a company's financial position. Prior to the adoption of these rules, public companies had weeks to disclose certain information, and no requirement to disclose others. The SEC now requires that information be reported to the public within four business days of the "triggering event." These new accelerated disclosure obligations took effect in August 2004.

Directors need to be able to identify the events that will require disclosure in order to make certain that there is a process to properly respond in a timely manner. The SEC added eight new items to the list of events requiring speedy reporting on SEC Form 8-K for a total of 17 de facto material reportable actions. These items are:

1. **Entry into a material definitive agreement.** This includes all material definitive agreements entered into by a company that are not made in the ordinary course of business. This would include such items as major purchase or sale of goods and services, related party contracts, acquisition or sale of property plant or equipment exceeding 15 percent of assets, material leases, management or compensation contracts with senior executives or directors, and business combinations. The guidance specifically excludes letters of intent and nonbinding agreements.

   Notice that the requirement to disclose management and director compensation is not held to a materiality standard. Directors must be careful to disclose all compensation, benefits, business dealings and those of family members received from the company. Shareholders are entitled to information regarding any relationships between a director and the company, including the employment of relatives, business with companies with which the director has an affiliation, and any perks or compensation in lieu of payment such as providing secretarial services, and so forth.

   The SEC recently reached a settlement with the Walt Disney Company over the company's failure to properly disclose relationships with its directors. At Disney, three directors had children working at the company earning salaries ranging from $60,000 to $150,000. Another director was provided a leased car, a driver, and secretarial services. Yet another director leased an airplane to Disney through his company, Air Shamrock. These lease payments accounted for more than 5 percent of Air Shamrock's revenues. Each of these omissions potentially impacted director independence and required disclosure.[1]

2. **Termination of a material definitive agreement.** Just as entry into such agreements is considered necessary investor information, so is their termination. The disclosure must not only identify the parties to the agreement and a brief description of terms and conditions—as would be the case when entering an agreement—but any costs associated with the termination must also be disclosed. The termination of a multiple aircraft order, given its

magnitude, might be an example of a material termination. The expiration of a license agreement, such as when Jones Apparel and Ralph Lauren discontinued their relationship (which was likely a material event to both companies), is another possible example. In that case, Jones licensed the Polo brand and manufactured products leveraging the Polo name. It accounted for a large portion of its sales, so when the contract was not renewed, it was a reportable event.

3. **Bankruptcy or receivership.** Every director would recognize this category as reportable. What needs to be disclosed will, in part, be determined if the company is reorganizing or if a receiver or similar officer is appointed and has jurisdiction over substantially all of the business's assets. Bankruptcy brings new responsibilities for directors that includes doing what is right for debtors. At this point, the board should have its own counsel to determine not only what should be disclosed, but also how to discharge its duties to debtors and stockholders.

4. **Completion of acquisition or disposition of assets.** Certain companies are constantly buying and selling assets. Once a material acquisition or disposition transaction has been completed, the company must report the date of completion, a brief description of the assets involved, the identity of the counterparty, the nature and amount of the consideration, and the source of the financing (with certain exemptions available) if the transaction represents more than 10 percent of the company's assets. Since most of these events also qualified earlier as a definitive agreement, for many of these transactions the company will make two disclosures, first when it enters into an agreement, and again when it is completed.

   By way of example, the board of PeopleSoft recently accepted an offer by Oracle to purchase the company. Not only is the agreement reportable, the closing of the deal will also need to be reported, together with the final terms of the purchase.

5. **Results of operations and financial condition.** Any dissemination of operating and/or financial information should also be reported on Form 8-K. This includes more than the annual and quarterly earnings announcements, and any material nonpublic operating or financial information or updates to earlier releases. The date and identity of the announcement must be disclosed together with the text as an exhibit.

One issue that concerned Congress was the widespread practice of reporting pro forma financial information that bore no resemblance to generally accepted accounting principles (GAAP). In many cases, the information provided may have better reflected drivers of the business; in others, it was simply window dressing. To address this issue, Section 401 of the Sarbanes-Oxley Act required the presentation of pro forma financial information with reconciliation to results under GAAP. The information must be "presented in a manner that (1) does not contain an untrue statement of material fact or omit to state a material fact necessary in order to make the 'pro forma financial information,' in light of the circumstances under which it is presented, not misleading; and (2) reconciles the 'pro forma financial information' presented with the financial condition and results of operations of the company under Generally Accepted Accounting Principals (GAAP)."[2] While there is certain information that a company or industry believes better reflects the effectiveness of its operating results, any numerical measure of a company's performance that is not sourced from financial statements prepared in accordance with GAAP will need to be reconciled to the company's GAAP financial results. Statistical and operating measures are excluded from the reconciliation requirement.

The PeopleSoft transaction with Oracle again provides us with a useful example, this time regarding how misstating the true financial position of a company can lead to trouble. Craig Conway, PeopleSoft's CEO, was fired because he made comments at an analyst conference that implied the Oracle bid had not hurt business. Later, in a lawsuit brought by Oracle to block PeopleSoft from using defensive measures, Conway admitted in a deposition that his statement was not true. A correction was filed with the SEC the next day, but the board, upon viewing the deposition, came to the conclusion that Conway's remarks were deliberate rather than inarticulate as previously stated. In fact, the remarks directly contradict a $1 billion claim made by PeopleSoft in a California court that their business had been harmed. Within two weeks of viewing the tape, the board announced they fired Conway for making false statements.[3]

6. **Creation of a direct financial obligation or an obligation under an off-balance sheet arrangement.** This includes long-term debt, a capital lease, an operating lease obligation, and short-term debt that arises other than in the ordinary course of business. Operating leases for a copy machine in a regional office would not qualify for disclosure, as it would be considered incurred in the ordinary course of business; however, the replacement of all copiers with a global reprographics and document management services contract might qualify. Off-balance sheet arrangements (think Enron special purpose entities) also require disclosure regarding contingent liabilities.

7. **Triggering events for direct and indirect financial obligations.** Many off-balance sheet agreements contain guarantees from third parties to ensure repayment of an obligation. If there is a default or similar event, a registrant that is now liable must describe the triggering event, the nature and amount of the obligation, and the impact the triggering event may have on other material obligations.

8. **Costs associated with exit or disposal activities.** There are times when, lacking a buyer, a company simply closes a facility or business. When a facility is shuttered, there are often substantial costs required to safely cease operations. Other times, there may be a buyer, but there are substantial costs in preparing the asset for sale. This may include carving it out of existing operations, rarely an inexpensive endeavor. Any plan of exit or disposal that will result in material charges under GAAP must be disclosed. The report will include the facts and circumstances leading up to the decision, expected completion date, an estimate of the amount or range of amounts for each major cost type, an estimate of total costs, and future cash expenditures associated with the plan. If costs cannot be estimated, guidance allows it to be omitted until a determination can be made, at which time an amended report is due within four days.

9. **Material impairments.** At times, a change in the business environment makes assets significantly less valuable. A company holding stock in a company that declares bankruptcy, owning a subsidiary whose market has shifted against it preventing a return on its purchase price, or maintaining significant inventory

that is now obsolete are examples of impaired assets. If securities, goodwill, or assets are impaired, the date that conclusion was made, the estimate of the impairment, and future cash requirements of the impairment should be disclosed.

10. **Notice of delisting or failure to satisfy a continued listing rule or standard; transfer of listing.** If the company is notified by an exchange or national securities association that it does not satisfy listing standards, the exchange has moved to delist the company's securities, or the association has taken all necessary steps to delist the security from quotation systems, the company must disclose these actions including what rules it failed to satisfy and any action the company plans to take. The company must also disclose any reprimand letters received.

    Companies may also choose to de-list or transfer their securities, which also require disclosure. Lastminute.com, an online travel group, recently announced that it planned to de-list from the NASDAQ. The reason cited was the cost of maintaining, what was for them, a secondary listing (the primary listing was on the London Stock Exchange). The company reported its listing cost approximately $2.78 million a year and it is seeking ways to eliminate its reporting obligations under the U.S. Securities and Exchange Act.[4]

11. **Unregistered sales of equity securities.** The sale of unregistered securities that constitute, in the aggregate, more than 1 percent of the class's outstanding shares since the last periodic report must be disclosed (5 percent for small business issuers). Directors should be aware this can result from approving the issuance of a convertible security. Convertible bonds are issued at a discount because they contain a feature allowing the holder to exchange the bonds for stock in a future period. When conditions are ripe, a company may experience a number of conversions. A company must capture and report this activity.

12. **Material modifications to rights of security holders.** Disclosure is required of all modifications or limitations to the rights of any class of shareholders, even if the event occurs by the issuance of another class of security. The issuance of new classes of stock, whether they be super-voting or only tracking stocks, can have an impact on the value of stock already issued and outstanding. Any changes to the rights of existing stockholders, whether

directly by re-defining their rights, or indirectly through issuance of different classes of stock, needs to be reported, as does any restriction on working capital or payment of dividends that might occur through an agreement with a lender.

13. **Changes in registrants certifying accountant.** One trend resulting from the passage of the Sarbanes-Oxley Act is the shift in the client base of the certifying accountants. The larger firms are charging their largest customers more and severing their relationships with smaller, less profitable companies. The smaller companies, in turn, are retaining the second-tier firms. This shift has resulted in a number of announcements relating to the resignation and retention of auditors. Reporting the retention, resignation, or dismissal of the independent accountant is required. If the accountant was dismissed, it must be disclosed whether the change was recommended or approved by the audit committee or the full board. Any disagreements with the auditors together with any adverse, disclaimed, modified, or qualified opinions and their nature for the past two years is to be disclosed. The company must provide the former accountants with a copy of the disclosures made and ask them to send a letter to the SEC stating whether or not they agree with its contents. A current example relates to the firing of KPMG as Fannie Mae's auditors after an accounting scandal erupted at that company. In the regulatory filing, Fannie Mae reported that KPMG did in fact observe accounting deficiencies in the company's third-quarter bookkeeping that required post-closing entries to correct. KPMG, in an attachment to the filing, concurred with Fannie Mae's statement.

14. **Nonreliance on previously issued financial statements or a related audit report or completed interim review.** One aspect of the financial crisis of 2001 and 2002 was the number of corporate announcements stating that a company could no longer rely on previously issued financial statements. If the board concludes it cannot rely on interim or annual financial statements, it must immediately identify the financial statements in question and the periods covered. If the company is advised by its outside accountant that it should take action to prevent reliance on the financial statements, then a brief description of the information provided by the accountant must also be incorporated within the disclosure including whether the accountant discussed the issue with

the audit committee or board of directors. In such a case the company must also provide a copy of the disclosure to the independent accountant and cause the independent accountant to prepare a letter to the SEC stating whether or not it agrees with the statements made in the disclosure.

By way of example, in August 2002, Gemstar-TV Guide International reported on Form 8-K that "based on a review conducted by the audit committee of the board of directors, the Company will delay the release of second quarter 2002 earnings and the filing of its Form 10-Q with the SEC." The company determined the collection of a large receivable was no longer reasonably assured and it intended to fully reserve for the amount. The company further described that it had retained another independent accounting firm. With the new firm, it was determined that the statements for 2001 needed to be restated by $20 million. Gemstar then relayed the impact this had on cash flow, how they notified KPMG (its certifying accountants), of its decision to restate, and that the investigation into other accounting practices continued. Interestingly, the company reported that KPMG informed Gemstar that it did not believe enough information was provided to support the change in accounting treatment.

The company presented what it knew at that point in its investigation together with the disagreement with its auditors regarding accounting treatment (even though the SEC's new Form 8-K reporting requirements had not yet been adopted). In a later filing, the company reported KPMG did not believe the information sufficient to support a change in accounting treatment and that the company sought guidance from the SEC. Eventually, the investigation led to the recognition of over $152 million of licensing revenue and $60 million of advertising revenue improperly reported in 2000, 2001, and 2002.

The SEC brought action against KPMG, selected partners, and a senior manager on the engagement for allowing the improper accounting treatment. An important finding was that KPMG's reliance on quantitative materiality thresholds was not sufficient given the visibility and performance of the business line affected. The business segment was emphasized by the company and closely watched by securities analysts. The settlement with the SEC cost KPMG $10 million together with a commitment to provide remedial training for its partners and managers regarding quantitative materiality and appropriate disclosures, among other items. The partners and manager working on the Gemstar-TV Guide engagement were barred from practicing before the commission for one to three years.

15. **Changes in control of the registrant.** The board must disclose the identity of the person or entity that, to its knowledge, has taken a controlling interest in the company. The percentage ownership, amount paid, source of funds, the identity of the person from whom control was assumed, and any arrangements between the former and new control groups regarding the election of directors or other matters must also be disclosed.

   You would think that a board would know when someone has effectively bought control of its company, but the board of Aksys Ltd. was unaware that Duras Capital Management had acquired 78.5 percent of its company. According to Duras, it was also unaware that it had taken control. The company claimed that software failures lead to the unintended purchase of Aksys' stock. Therefore, none of the 13-D filings (required when a person or company acquires more than a 5 percent stake in a company) was transmitted to the SEC.[5] This example is an isolated incident, but nevertheless illustrates the need to disclose this type of information to the public. The remaining shareholders of Aksys had no idea that a single buyer was supporting the market for the stock. Furthermore, management and the board of the company had no idea that they had lost control of their company, and no doubt were not amused by Duras' internal control problems.

16. **Departure of directors of principal officers, election of directors, appointment of principal officers.** Changes in the composition of the board of directors or principal officers of the company are important to most investors, particularly if a director leaves due to a serious disagreement with management, the board, or both. Any changes in the composition of the board or to executive management should be reported together with the circumstances surrounding the change. If a director provides any written correspondence regarding a resignation, refusal, or removal, the company must also file a copy as an exhibit to the Form 8-K. The

company is obligated to provide the director with a copy of the disclosures it is making and allow the director to respond, which will also be filed with the SEC.

17. **Amendments to articles of incorporation or by-laws; change in fiscal year.** Any changes to the company by-laws or articles of incorporation not disclosed in the proxy statement must be filed. The changes can be minor, but still require disclosure and so should be done with care.

In addition to these 17 events, there are two other required disclosures regarding the temporary suspension of trading under the company's employee benefit plans required under the Sarbanes-Oxley Act Section 306 and amendments to or waivers of the company's code of ethics under Section 406. We covered these two subjects in some detail earlier. In response to the selling of company stock by Enron's executives and directors while employee stock in pension assets were frozen, Congress required that *pension blackout periods* had to be widely communicated, and restricted executives and directors from selling company stock during this period. The blackout period has to be reported to the SEC on Form 8-K on the same day the notice is transmitted to directors and executive officers. In most cases, this will be within five days following receipt of a blackout notice from the plan administrator.

In a move that appears to be a bit like the kettle calling the pot black (When was the last time someone used the word *ethical* to describe a politician?), Congress was highly critical of the ethical conduct of certain public company executives. Now, in addition to requiring each company to maintain a code of ethics for senior financial executives (or explain why not), Congress also explicitly obliges companies to report, via Form 8-K, any changes or waivers to the code of ethics. The company may disseminate any change or waiver via its Internet website instead of on Form 8-K if it is included within its most recently filed 10-K:

■ Its intention to disclose these events on its Internet website
■ Its Internet website address

Otherwise, the disclosure must be reported on Form 8-K within five business days after it amends its ethics code or grants a waiver.

The value of this disclosure was illustrated by Congress itself when the majority party recently tried to implement new ethics rules that would let an indicted party leader retain his position. Members of Congress also proposed a change that would have effectively eliminated the standard that members of Congress not engage in conduct that discredits the House of Representatives. The public outcries eventually lead to a retrenchment, with the House adopting a weaker rule and eventually a full retrenchment. Nevertheless, this example shows that without transparency, there will be motivation to water down or waive ethics rules to accomplish specific objectives. Public disclosure and transparency help prevent such actions.

A brief summary of the various items required to be reported on SEC Form 8-K has been provided, and indeed, there are many details that must also be incorporated for each item identified above that we have not presented here. What is important is that directors are aware of the company's duty to report on these issues, and that there is a process to capture these events at the C-level, that the right people are brought together to prepare a response, and that counsel is involved in reviewing the communication prior to its filing with the SEC. Given that the company has only four days to ensure timely filing, the importance of quickly identifying the reportable items presented above must be repeatedly communicated to those in a position to know.

Therefore, the first step a board should take is to ensure management has identified those who are on the front lines of reportable events and ensure that they are properly trained and informed. This includes human resources for blackout periods or turnover of executives and directors, senior business unit managers who can commit the company to large operating leases or may be holding impaired assets in inventory, the treasurer or other party responsible for tracking outstanding securities for issuance of unregistered stock or change in control, and, of course, the CFO and general counsel.

The second step is to appoint a rapid-response team well in advance of its need. Such a team will nearly always include the general counsel or their staff to make certain communications meet the guidelines laid out by the SEC and to file the Form 8-K, a public/investor relations specialist to help draft the release, putting any negative news into appropriate context so that markets do not over-react, the CEO and CFO to ensure that any numbers or strategy issues are correctly presented, and oversight from the board. Others will likely be asked to participate depending on the event, such as the head of the business unit or department from which the triggering event emanated.

Third, the rapid-response team should establish guidelines for reporting issues. Such concepts as what is material and when the company deems the event to have occurred are important and should be formally documented for each occurrence. By way of example, is the announcement of a new officer to be made when the offer has been accepted, when the executive starts, or both? These issues, and others, should be hashed out in advance and not during the four-day reporting window.

Finally, agree on the process of preparation, approvals, and distribution of the disclosure. A series of sign-offs by the CEO, CFO, general counsel, and so forth as well as representatives of the board should be required for every report before it is filed. The board's role is to make certain the process has been carried out properly and on-time. In the spirit of continuous improvement, a post-mortem conducted by management with an eye to improving the process makes the board's role easier.

OTHER NEW REPORTING REQUIREMENTS

The SEC has spent much time considering new disclosure requirements that will help investors evaluate the corporate governance operations of public companies. It paid particular attention to the operations of audit and nominating committees, the ability of shareholders to communicate directly with the board of directors, and director and officer trading in company stock.

Audit Committee Disclosures

As mentioned in Chapter 5, the company is obligated to speak about its audit committee in the annual report. This will include such information as the committee's members, the number of meetings held, and the functions performed. A company is also required to disclose in its proxy statement whether the "audit committee has reviewed and discussed the audited financial statements with management and discussed certain matters with the independent auditors" as well as "disclose whether the audit committee is governed by a charter and, if so, to provide a copy of the charter as an appendix to the proxy statement once every three years."[6] The company must also disclose if the audit committee members are independent under the relevant listing standards. Issuers that do not belong to a national exchange must select any one of the definitions from the NYSE, NASDAQ, or AMEX listing standards.

The U.S. Congress, recognizing the important oversight role audit committees perform in the financial reporting process, determined that each should have a financial expert (Sarbanes-Oxley Act, Section 407). The company must disclose in its annual report that its board of directors has determined that the company has at least one audit committee financial expert serving on its audit committee and the name of that director. If there is no financial expert, the company must explain why. Furthermore, companies are also obligated to report whether the audit committee financial expert is independent of management. The SEC decided to require this, listing requirements notwithstanding, because not all public companies are listed on a national exchange.

Section 406 of the Sarbanes-Oxley Act requires the company disclose whether or not it has adopted a code of ethics for its senior financial officers. The SEC expanded this disclosure to include the principal financial officer (CFO). The SEC defined a code of ethics to mean "written standards that are reasonably designed to deter wrongdoing and to promote:

- Honest and ethical conduct, including the ethical handling of actual or apparent conflicts of interest between personal and professional relationships;
- Full, fair, accurate, timely, and understandable disclosure in reports and documents that a registrant files with, or submits to, the commission and in other public communications made by the registrant;
- Compliance with applicable governmental laws, rules and regulations;
- The prompt internal reporting to an appropriate person or persons identified in the code of violations of the code; and
- Accountability for adherence to the code."[7]

The last two bullets were broader than required by the Sarbanes-Oxley Act, and were added by the SEC to improve enforcement of the code. This disclosure must be made in the annual report. As mentioned earlier in this chapter, the Act also requires that any change or waiver to the code of ethics be immediately disclosed either via the company's website or SEC Form 8-K.

There are certain exemptions under SEC rules afforded the audit committees for certain issuers. For example, countries such as Germany have a practice of employees sitting on their supervisory boards and audit committees. These employees provide an independent check on management and the SEC does not want to discourage this practice and, therefore, considers the employees to be independent for audit committee purposes. Additionally, certain foreign jurisdictions require an independent board of auditors or similar body rather than an audit committee. In such cases the SEC exempts issuers from all audit committee requirements if:

- The foreign issuer has a board of auditors established pursuant to home country legal or listing provisions expressly requiring or permitting such a board.
- The board of auditors is either required to be separate from the board of directors or a mix of board and nonboard members.
- The board of auditors is not elected by management and no executive officer is a member.
- Home country listing provisions set standards for board of auditor independence.
- The board of auditors is responsible for the appointment, retention, and oversight of a registered public accounting firm engaged for the purpose of preparing or issuing an audit report or other audit, review, or attest services.
- Other responsibilities of Exchange Act Rule 10A-3, such as the complaint procedure, advisors, and funding requirements, apply to the board of auditors as permitted by law.

Some other independence exemptions include representation from controlling shareholders, government representatives, and government issuers. For instance, many foreign-based companies either have government representatives on their board, or the issuers themselves are foreign governments. Government representatives may be exempted from the independence requirements for audit committee purposes so long as they are in compliance with the "no compensation" rules. Likewise, governments themselves can be exempted. A company utilizing these exemptions, among others, is required to disclose this to shareholders in the annual report and proxy statements.

Nominating Committee Disclosures

In Chapter 7, we tackled the director nomination process and related best practices. Emanating from a growing concern among stockholders that they lacked sufficient means to communicate to and affect decisions made by the board of directors, the SEC adopted new disclosure rules regarding a company's director candidate nomination process and avenues available to shareholders to contact board members. The SEC now requires that a company disclose in its proxy statement:

- Whether the company has a nominating committee and, if not, the basis for the view of the board that the company not have one, together with the identification of those directors involved in the nomination process.
- The nominating committee's charter and if it is available on the company's website (and the website address, if applicable). If a charter is not readily available on a website, then the company must include it as an appendix to the proxy statement once every three years, and identify the prior fiscal year when it was included. If there is no charter, the company must say so.
- Whether the members of the nominating committee are independent under the relevant listing standards, and if not a listed issuer, which listing standards are used to evaluate independence.
- Whether the nominating committee will consider director candidates recommended by shareholders, and if so, a description of the material elements of such a policy and the procedures for shareholders to submit such recommendations. If there is no policy, the view of the board regarding why they believe this is appropriate must be provided.

- The nominating committee's processes for identifying and evaluating candidates; and any differences in the process, if the recommendation comes from a shareholder.
- The minimum qualifications for a nominating committee-recommended nominee and any qualities and skills that the nominating committee believes are necessary or desirable for board members to possess.
- The source category of the recommendation for each nominee approved by the nominating committee. These categories are security holder, nonmanagement director, chief executive officer, other executive officer, third-party search firm, or other, specified source.
- Any fees to third parties for the identification, evaluation or assistance of potential nominees and the function performed by each.
- Identity of any candidates emanating from investors (or investor groups) beneficially owing more than five percent of the company's voting stock (with consent of the security holder and the candidate).[8]

If a company makes material changes in the process for shareholders to submit director nominations, it also must be reported in the quarterly or annual reports. These disclosures help remove the veil covering director nominations as a first step to providing more investor transparency and participation. But just as important, the SEC has made provisions to afford better investor access to board members.

Shareholder Access to the Board of Directors

The SEC adopted new disclosure standards intended to aid a shareholder's ability to communicate with the board of directors. These disclosures will enable shareholders to evaluate the nature and quality of a board's communication process. Companies are required to provide:

- A statement as to whether or not the company's board of directors provides a process for security holders to send communications to the board of directors, and if not, the board's view on why this is appropriate

- If the company has a process:
  - A description of the manner in which security holders can send communications to the board or to specified individual directors
  - If all security holder communications are not sent directly to board members, a description of the company's process for determining which communications will be relayed to board members
- A description of the company's policy, if any, with regard to board members' attendance at annual meetings and a statement of the number of board members who attended the prior year's annual meeting

According to SEC guidance, correspondence from officers of the company is exempt, but employee correspondence must be captured if it is made solely in their capacity as a security holder. The disclosure requirements also include a description of how a shareholder can communicate to the board and how the company determines what is forwarded to board members. Obviously, the company will want to put a process in place to capture and disseminate shareholder communications to the board. Not all correspondence may be appropriate, and you do not want to overwhelm the board with vendor solicitations, customer requests, rants, minutiae, or irrelevant streams of consciousness. The detailed process for collecting and organizing communications need not be disclosed as long as it is approved by a majority of the independent directors.

An obvious concern for shareholders and directors will be that the company filters "appropriate" communications to the board. Best practice would dictate that the boards periodically tap an independent advisor to review the triage process and correspondence discarded to ensure it is being executed properly. The last thing a director needs is to have been informed of a fraud in an intercepted communication. The next step would be for a plaintiff's attorney to questions a director's oversight of the process.

The SEC recognized that by attending annual meetings, directors will have an opportunity to assess shareholder attitudes and shareholders will have the opportunity to communicate directly with directors. To encourage attendance, the SEC requires that companies disclose director attendance policies.

Securities Trading Disclosures

The importance of monitoring management and director trading was mentioned earlier. Well, there are also important disclosures that have to be made regarding securities trading. In fact, there were pre-existing disclosure requirements, but Congress determined this information was not timely. Previously, activity had to be reported 10 days after the close of each calendar month in which the transaction occurred. This could be weeks after the transaction was executed. Changes in director, officer, and principal stockholder holdings now have to be reported within two days on SEC Form 4 with exceptions for certain transactions where the reporting person does not select the date of execution. As required by the Sarbanes-Oxley Act Section 403, these communications will be posted on the SEC's website, and if the issuer maintains a website, it must be posted there, as well, no later than the business day following the filing.

Fair Disclosure

Even though Regulation FD (fair disclosure) was implemented well before the passage of the Sarbanes-Oxley Act, its importance to directors is still substantial and relevant. FD requires that companies cannot be selective about with whom they share material information. If a company decides to have a conference call for banking analysts, they must allow access to others who wish to participate or otherwise simultaneously disseminate the information. The reason this is particularly important to directors is that they are privy to material information that is not widely distributed. Even the inadvertent disclosure of this information, say, over lunch with an investor, could expose the company to a SEC enforcement action. If a director does slip, it is imperative that he or she immediately notifies company counsel and that the company disseminate the information as quickly as possible. The SEC has, to date, not used a heavy hand to enforce the rule, so quick mitigation can be effective.

Amazingly, Siebal Systems has been the subject of two FD enforcement actions. After agreeing to a cease-and-desist order, the company privately shared material information with certain investors who bought stock on the information. Among other defenses, Siebal claims that it should not be penalized even if it did share material information and the Chamber of Commerce of the United States agrees with them. The Chamber, in a friend of the court brief, defends Siebal's position because it believes it is a threat to "a free, robust, orderly, and democratic society." It goes on to say that required disclosures either "chills protected expression" or "mandates unwanted speech."[9] Putting the law aside, these arguments are simply unethical and morally wrong. It harkens back to the days when favored insiders and their friends were allowed to profitably trade ahead of market moving news to the detriment of other shareholders. One suspects that everyone reading this book believes in the capitalist system and in its wealth creating capability. However, for the system to survive, it must be viewed as fair. The U.S. Chamber of Commerce has soiled its name and the integrity of U.S. business by adopting this position.

The reporting requirements of public companies are substantial and increasing. Not all reporting requirements have been addressed here; on the contrary, only those recent changes that are relevant to the board of directors (rather than solely the company or its management) have been included. In total, these new and revised disclosure requirements are significant and provide greater transparency of governance operations. Directors need to be aware of them and ensure that appropriate steps are taken to address events or triggers that create or change a reporting requirement. Directors also need independent, periodic review of shareholder communications that were triaged out of the board's queue. This procedure provides some assurance that management is not inadvertently or purposely blocking relevant information. The issues discussed above will help a director prepare for this challenge.

KEY CONCEPTS

- Be familiar with the 17 events triggering reporting to the SEC on Form 8-K within four days as well as reporting rules concerning pension blackout periods and changes to the company's code of ethics.
- Assign to specific individuals responsibility to monitor and report a triggering event.
- Ensure that management has appointed a rapid response team comprised of core members who are prepared to respond to reporting triggers.
- Establish guidelines describing what constitutes an event in advance and make certain that it is communicated to front line employees assigned to monitor the environment for these events.
- Prepare and document an approval process for event reporting in advance.
- Be aware of company requirements to disclose audit committees' participation in review and discussion of the financial reports with management and the independent auditors.
- Make certain other audit committee disclosures are made such as whether it is governed by a charter, all members are independent, the name of the director designated as the audit committee financial expert, and if there is a code of ethics for financial personnel.
- Be aware that the company must make disclosures regarding:
  - Whether it has a nominating committee
  - Its charter
  - The committees' independence
  - The process for identifying and evaluating candidates
  - Any difference in the process if a recommendation comes from a shareholder
  - Minimum qualifications for candidates
  - Source of recommendation for approved candidates
  - Fees paid to search firms
  - Identity of candidates emanating from large shareholders
- Be aware that the company must also report on shareholder access to the board of directors including the process for

security holders to send communications to the board and director attendance at board meetings.

■ Independently review the vetting process over communications to board members on a periodic basis to ensure directors are receiving everything they should.

■ Know that directors now have two days to report security transactions on Form 4 to the SEC.

ENDNOTES

1. Geraldine Fabrikant, "Disney Settles S.E.C. Complaint on Directors," *New York Times*, 21 December 2004, C4.
2. Securities and Exchange Commission, *SEC Adopts Rules on Provisions of Sarbanes-Oxley Act: Actions Cover Non-GAAP Financials, Form 8-K Amendments, Trading During Blackout Periods, Audit Committee Financial Expert Requirements*, Release 2003-6, January 15, 2003.
3. Rita Farrell, "PeopleSoft Chief's Remarks Cited as Cause of Dismissal," *New York Times*, 5 October 2004, C4.
4. Louisa Hearn, "Lastminute.com Plans to Quit Nasdaq," *FT.com* [*Financial Times*], 15 July 2004. http://news.ft.com/s01/servlet/ContentServer?pagename=FT.com/StoryFT/FullStory/&c=StoryFT&cid=1087373743806&p=1012571727251.
5. Floyd Norris, "Investor Says He Bought Stock and Didn't Know It," *New York Times*, 30 July 2003, C1.
6. Securities and Exchange Commission, *Final Rule: Standards Relating to Listed Company Audit Committees*, 17 CFR Parts 228, 229, 240, 249 and 274, Release Nos. 33-8220; 34-47654; IC-26001; File No. S7-02-03, 37.
7. Securities and Exchange Commission, *Final Rule: Disclosure Required by Section 406 and 407 of the Sarbanes-Oxley Act of 2002*, 17 CFR Parts 228, 229 and 249. Release Nos. 33-8177; 34-47235; File No. S7-40-03.
8. Securities and Exchange Commission, *Final Rule: Disclosure Regarding Nominating Committee Functions and Communications Between Security Holders and Boards of Directors*, 17

CFR Parts 228, 229, 240, 249 and 274, Release Nos. 33-8340; 34-48825; IC-26262; File No. S7-14-03.

9. Floyd Norris, "Does the 'Voice of Business' Think the Bill of Rights Covers Insider Tips?" *New York Times*, 4 February 2005, C1.

Other Useful Advice and Conclusions

There are a large number of directors who do not sit on the boards of large public companies. Instead, they sit on investment company, not-for-profit, advisory, or small public company boards. These organizations have some unique governance issues. Since these topics are not relevant to all directors, they are not included in the High-Impact Governance Framework. However, there are some important topics tackled that most directors will be able to learn from and can apply to their oversight responsibilities. In this section, we will explore these specific issues.

Finally, a call to service is proposed. It is in everyone's best interests to heed the call of good governance, and by embracing the practices contained in this book, we can contribute to the greater good by improving those areas over which we have influence.

CHAPTER 15

Big Money, Little Money, No Money

L arge public companies, although they compete in a number of industries, face many similar governance issues that can be addressed structurally. There are, however, other types of organizations that have unique characteristics and resist the highly structured governance templates utilized by large public companies. These include investment companies, not-for-profit entities, advisory boards, and even very small public companies. The number of people serving on the boards of these organizations is relatively large. Therefore, the purpose of this chapter is to address many of the issues specific to these directors.

THE MONEYMAKERS

John Bogel, the revered founder of the Vanguard Group of mutual funds, said recently: "When we have strong managers, weak directors and passive owners, it's only a matter of time before the looting begins."[1] Having long been a critic of investment company governance, he is acutely aware that this is particularly true of mutual funds.

Investment companies are different from public corporations in that they are regulated under the Investment Company Act of 1940 and the Investment Advisors Act of 1940. Congress passed these acts in response to investment company abuses stemming from conflicts of interest that arise in the operations of these companies. They regulate entities that exist primarily to invest in securities of other companies. Mutual funds are one type of an investment company covered under these acts. Congress correctly recognized that advisors have a near monopoly over information and an inherent conflict regarding the advisory fees paid to them by the funds they manage. Independent director oversight was seen as a way to keep these conflicts in check.

Growth in the mutual fund business has truly been meteoric. From just 564 funds in 1980 with assets of less than $200 billion, they are now the largest segment of the investment company industry with approximately $7 trillion in assets invested in over 8,000 mutual fund companies that are managed by over 900 investment company advisors. The variety of assets is also diverse and includes money market, equity, fixed income, hybrid, and tax advantaged funds. Within each of these categories exists further diversity such as large cap versus small cap, international versus domestic, government versus corporate, and so on. Add to this another 8,000 registered investment advisors who manage over $20 trillion in assets (including mutual funds) and you can get a sense of the magnitude of the industry. The SEC exercises oversight of the industry and is authorized to examine the records of mutual funds, yet prior to 2003, the SEC had only 370 members on its staff to examine all of these funds and fund advisors.

Eliot Spitzer, New York's Attorney General, recently set the mutual fund industry on its ear when he implicated a number of advisors, hedge fund managers, and mutual funds in late trading and market timing practices that were to the detriment of the nation's small investors. Market timing itself is not illegal; however, it may dilute the value of long-term shareholders' interests if the fund calculates *net asset value* (NAV) using stale closing prices. The list of financial institutions that had employees investigated is truly shocking. These organizations read like a who's who of the financial community: Bank of America, Janus, Alliance, Pilgrim, Wellington, PIMCO, Putnam, Massachusetts Mutual, CSFB, Invesco, Fred Alger, Prudential, U.S. Trust, Merrill Lynch, Bank One, Citigroup, Millennium Partners, Canary Capital Partners, Heartland Advisors, and others.

Concerned that the number of enforcement actions reflected a serious and widespread breakdown in management controls, the SEC adopted a number of new rules. These include:

- A requirement that board composition include at least 75 percent independent directors (except for small boards of three, in which case two must be independent)
- That the chairperson of the board must be an independent director

- That independent directors must meet at least once a quarter
- A requirement that the board perform a self-assessment at least once annually
- That the independent directors must be affirmatively authorized to hire their own staff

These initiatives are designed to improve the independence of the board and quality of oversight. Some analysts estimate that, prior to the new rules, over 80 percent of U.S. mutual funds had chairmen who were also executives of the advisor or management company.[2] So this change is nothing short of revolutionary. Investment companies have until January 16, 2006 to comply with these new rules.

Additionally, in December 2003, the SEC adopted a rule requiring all funds and advisors to implement and maintain written compliance policies and procedures reasonably designed to prevent and detect violations. They also require funds and fund advisors to designate a chief compliance officer to administer the policies and procedures and report annually to the board of directors regarding compliance matters. It will become evident as we analyze what has recently gone wrong in this industry, a strong compliance officer can be a director's best defense against fraudulent behavior. Fund compliance activities fall into 12 basic categories:

Portfolio management	Advertising
Execution arrangements	Safeguarding assets
Trade allocation	Transaction processing
Personal trading	Antilaundering
Pricing and value calculations	Governance
Books and records	Money market safety

Investment company board members should be aware of these issues and be prepared to ask good questions and provide strong oversight.

Portfolio Management

Portfolio management considers whether investments are consistent with client objectives. For instance, it would not be appropriate to place a substantial portion of a retiree's savings in a high-yield bond portfolio if their primary objective is safety. Normally, compliance will play a role in this oversight. Some good questions for the compliance officer might be whether there are any required client documents that have been outstanding for more than 30 days, and how they ensure that only appropriate investments are made in accordance with those objectives.

Execution, Costs, and Fees

Mutual funds are allowed to charge a small fee from investors, called *12b-1 fees*, for promotions, sales, or any other activity connected with the distribution of the fund's shares. The fee must be reasonable, which is normally considered to be 0.5 to 1 percent of the fund's net assets. The theory behind the 12b-1 fee was that by marketing a mutual fund, its assets would increase. This would, in turn, lower management expenses because the cost would be spread out among more investors. However, there is concern by regulators that mutual fund investors are paying for a fund's aggressive expansion plans. For example, Capital Research and Management, the advisor for the American Funds, the third largest fund family in the country, is under investigation for rewarding "brokerage firms that aggressively sold its funds by funneling commissions on securities trades to those firms."[3] If true, it is not hard to imagine that the commissions paid may not be competitive, and shareholders pay those costs.

The SEC also took action fining Morgan Stanley $50 million for buying "shelf space." The SEC contended that Morgan's customers did not know that they were paying brokerage companies to push Morgan's funds. The SEC levied the largest penalty for nondisclosure of revenue sharing agreements against Edward D. Jones & Company for failing to disclose hidden marketing deals and the company was fined $75 million. They marketed seven preferred investments, but did not tell investors that the company was being paid to make the recommendation.[4] Had they done so, investors may have been more careful about buying a fund solely on the recommendation of a sales representative. One would question whether the fund was being recommended because it was well managed, or because the agent was being well paid to push it.

Advisors are also required to seek the best price for execution of their security purchases and expected to negotiate the best deals possible to keep brokerage costs low. To control these risks, a director should ensure that broker share and commission pricing are periodically reviewed by compliance, internal audit, or outside consultants and any off-market pricing investigated further.

Allocation

Allocation of trades considers whether block trades or *initial public offerings* (IPOs) are fairly distributed. For instance, in 2004, Alan Bond, an investment advisor and well-known guest on *Wall Street Week* with Louis Rukeyser, was accused by the SEC of "cherry-picking" where he allocated profitable trades to himself while shedding losing trades to his clients. Bond realized $6.6 million in profits while his customers lost over $56 million. In related criminal actions, he was convicted of fraud by a jury and is serving a 12-and-a-half-year prison term.[5] The only way to identify such behavior is by detailed analysis of how trades are allocated. As a director, you will want to ensure that someone independent of the portfolio manager is reviewing the allocations on a regular basis. This would normally be performed by the designated compliance officer, but it is also a best practice to have auditors regularly review and report on allocation controls.

Transaction Processing

After hours trading has become the most recent mutual fund scandal capturing headlines. Orders received after the close should be priced using the next day's asset value. However, several investment advisors were found to permit after hours trading at the closing price, allowing certain favored clients to benefit from information available only after the close. Knowing that foreign markets are rallying, and having the ability to buy a U.S. fund invested in foreign stocks at its previous closing price is virtually a sure thing. Massachusetts Financial Services, Co. (MFS) was one such advisor allowing after hours trading. MFS allowed Security Brokerage, Inc. (SBI) to trade late and engage in market timing that netted profits of approximately $175 million for SBI's president and majority owner. MFS was forced to disgorge over $225 million that will be distributed back to injured shareholders. The courts have frozen the assets of SBI and its president while the investigation against them continues.

The SEC also recently focused on "breakpoints" or discounts for larger purchases. During their examinations, they found that such discounts were not awarded uniformly and have taken action against 15 funds.

It is imperative that mutual fund organizations have a strong compliance function to monitor transactions. Automated tools can easily identify trades received after 4 P.M. as well as automatically calculate breakpoints. Directors can reduce this exposure by requiring appropriate investment in automated monitoring tools and making certain that procedures require exceptions to be reported, vetted and cleared. Directors should get close to the compliance officer as he or she is the best line of defense against unethical or illegal activity.

Personal Trading

Investment advisors of large mutual funds are in a unique position of knowing what the fund will be buying (or selling), and how they are positioned against world markets. As such, they can use this knowledge to time trades into and out of the funds they manage to the detriment of other shareholders. Richard Strong, investment advisor to Strong Capital Management, used his position to time trades in and out of Strong funds, including those where he was a portfolio manager. Incredibly, it was reported that Strong had been warned by in-house counsel that his trades could disadvantage customers and that he should cease the practice. Unfortunately, it appears this advice was ignored. The SEC accused him of trading 10 Strong funds in 40 accounts that he managed for himself, family, and friends. He would invest huge amounts in single positions, some that he would hold for only one day. Not surprisingly, Strong never disclosed his frequent trading to his board of directors. The SEC has barred Strong from the industry for life and he must pay $60 million in disgorgement and civil penalties.

This case is particularly frustrating from a director's point of view, since in-house counsel and compliance were aware of the trading patterns. Directors can reduce this risk by having management certify that they are not aware of any breaches in the personal trading policy. They can include this in the annual attestation of compliance with other company policies such as confidentiality and computer use certifications. Directors can encourage counsel to proactively share concerns and, at least annually, directly question and document responses from counsel and the compliance officer about their knowledge of any policy breaches.

Pricing and Valuation

One of the oldest tricks in the book is to mismark a portfolio, making it seem more valuable than it really is. As an example, Piper Capital management was found to have overridden dealer quotations with their own valuations in a plan to gradually lower net asset value instead of recognizing the rapid and deep losses actually experienced. It seems that by gradually reducing the NAV, the fund hoped to avoid a corresponding upswing in redemption activity. The Commission revoked Piper's registration and caused it to pay over $2 million in penalties. Directors should inquire if securities and NAV are priced and calculated by a back-office team independent from the portfolio manager. If the managers themselves are calculating NAV, there is potential for manipulation.

Antilaundering

Money laundering is the introduction of illegally gained funds into the legitimate financial system in an attempt to cover up their origin. The problem is significant as the International Monetary Fund has stated that the aggregate size of money laundering in the world could be somewhere between 2 percent and 5 percent of the world's gross domestic product. The key is to have an entry into the legitimate financial system.

The recent investigation into Riggs Bank shows how some of the most powerful people in the world launder their ill-gotten gains. Washington D.C. based Riggs once billed itself as "the most important bank in the most important city in the world." More recently, it has come under fire by the U.S. Senate's Permanent Subcommittee on Investigations for failing to monitor suspicious transactions, even in the wake of the terrorist attacks on September 11, 2001. One of the more prominent accounts at issue is that of General Augusto Pinochet, the former dictator of Chile. Pinochet took power forcibly in 1973, and opened accounts at Riggs Bank in 1985. The Chilean military has notoriously low wages, even for a general (never more than $40,000), but somehow, Pinochet amassed as much as $8 million in the accounts.[6] In a report issued by U.S. Senate investigators, it is alleged that Riggs Bank officials not only accepted the money, but helped Pinochet hide it for years by moving it around the world, even after his human rights accusations and arrest became well known. Some other accounts at Riggs that concern regulators include those of the leaders of Equatorial New Guinea who have amassed approximately $700 million and over 150 Saudi Arabian Embassy accounts that lacked appropriate background information on their owners.[7]

One defense against laundering is the "know your customer" rules. It is important that a financial institution not only know who their customers are, but also the source of their money. Clearly, General Pinochet would have had difficulty explaining the source of his wealth.

Books and Records

This category generally concerns keeping current books and filing regulatory reports on time as well as the security over personal client information to prevent unauthorized use. Books and records can be altered or improperly used to hide unethical or illegal activity. Take Security Trust Corporation as an example. STC enabled the hedge fund Canary Partners to trade after hours by disguising the trades as retirement accounts. Prior to recent rule proposals, brokers and managers of retirement funds, who might receive an order at 3:59 P.M., but still needed to buy the shares from the fund, would be allowed to complete the transaction, even if received by the fund after 4 P.M. If current proposals are adopted these investors will receive the closing price the following day. The Office of the Comptroller shut down STC costing some 130 employees their jobs, and Eliot Spitzer brought charges against management. Obviously, proper internal controls play an important role in maintaining and securing books and records. The public accountants and internal auditors can provide some comfort to a director that the control environment is adequate, but a robust compliance program to "know your customer," their accounts, and the activity in the accounts is a key component to discouraging games that impair the integrity of the books and records. This requires a competent and objective compliance officer to ensure accounts are properly documented and monitored.

Advertising

The SEC is concerned that investors have accurate information when making investment decisions, and monitors advisor advertising to ensure it is truthful. The most common concern is where an advisor inflates their investment returns. For instance, the Commission found that Merrimac Advisors claimed they had annual five-year returns of over 20 percent, which was untrue. They also overstated the number of clients and the amount of money under management. Merrimac's registration was yanked, the principal barred from the industry and fined $50,000. A direct question about the type of fact-checking performed on advertisements before they are released may uncover poor control over the inadvertent or purposeful release of inaccurate information.

Safeguarding Assets

There are rules designed to protect customer assets such as ensuring proper custody arrangements and having independent auditors conduct surprise security counts if they are kept by the advisor. Directors should ensure that assets are regularly reconciled to custodian accounts.

Governance

Not surprisingly, this category has to do with how a board is constituted and whether it is carrying out its fiduciary duties to shareholders.

When Eliot Spitzer settled charges with Bank of America for over $675 million and extracted an agreement to exit the securities clearing business, he also forced the ouster of eight directors. This is the first settlement to hold a board responsible. Spitzer pointed to the directors' knowledge of the harmful results from market timing, but nevertheless allowing a favored client an exemption.[8]

Money Market Safety

Money market funds are considered a safe, conservative investment. An important aspect of money market funds is that they are required to maintain a NAV of $1. Investments must be conservative as a fund that sustains losses will be unable to maintain an NAV of $1. The Commission found that John Backland invested up to 27 percent of a money market fund in structured notes, a volatile derivative. Despite knowing about steep losses resulting from the derivative, the board continued to allow shares to be sold and redeemed at $1 a share. The fund was eventually liquidated at 96 cents per share. A director can reduce this risk by periodically reviewing the components of the portfolio. Ask questions about anything that is not familiar or that looks aggressive.

Effects of the Sarbanes-Oxley Act
on Investment Companies

Despite being regulated under the Investment Company Act of 1940, investment companies were impacted by the passage of the Sarbanes-Oxley Act of 2002. Specifically, the SEC amended their rules to require a registered management investment company's principal executive and financial officers to certify the information contained in the shareholder reports (Form N-CSR) filed with the SEC. This is akin to CEOs and CFOs certifying their financial statements filed on 10-Ks and 10-Qs with the Commission.

As required under Sections 406 and 407 of the Sarbanes-Oxley Act, a registered management investment company must divulge "whether it has adopted a code of ethics that applies to the company's principal executive officer and senior financial officers. An investment company revealing that it has not adopted such a code must disclose this fact and explain why it has not done so." They are also required to make public amendments or waivers to such a code. The rules also necessitate that the registered management investment company make known whether it has at least one "audit committee financial expert" serving on its audit committee and whether that person is independent. An investment company that does not have such an expert must disclose this fact and explain why.

TIAA-CREF is one of the United States' largest institutional investors that includes Teachers Insurance and Annuity Association, College Retirement Equities Fund, and various affiliates. They have made their presence felt by pressing the boards of directors of companies in which they have invested to adopt good governance practices. To their credit, they have stepped up to eat their own cooking. In response to the recent mutual fund scandals, TIAA-CREF issued Principles for Fund Governance and Practices. They are investor-friendly principles to which they aspire and to which they will hold other fund providers whose funds they offer. They have generously agreed to allow them to be reprinted in Appendix F of this book so that we can all benefit from their experience.

Pension Funds

On the burner with the SEC are those conflicts that can exist between a pension fund and its consultants. The boards of many pension funds hire advisors to help develop investment strategies and select the managers that will invest their funds. When those consultants work for a brokerage or an investment company that also manages money, the potential for conflicts are ripe. Consultants can be paid directly, or in some cases, agree for those fees to be offset by trading commissions (which would guarantee deal flow and revenue to the financial institution for which the consultant works). This particular conflict resembles that experienced by the independent auditors prior to the enactment of the Sarbanes-Oxley Act. Just as it would be difficult for an auditor to objectively assess a system or internal control structure that their consulting firm implemented, it would also be difficult for an advisor to objectively assess the effectiveness and efficiency of brokerage services or money managers working for their firm.

A case involving the Chattanooga Pension Fund underscores this potential conflict. Its advisor, William Keith Phillips, was a top broker at Paine Webber and offered for the fund to pay for his consulting services directly, or agree to allocate a portion of its trading commissions to cover fees. Mr. Phillips allegedly told the trustees that the commission arrangement would leave more money to invest for its beneficiaries. Seven years later, the pension plan filed an arbitration suit against Mr. Phillips as they learned the commission arrangement lead to "$20 million in losses, undisclosed commissions, and fees."[9] The pension fund argues that the commission agreement put Mr. Phillip's interests ahead of his client's, thus breaching his fiduciary duty to the fund.

Boards often view, quite correctly, that consultants can bring specialized expertise and objectivity to sensitive issues such as compensation, sourcing new directors, reviewing potential transactions

KEY CONCEPTS: INVESTMENT COMPANY

- Directors must get close to the compliance officer. In some cases, they are your best chance to identify and address a threat before it takes hold and grows.
- Evaluate costs independently and pay for services directly rather than trading services for guaranteed deal or trading flow.
- Make certain that allocations are periodically reviewed for "cherry picking" by the internal or external auditors.
- Support the use of automated control tools wherever possible.
- Directly question the compliance officer and general counsel regarding their knowledge of any policy breaches or potential concerns.
- Make sure that portfolio pricing is performed independent of the front office or fund managers.
- Periodically query the compliance officer regarding the completeness of the "know-your-customer" documentation.
- Assess the fact checking process for advertising claims.
- Ensure that the company has an enforceable code of ethics— resist efforts to provide waivers to the code.

and investigating management, but there is still the potential for conflict. The board has to remain vigilant when retaining a consultant. This can be difficult as you do not always know that there may be a conflict until the consultant has breached their duty and damage has been done, but understanding the potential given the person's position and relationships can go a long way towards controlling this risk. Pay directly for services. Evaluate each cost independently. Continually monitor results and compare the cost of services to the market. While soft costs sound appealing, just like Chattanooga Pension Fund, the siren song can become an expensive lesson.

NOT-FOR-PROFIT BOARDS

Many consider the not-for-profit corporation the informal and immaterial cousin of the for-profit corporation, but in reality, they can be quite substantial. Not-for-profits control over $2 trillion in assets and transact over $900 billion in revenue annually. The mission of not-for-profit boards is much different from their for-profit counterparts. While for-profit corporations exist to make a return for their shareholders, not-for-profit corporations exist to provide a service to a particular institution, constituency, or social program. Their boards are usually much larger than their corporate cousins, and directors are generally not paid, rather they are usually expected to be a source of service, talent, and fundraising. It can be as star-studded as any for-profit corporation as over two thirds of CEOs and corporate directors serve on at least one not-for-profit board of directors.

Not-for-profit boards have some unique issues. They are regulated by the Internal Revenue Service (IRS), and the IRS will not hesitate to hold directors directly accountable for awarding executive compensation in excess of market. No show directors are another distinctive problem associated with these boards. Too many directors are attracted to the position due to its social status with little consideration to the time commitment. These directors often appear to be the most qualified, because they sit on numerous boards, but in reality, they are not committing adequate time to any of them. A good practice for not-for-profits is to disqualify up front those candidates who sit on too many boards. Once invited, it is hard to remove a director who is not performing. While there are usually attendance rules in most board by-laws, in reality boards are reticent to enforce them. A process of annual self-evaluation can be effective because directors will usually discern their own shortcomings. Then a real discussion can occur regarding commitment to the board. Introducing this concept should become easier now that it is a required feature of many public companies. Directors should also be made aware that they are liable for decisions made by the board in their absence.

Just because boards are populated with volunteers does not mean they are risk-free. It is not difficult to recall some large frauds involving not-for-profits. The sexual and financial scandals at Covenant House, the forced resignation of Bishop Estate Trustees for their million dollar salaries and legislative intimidation, and the excesses at the United Way that lead to prison for its chief are some examples that come to mind. The most recent addition to this infamous list is the unpaid president of the James Beard House, a culinary organization named after the celebrated chef who died in 1985. Leonard F. Pickell Jr., has pleaded guilty to using foundation funds to pay credit card bills for himself and his brother. The investigation began after the board of trustees learned that tax filings were delinquent. An internal audit then uncovered what appeared to be misuse of foundation money to the tune of hundreds of thousands of dollars. Documents provided to back up these expenses were also at issue. These documents, which apparently gave board approval for these expenses, appeared to be forgeries.[10] This example should enlighten any not-for-profit director to the need for checks and balances that are independent from the senior management team. Internal audit can be just as important to these organizations as for their for-profit cousins.

Directors of not-for-profit corporations are held to the same duties of care and loyalty as for-profit directors. Unfortunately, for many of these boards when things go wrong, the initial instinct is to circle the wagons and deny the problem. That is the most unadvised action a board can take. The resulting investigation can be damaging to a director's reputation and result in a costly legal defense. When allegations surface, the board should aggressively investigate them, and honestly deal with the findings. This is easier said than done.

A useful example of the difficulties faced by not-for-profits comes from the Milton Hershey School Trust. The Trust, founded by Milton Hershey, the benevolent candy manufacturer, was set up to fund a school for orphaned children. He donated 486 acres of land and $60 million in Hershey Candy stock. By 2002, the endowment had grown to $5.9 billion, all in Hershey stock representing a 77 percent voting interest in the company. The board, at the behest of the deputy attorney general of Pennsylvania, and recognizing their fiduciary responsibility, determined it would be prudent to diversify their financial holdings.

Unsurprisingly, the prospect of selling a controlling interest spread fear throughout the local community where the school and many Hershey employees coexisted. Competitors of the candy company were interested in acquiring the large stockholdings and the community knew that unfriendly owners could shutter local operations.

In an about-face, the State of Pennsylvania's attorney general sued to stop the sale and won a preliminary ruling in Orphan's Court. Interestingly, the judge in the case admonished the Trust to reduce the number of board members and increase the percentage that were from the Hershey community. Where some see creating a greater conflict of interest, the judge saw a disconnect from the interests the Trust served. The foundation backed off and agreed to inform the attorney general's office before they sold any Hershey equities. The stock fell $24 on the news costing the Trust over $1 billion.

This example shows how difficult it often is for directors to do what is right for their not-for-profit. There are countervailing forces that will selfishly try to block what is right for the organization to further their individual interests. What is clear from this case is that now, at least in Pennsylvania, trustees have to look beyond their traditional role as prudent stewards of the trust and be aware of other indirect stakeholders.[11] It is understandable that there would be local opposition to selling a controlling stake as jobs might have been lost. Perhaps the board should have taken this into consideration by selling less than a controlling interest to diverse parties that would have helped them realize their diversification goals without creating a crisis. Instead, the organization was quickly consumed by events set in motion by their desire to sell.

The experience of the University of Idaho Foundation (UIF) detailed in the Case Study *A Board of Vandals*, provides us with another example of a not-for-profit board facing a crisis. All too often, boards are either unresponsive or react too late to save the organization and stem losses. The reaction by the volunteer directors of the UIF is one that could serve as a model to many of our paid public corporation boards.

CASE STUDY: A BOARD OF VANDALS

The University of Idaho is a picturesque, secluded, residential campus located among the rolling hills of the Palouse in northern Idaho. Founded as a land-grant university in 1889, the campus is replete with gothic architecture normally found at Ivy League schools.[a] The institution has a reputation for academic excellence in agriculture and biological science, engineering and computer security, wildlife conservation, and, surprisingly, a state of the art training facility for securities trading. Every February, the campus is transformed as it hosts the world renowned Lionel Hampton Jazz Festival, which brings elementary through high school students together with jazz greats. Given its isolation and residential characteristics, the community is tight knit, much more so than big-city commuter schools. People get to know each other well and build lifelong friendships.

There has generally been a healthy rivalry between the University of Idaho and other states schools. Many alumni believe support for the school is greater than you normally find elsewhere, a phenomenon some dub "Vandal Pride" in reference to the university's sport team nickname. The Vandal community as a whole, however, can also be defensive of their institution due to the northern perception that the political appointees of the State Board of Education, which oversees all of the public institutions of higher learning, and the press favor the institutions in the southern part of the state.

The University of Idaho Foundation (UIF) is a private, nonprofit organization founded for the purpose of soliciting financial support for the University of Idaho. The Foundation also manages millions of dollars in funds, trusts, and endowments for the benefit of the university. The largely volunteer board consists of some of the best and brightest graduates of the University and includes former CEOs of large public companies, some of the best legal minds in the state, and dot.com millionaires, among others. Board members are unusually dedicated and will collectively spend hundreds of hours advancing the interests of the university simply because of their love for the institution.

As a land grant institution, the University of Idaho is required to provide community outreach throughout the state. To continue this mission, the university originally planned on a four-building complex in Boise, home of Boise State University, with the initial facility focused on water-related research and programs. The University of Idaho had been offering outreach programs and services to the Boise area for over 75 years, yet not everyone was happy that they were expanding their presence there. Nevertheless, the President of the University called on the UIF to purchase the land and provide interim financing for the development of the complex, which they did.

The UIF took on debt for land acquisition and preconstruction costs that they believed would be reimbursed from the sale of state-backed bonds. However, the

Idaho State Building Authority, the state agency responsible for issuing the debt, held back reimbursement to the UIF until they were confident that the project was properly defined and that there were enough funds to complete the project. These were valid concerns as construction and operating costs for the project skyrocketed and the rental market in the Boise area softened. About the same time, the local newspaper, the *Idaho Statesman,* caught wind of brewing financial crisis and began running a series of exposés. Soon, the State Board of Education was calling on university officials to explain and for an independent investigation into the project to be funded by the institution. Unsurprisingly, the investigation found poor management of the project. The fallout led to the resignation of the university's president and dismissal of its CFO. Importantly, the investigators believed they had found a "likely breach of fiduciary duty of loyalty" and a "possible breach of the fiduciary duty of care" stemming from the UIF's actions.[b]

Naturally, "likely" and "possible" are far from convictions, but such comments sell newspapers, and the *Idaho Statesman* ran with it. Vandal Pride was recast by nonalumni as cult-like behavior embarrassing the school. The State Board of Education began detailed oversight of university operations, and not to be left behind, federal, state, and county prosecutors began their own investigations. The UIF was facing a full-scale crisis.

Imagine, you are at the pinnacle of your career, you join a prestigious board as a volunteer, rely on the financial information furnished you by a popular CEO and long-time CFO, and suddenly people are accusing you of breaching your fiduciary duties. Most volunteers would have packed their bags and gone home, but the directors of the UIF correctly responded with a sense of urgency to right the ship.

While the board did not believe they were getting unbiased treatment from the press or the State Board of Education, they resisted the temptation to pick a fight with either. They correctly assessed that you cannot win a fight with someone who buys ink by the barrel, or a political board empowered to control the institution you are trying to support. Rather, they rightly focused on the cause of the problem identified by investigators: the debt and related financial pressures that threatened to undo the Foundation. And led by Jim Hawkins and Mike Wilson, the Foundation President and Executive Director, respectively, they pursued solutions as if their collective hair was on fire. Over the course of a year, the president called 33 board meetings (of which 28 were by telephone) and, amazingly, only one did not meet the requirements for a quorum (11 of the 21 board members). The board also decided that they needed their own legal counsel. Finding that most in-state attorneys had deep conflicts of interest, the board went out-of-state to retain counsel.

The University of Idaho Foundation acquired $26 million in debt associated with the Boise project, however, in less than a year, the Foundation had cut their debt load in half and regained solvency by completing the first building (freeing up $4.5 million held back by the Idaho State Building Authority), selling unneeded land at the Boise site, and selling other underproducing real estate investments. According to the *Idaho Statesman,* the board also filed an insurance claim with the

State to recover losses due to disclosures that were not made to the board by a university official and filed a lawsuit against the developer of the Boise project. Finally, they engaged independent governance experts to help them restructure and ensure their independence from the university. These results also built credibility with certain members of the State Board of Education. In total, the aggressive activity of the board has been so successful that they are now turning their attention back to their original mission, and believe that they are in a position to once again contribute over $2 million annually to help fund university operations possibly as early as their next fiscal year.

Key success factors for this turnaround lay squarely in a few important concepts:

- **Character:** Despite their volunteer status, many directors worked at the problem as a full time job.
- **Urgency:** They worked at the problem as if their own livelihood depended on the result.
- **Focused:** They targeted the root cause of the problem rather than wasting energy on fights they could not win.
- **Loyalty:** They made decisions that were right for the Foundation they served, even if it meant giving up on the grand plans envisioned by the University.
- **Independence:** They brought in experts to ensure that they received objective, independent feedback.

A list of qualities worthy of any board.

---

[a]The author is a graduate of the University of Idaho. He has also served as President of the University's National Alumni Board of Directors, an organization unaffiliated with the Foundation. While attempting to be as objective as possible while developing this case, some at the University of Idaho and others who have an interest, may or may not come to the same conclusions as the author. The lessons are important and the author would encourage readers to review the report of the independent investigators which can be accessed on the University's website: www.uidaho.edu.

[b]Holland & Hart. University Place Management Review: A Report of the Special Deputy Attorney General to the Idaho State Board of Education. December 5, 2003.

A final word regarding non-profit regulatory initiatives. As this book goes to press, the U.S. Senate Finance Committee is considering legislation designed to strengthen penalties for executives that commit crimes and require stricter corporate governance practices for nonprofit corporations. It is worthwhile for the management and boards of directors for not-for-profit corporations to research and engage in the debate surrounding this proposed legislation.

KEY CONCEPTS: NOT-FOR-PROFIT

- Disqualify candidates who already sit on a number of boards.
- Know that directors serving on non-profit boards also have many of the same liabilities as for-profit companies, even if they do not show up.
- Understand that nonprofit boards can be held liable by the IRS for excessive CEO compensation.
- Recognize that not-for-profits experience many of the same frauds as for-profit companies and also need a formalized system of internal control.
- Directors may have to consider stakeholders beyond their traditional constituencies when considering important decisions.
- Keep current of legislative initiatives. The U.S. Senate is considering legislation that could significantly impact the corporate governance practices of not-for-profits.

SERVING ON ADVISORY BOARDS

An additional source of expert opinion complementary to the board of directors is the advisory board. These boards were popular in the 1970s with multinational companies seeking understanding of foreign markets. A group of advisors can bring that critical local knowledge necessary to penetrate and compete in far away lands. But advisory boards can be created for any number of reasons.

Companies such as U.S. Bank, Avon, and Merrill Lynch still maintain advisory boards to obtain objective, independent advice regarding their operations. Many high-tech startups also use advisory boards to help them negotiate the various minefields encountered on their way to corporate maturity. There may be a permanent body such as an international advisory board, or a temporarily established committee in response to a specific issue such as the formation and oversight of a diversity program. Some advisory positions are compensated, while others can be honorary. Regardless of the form or purpose, advisory boards can deliver a vault stuffed with experience and good judgment to the corporate neighborhood where it is most needed.

U.S. Bank, one of the largest bank holding companies in the country, maintains advisory boards for every consumer banking region where it does business. There could be a number of these regions in a single state. In general, the boards consist of local leaders that meet several times a year for the purpose of keeping the bank informed of activity in the community. That might include new construction activity, the opening of new businesses, and so on. The bank does compensate the advisory board members each meeting for their time and effort. But the communication is not only directed one way, the bank also uses the occasion to inform the community leaders of new products and special promotions. Periodically, they also use these meetings as an opportunity to introduce senior managers of the bank.

The best advisory boards are not filled with CEOs or directors, but with experts from various fields. They are in the trenches and received recognition, not because of their title, but from what they have accomplished and the specific knowledge that they can bring to the table. Some of the most effective advisory boards have a limited life, a well-defined mission, and a mandate to produce a deliverable, generally a report.

Advisory boards usually are not empowered to make binding decisions for companies but exist to dispense advice to directors and management. These boards rarely go beyond making recommendations, and because of this limitation, are not normally exposed to the same liability risks as the board of directors. Nevertheless, some believe it is conceivable that a court could hold compensated advisors on whose advice the company relies to the same standards of good faith as directors. Even in the absence of such a ruling, just defending yourself against such a claim could be an expensive proposition.

Companies can reduce the risk of serving on an advisory board by having a charter or policies regarding the advisory board adopted by the board of directors. Such written documents must make it clear that advisors are not directors and cannot act on behalf of the company. Advisory board members should also ensure that they are covered under the company's D&O insurance. In addition to insurance, the company may also be able to indemnify advisory board members from third-party lawsuits and related costs, depending on the state of incorporation. Most organizations offer broad indemnification provisions in their charter or by-laws.

It is critical for any potential advisory board member to approach joining such a board in the same way they would the board of directors. While the liability associated with serving on such a board is not clear, protecting your wealth is worth investigating these issues.

KEY CONCEPTS: ADVISORY BOARD

- Liability for members of advisory boards is not clear.
- Have the board of directors adopt an advisory board charter that clearly indicates that its members may not act on behalf of the company.
- Make certain that advisory board members are covered by D&O insurance.
- Determine if the company can indemnify advisory board members.

A WORD ABOUT SMALL PUBLIC COMPANIES*

From a regulatory point of view, small public companies are similar to large companies. There are, however, differences, and they are important to consider when applying new legislation with a trawl to all public companies. I expect that most CEOs and CFOs are honest people. So when Congress passed legislation requiring the certification of financial statements, no conscientious CEO wanted his or her name associated with statements that did not properly reflect the financial position of the company. Procedures were efficiently and rapidly implemented to ensure that what was filed with the SEC was accurate. These officers certified the statements knowing there were criminal and financial penalties associated with falsification.

Congress did not stop there. They also legislated the documentation and reporting of financial reporting controls. While this may

---

*Scott Green, "The Limitations of the Sarbanes-Oxley Act," *USA Today Magazine*, March 2005, 66–68. Reprinted from *USA Today Magazine*, March 2005. Copyrighted by the Society for the Advancement of Education, Inc. All rights reserved.

lend even more confidence to the financial reports emanating from public companies, the cost of this marginal benefit is high. Risks can migrate from deep in an organization to the financial statements. For a multinational company to document the control structure for all of these potential sources at a detailed level is a tremendous undertaking. In many cases, internal swat teams are added to consulting resources as they scope, document, and test controls across the company. Since a material deficiency would be reported to the public, smart companies err on the side of caution and include any system or process that could remotely contribute to financial presentation misstatements. In effect, Congress is underwriting an environment of corporate risk aversion as opposed to prudent risk-taking.

According to AMR Research Inc., U.S. companies will spend $5.5 billion on Sarbanes-Oxley compliance in 2004. Financial and system consultants, tracking software, and increased audit fees can quickly add up to millions of dollars. Yet it is unlikely that these efforts will stop a management team determined to circumvent existing controls. Clearly Congress believed the benefits of ensuring a strong control structure outweighed the cost borne by our public companies. Or it could be that they did not foresee how expensive Section 404 could be or the full impact its implementation could have on our companies? Regardless, it is now law.

While the largest companies have the resources to comply, smaller companies may have to make some hard choices between the costs of compliance and the need to access public markets. According to a survey by Foley & Lardner LLP, "the average cost of being a public company with revenue under $1 billion in the wake of corporate governance reform has increased 130 percent from the inception of Sarbanes-Oxley through 2003." Survey participants overwhelmingly cited Section 404 as having the most significant financial impact. And this is before the full costs of Section 404 have been tabulated. Companies are still preparing, and still spending. The deadline for large companies is their first filing after November 15, 2004, and after July 15, 2005 for public companies with a market cap less than $75 million (recently delayed to November 15, 2005).

Even if one is supportive of the Sarbanes-Oxley Act as a whole, we need to closely monitor the impact Section 404 will have on our small companies and private entities wishing to go public. If the regulatory environment has become too burdensome, then policy makers need to exempt small companies from Section 404 of the Act or risk losing this engine of growth. We may already have evidence that this is occurring. A study cosponsored by the Wharton School and the University of Maryland revealed that the number of companies delisting from U.S. exchanges nearly tripled in 2003. The study found that most companies did so to avoid the high cost associated with complying with the Sarbanes-Oxley Act. Even Mike Oxley, the Ohio Congressman who was the cosponsor of the Sarbanes-Oxley Act, recognizes this problem. In a recent interview, he was asked if he could change one thing about the law, what he would do differently. He replied, "I would make it more flexible for the SEC and the Public Accounting Oversight Board relating to small- and medium-sized companies."[12]

However, reversing such legislation will not be easy. It took over 70 years to address the overly onerous sections of the Glass-Steagall Act. It stood for decades despite widespread recognition that it was too broad a solution for the particular problem it was designed to address. That put our banking system at a competitive disadvantage compared to our foreign competitors. The reason for lack of action may have been the absence of competition in the wake of World War II, but the emergence of European banking powerhouses by the late 1990s had made the case for reform more acute.

One of the United States' greatest competitive advantages lies in our small public companies. While heavily regulated European companies tend to be quite large before they can afford the costs associated with going public, the United States has been able to provide relatively low-cost access to liquid markets for thousands of small- and mid-cap public companies. Money to a business is like water to a plant. In good soil and climate, the plant may grow from rainwater alone, but add irrigation, and crop yields dramatically improve. Likewise, choke off access to capital, and you inhibit the growth of our small companies. Provide access to public markets for companies of this size and you not only get the opportunity for faster growth, but also job creation, more tax revenues into public coffers, and better, cheaper goods and services to consumers.

The key is legislative restraint. Let the markets self-correct wherever possible, and legislate where business is incapable of self-policing or cannot meet society's safety goals. Objectives, such as board independence, benefited from Congressional guidance. It is unlikely that independence on our board of directors of public companies would have increased to the point they have without the passage of the Sarbanes-Oxley Act. Looking forward, it is also unlikely that many "imperial CEOs" would willingly give up one of these positions despite the clear conflict of interest. Shareholder activists are continuing to put pressure on boards to increase their independence from management, but they tend to focus on larger companies and seem to be fighting on too many fronts to be effective. This is an example of where legislation, in the absence of an effective self-correcting mechanism, can help create needed structural change at reasonable cost. Competent, independent oversight of management will do more to deter fraud at small companies then a mandated system of internal control ever could.

The response to the recent market timing frauds experienced in the mutual fund industry provides a lesson in restraint. Rather than rushing new legislation through Congress, cooler minds are waiting to gauge the impact of the SEC's response to the crisis. When the next scandal presents itself, we should continue to exercise legislative restraint. Confidence building, yes. Aggressive prosecution, yes. More independent supervision, yes. Layering extensive and costly requirements of marginal benefit on our public companies, *no*. If we ignore the competitive threat in an irrational attempt to eliminate all corporate fraud, the ticking we hear may not be legislation's biological clock, rather it may be the sound of a well-meaning but dangerous weapon delivered to an important pillar of the U.S. economy. Sarbanes-Oxley is good legislation. It could be better by being less. As long as there are fallible people at the helm, no amount of legislation can eliminate fraud from our nation's corporations. Let us not destroy our competitiveness trying.

As directors, we need to work closely with our small companies to implement strong, inexpensive controls. It is neither cost-efficient nor necessary to force a highly formalized control structure on a small firm. Where big companies may have preventive controls that are systemically enforced, small companies may have to rely on segregation of duties and detective controls such as managerial oversight. Rather than fancy documentation systems, smaller organizations will have to rely on spreadsheets. Instead of a legion of consultants lining up the compliance documentation, managers may have to document their control structure themselves. Regardless, directors need to understand what the company is doing to comply with the internal control requirements of the Sarbanes-Oxley Act and monitor progress. A reported deficiency may result in a reduction of the company's stock price and, by association, an increase in litigation risk for sitting directors. Smart directors will make certain that they corroborate progress from more than one source, including their own internal control consultant if necessary.

It is also vital that our newly invigorated public accountants provide sound feedback regarding what a small client has to do to improve controls. The fear to say anything has proved obstructive to improvements at larger companies and we cannot afford to let it happen to the resource-constrained small caps. And the regulators have to step up to the plate. To date, the SEC has effectively punted on the small corporation issue. But there are signs that the SEC intends to bring focus to the impact the Act is having on small companies. They recently delayed the implementation of Section 404 for small companies until mid-2006 and announced the creation of a small business advisory committee to assess the impact of the Sarbanes-Oxley Act on these organizations. They also plan to hold a public roundtable to discuss small company concerns about the internal control component of the Act. Companies and auditors are desperately looking for some guidelines that reflect size and cost structure. There has been enough procrastination. Perhaps this new SEC initiative will finally address these issues. Regardless, it is time for our legislators, regulators, and gatekeepers to spend the time necessary to get the regulatory balance right for our small companies.

KEY CONCEPTS: SMALL COMPANY

- Small companies will be impacted to a greater extent than larger companies by implementation of Section 404 of the Sarbanes-Oxley Act.
- Small companies have to rely more on manual controls.
- Whistle-blowers are just as important for small companies. Ensure that that a valid reporting process is operational.
- Smart directors will make certain that key management assertions are independently corroborated.

ENDNOTES

1. John C. Bogel, "Scandal and Reform," *Forbes*, 13 October 2003, 44.
2. Stephen Labaton, "S.E.C. Backs Rules on Fund Ethics and Disclosure," *New York Times*, 27 May 2004, C1.
3. Gretchen Morgenson, "Funds Manager Is Said to Face S.E.C. Inquiry," *New York Times*, 29 June 2004, C1.
4. Bloomberg News, "Edward Jones Agrees to Settle Marketing Charge," *New York Times*, 21 December 2004, C7.
5. U. S. Securities and Exchange Commission, "Litigation Release No. 18923," *SEC.gov.* http://www.sec.gov/litigation/litreleases/lr18923.htm (7 October 2004).
6. Timothy L. O'Brien and Larry Rohter, "The Pinochet Money Trail," *New York Times*, 12 December 2004, C1.
7. Timothy L. O'Brien, "At Riggs Bank, A Tangled Path Led to Scandal," *New York Times*, 19 July 2004, A1.
8. Jenny Anderson, "B of A Slammed," *New York Post*, 16 March 2004, 33.
9. Gretchen Morgenson and Mary Williams Walsh, "How Consultants Can Retire on Your Pension," *New York Times*, 12 December 2004, C13.
10. Julia Moskin, "Ex-President of Foundation Held in Theft," *New York Times*, 14 December 2004, B1.
11. Christopher H. Gadsden, "The Hershey Power Play," *Trusts and Estates* 8 (November 2002). http://www.trustsandestates.com (11 November 2002).
12. Editorial Staff, "Inside View of Sarbanes-Oxley," *Catalyst* (January–February 2005): 13.

CHAPTER 16

A Call to Service

We have covered a lot of ground together. I developed the High-Impact Governance Framework with the view toward providing the tools that conscientious directors seek in an easy to assimilate format. Being a director in the post-Sarbanes-Oxley world can be daunting. Armed with a rock solid framework, directors now have a resource they can reference to take measure of the boards on which they serve. As demonstrated in Exhibit 16.1, we have reviewed in some detail the framework's five governance factors which are: Insist on High Standards, Build a Strong Foundation, Organize to Lead, Let Them Know You're Watching, and Communicate Clearly.

Each factor contains useful information to not only comply with current laws and regulations emanating from the Sarbanes-Oxley Act, but also best practice objectives that every board can attain. Some best practices, such as separating the role of CEO and chairman, are controversial. But whether you agree with certain practices or not, you are versed in these emerging issues and ready to join the debate. All that is now needed are well-intentioned directors set upon a course of actively doing what is right for the shareholders they represent.

Service to a public corporation in the form of a directorship is a high calling. The reputation of directors has been sullied from the many financial reporting frauds and the high-profile prosecutions that followed. Nevertheless, the board of directors remains the small shareholders' best hope for informed decision-making based on real results and adequate disclosures. They can take comfort in the fact that the board is looking out for their interests. Service to a public company used to be viewed with reverence and will again—*one day*. The biggest threat to our public companies lies in the reticence of our best and brightest to serve on the board of directors. For a stipend and the recognition that comes with being a director, you get added

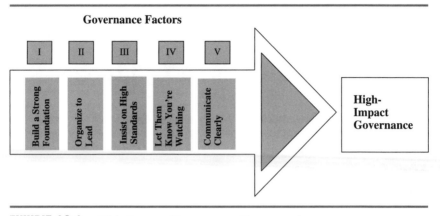

EXHIBIT 16.1   High-Impact Governance Framework

liability, potentially crippling demands on your time, and your reputation is put on the line. Once your reputation is damaged, none of the
benefits will seem worth the cost of service. There is little doubt that
there were good directors caught up with the bad at Enron,
WorldCom, and others. But all were painted with the same brush once
the financial frauds came to light. Granted, certain Enron directors did
not have to pay a penalty for trading Enron stock during the pension
plan blackout period. Do you believe most knowledgeable people
make that differentiation when it is disclosed that you were a director
of that company? Most likely not. The reputations of all are tainted.

Yet it is imperative that potential directors not only recognize
their liability, but also look to the importance of their contribution to
public service. The comparison of how some respond to jury duty
comes to mind. The right to a trial by jury is a cornerstone of our justice system. Our country can not properly support the right to a jury
trial if citizens are not willing to contribute their time. Likewise, if
our best business people refuse to serve, then eventually suboptimal
decisions and poor oversight will take its toll on our international
competitiveness. Worse yet, management unchecked may result in
more lost jobs and pensions. Littered among the debris of these
financial collapses are the thousands of jobs and retirement savings
destroyed. Despite a resilient American economy, these victims are
often least capable of recovering what was lost.

I recently attended the grand opening of Icahn Stadium on
Randall's Island in New York City. The event was notable because it

represented all that is right and good in our country. The site itself had a proud history. Randall's Island hosted the trials where Jesse Owens overcame negative forces and earned the right to represent the United States in the 1936 Olympics in Germany. It was at these games that Owens demonstrated to the world the fallacy of the Nazis' notion of superiority. The stadium and local playing fields had always been a resource for the community, however, they had fallen into disrepair, leaving the young men and women of Harlem and the South Bronx without facilities. One student at the event talked about running track on an asphalt playground littered with glass. Another related how he practiced by running through the halls of his school. My guess is that their experiences were not unique.

To address the problem, the not-for-profit Randall's Island Sports Foundation was formed and a board of highly successful and influential members constituted. In a unique partnership, they worked with the New York City Department of Parks and Recreation to replace the neglected ball fields and dilapidated Downing Stadium. Board members liberally gave their time, skills, contacts, and personal money to achieve this objective. This unselfishness was not limited to Carl and Gail Icahn, although their donation and Gail's substantial time commitment to board activities was an important catalyst. The untiring efforts of the many members of the board was truly inspiring. And it was not all smooth sailing. The Chairman of the RISF board confided in me some darker moments when value engineers, little by little, sliced away at the stadium to keep it under budget. But in the end, the hard work paid off and they delivered world-class track and stadium facilities. Athletes came from across the nation to help celebrate. Current and former World Champions such as Renaldo Nehemiah (110 meter hurdles), Al Oerter (four times discus gold), Bob Beamon (long jump), and the fastest man in the world, Justin Gatlin (100 meters) were in attendance. Jesse Owen's daughter, Marlene Owens Rankin, was on hand to announce the Jesse Owens Track & Field Club for underresourced children. Most importantly, the stadium served as host to the New York Relays that day, featuring local high school athletes. If there was any doubt about the worthiness of this cause, one only had to see the love-sick panic of a young discus athlete who was afraid she would not get to meet her inspiration, Al Oerter (she did), or the throngs of kids who threw themselves at Justin Gatlin as he crossed the finish line in a celebratory exhibition. Even the usually stoic Gatlin could not help but smile. He seemed to enjoy the admiration as much as the kids were excited for him being there. It was a magical day that would not have occurred if caring people had not given their time, effort, and yes, board leadership, to make it happen.

Even if you are not motivated by these high-minded arguments, consider then the new tools available to directors to help them perform their duties. While much of the focus has been on officer certifications and compliance with internal control disclosures, Congress, the SEC, and the self regulatory organizations (NYSE, NASDAQ, and AMEX) have increased the independence of key committees, placed the director-nomination process squarely with the board, reinforced the boards' authority regarding the selection, retention and compensation of the certifying public accountants and other advisors, and directed that a company provide the funds needed for a board to do their job. Boards have never been more directly empowered.

Some are saying that corporate governance initiatives have gone too far and that the pendulum is swinging back. While I agree, particularly for small public companies, that some of the regulations are unnecessarily burdensome, in total the changes will result in better transparency for investors, more empowered boards, fewer management conflicts of interest, and better performance from the nation's gatekeepers (the accountants, lawyers, security analysts, among others). It is my hope that instead of a pendulum, we are seeing a temporary but timely and healthy retrenchment in a continuum of voluntary improvement.

While there has been some second guessing and push back of reforms, perhaps the time is right to pause and evaluate how far we have come and where we should focus future attention. The problem is, unless there is a crisis, continuous improvement usually falls victim to the status quo. To combat the status quo, it is essential that large shareholder activists truly evaluate what they hope to accomplish and use their significant influence in a targeted manner to effect change. They must work smarter, not harder. At the Walt Disney Company, we may have glimpsed the future model that will force change in our boardrooms. Two strong-willed directors, Roy Disney and Stanley Gold (who led the revolt calling for Michael Eisner's resignation as CEO), and large shareholders stood together to force change. If shareholders can team with directors to better direct their energies, I expect the responsiveness of management will only improve.

Business, government, and investors need to work together to achieve balanced corporate governance. With the help of experienced directors willing to serve, business can recognize and negotiate most needed changes voluntarily. I have endeavored to write a book that provides directors with the knowledge necessary to succeed in their role and to improve the governance of their public company. It is when improvement yields to entrenched resistance that the potential for a crisis-induced regulatory initiative becomes most likely. Never has our business community needed the leadership of seasoned directors more than today. The tools are available. The call to service is made. We should all be concerned about who will answer.

GMI Corporate Governance Ratings*

Governance Metrics International (GMI), a corporate governance research and ratings agency, maintains ratings on the corporate governance practices of over 3,200 global companies. Such metrics are used not only by institutional investors, but also by credit rating agencies, lenders, and even regulators. GMI has granted reprint rights for their most recent release of those companies attaining a perfect score of 10.0, as well as some lessons learned from low-rated companies of the past.

Top Rated Companies—Score of 10.0

Company	Ticker	Country
3M Company	MMM	USA
Air Products & Chemicals	APD	USA
BCE Inc.	BCE	Canada
BP plc	BP	United Kingdom
CIT Group Inc.	CIT	USA
Colgate-Palmolive Company	CL	USA
Cooper Industries Ltd.	CBE	USA
Eastman Kodak Company	EK	USA
Entergy Corp.	ETR	USA
General Electric Co.	GE	USA
General Motors Corp.	GM	USA
Gillette Company	G	USA
Great Lakes Chemical Corporation	GLK	USA

---

*Top Rated Companies reprinted courtesy of Governance Metrics International. Low rated companies adapted from *GMI Ratings: What's Happened Since?* October 25, 2004.

Company	Ticker	Country
Johnson Controls	JCI	USA
Lockheed Martin Corporation	LMT	USA
Mattel Inc.	MAT	USA
Nexen, Inc.	NXY	Canada
Occidental Petroleum Corp.	OXY	USA
Peoples Energy Corporation	PGL	USA
PepsiCo, Inc.	PEP	USA
PG&E Corporation	PCG	USA
Praxair Inc.	PX	USA
Public Service Enterprise Group Inc.	PEG	USA
Regency Centers Corp.	REG	USA
Rohm & Haas Company	ROH	USA
SLM Corporation	SLM	USA
Smith & Nephew plc	SN	United Kingdom
The Dow Chemical Company	DOW	USA
The Procter & Gamble Company	PG	USA
TransCanada Corporation	TRP	Canada
United Technologies Corporation	UTX	USA
Vodafone Group plc	VOD	United Kingdom
Westpac Banking Corp.	WBC	Australia
Wisconsin Energy Corporation	WEC	USA

Each of the following companies had low reported governance ratings well in advance of experiencing severe difficulties.

Company	Score	Issue/Result
Parmalat Finanziaria	4.0	Issues about board accountability as only 3 of 13 directors were deemed independent. One of the largest frauds in history.
Freddie Mac	1.0	Lack of disclosures and board accountability were cited. Management was improperly managing earnings by billions of dollars.
Fannie Mae	2.0	Lack of financial transparency. Aggressive accounting deemed inappropriate causing the company to restate earnings and raise additional capital.
Biovail Corp.	3.0	Issues include board accountability, executive loans, related party transactions. The company later reported questionable accounting and the Ontario Securities Commission opened an investigation into suspicious trading activity.

Company	Score	Issue/Result
Interstate Bakeries	4.5	Issues flagged included financial disclosures, internal controls, corporate behavior, and lack of independence on the audit committee. Company eventually filed for bankruptcy protection after twice delaying the filing of their annual report.
Krispy Kreme Doughnuts Inc.	2.5	Lack of disclosure, poor corporate behavior, and independence issues relating to the compensation and governance committees. Shareholder lawsuits, SEC investigations, auditor refused to sign off on financial statements.

General Motors Corporation: Audit Committee of the Board of Directors Charter*

Purpose

The Audit Committee's primary function is assisting the GM Board with its responsibility for overseeing the integrity of GM's financial statements, GM's compliance with legal and regulatory requirements, the qualifications and independence of the independent accountants and the performance of GM's internal audit department and independent accountants.

In carrying out this function, the Committee shall independently and objectively monitor the performance of GM's financial reporting processes and systems of internal controls; review and appraise the audit efforts of GM's independent accountants and internal audit group; provide for open, ongoing communications concerning GM's financial position and affairs between the Board and the independent accountants, GM's financial and senior management, and GM's internal audit department; review GM's policies and compliance procedures regarding ethics; prepare the Audit Committee Report for the annual proxy statement; and report regularly to the Board regarding the execution of its duties.

Membership

The Committee shall be composed of three or more directors as determined by the Board. The duties and responsibilities of a

---

*Reprinted with permission of the General Motors Corporation.

Committee member are in addition to those required of a director. Each Committee member shall be an independent director as determined in accordance with the Corporation's Bylaws and as defined by all applicable laws and regulations. All members of the Committee shall be "financially literate" and the Committee will have at least one member qualified as an "audit committee financial expert" as defined by applicable regulations.

Meetings

The Committee shall meet approximately six times annually. Periodically, it shall meet in executive sessions with management, the General Auditor, the independent accountants, and other GM management members. Annually, it shall meet at its discretion with representatives of GM's major subsidiaries regarding their systems of internal control, results of audits, and integrity of financial reporting. The Committee shall periodically meet in executive session absent GM management.

The Committee shall maintain independence both in establishing its agenda and directly accessing management of GM and its subsidiaries. Annually, the Committee will reassess the adequacy of this charter, evaluate its performance, and report these and other actions to the Board of Directors with any recommendations.

Responsibilities and Duties

Financial management is responsible for preparing financial statements and related disclosures and communications; the Committee's primary responsibility is oversight. To carry out this responsibility, the Committee shall undertake the following common recurring activities:

Financial Statements
- Discuss with management and the independent accountants the annual audited financial statements and quarterly financial statements prior to filing including Management's Discussion and Analysis of Financial Condition and Results of Operations, GM's

earnings announcements as well as financial information and earnings guidance provided to analysts and rating agencies (NYSE), and the results of the independent accountants' reviews; these discussions may be general, covering types of information to be disclosed and the type of presentation to be made, and need not take place in advance. The Committee may be represented by the Chair or a subcommittee to review earnings announcements.

■ Review critical accounting policies, financial reporting and accounting standards and principles (including significant changes to those principles or their application), and key accounting decisions and judgments affecting the Corporation's financial statements. The review shall include the rationale for such choices and possible alternative accounting and reporting treatments.

■ Review the effect of regulatory initiatives and unusual or infrequently occurring transactions, as well as off-balance sheet structures, on the financial statements.

■ Review with the independent accountants difficulties in performing the audit or disagreements with management.

■ Review GM's financial reporting processes, including the systems of internal control, and the independent accountant's audit of GM's internal controls.

■ Discuss with the independent accountants the matters required to be discussed by Statement on Auditing Standards No. 61 relating to the conduct of the audit.

■ Review any disclosure of significant deficiencies in the design or operation of internal controls and any special audit steps adopted.

Independent Accountants

■ Select, evaluate, and, if appropriate, terminate or replace the independent accountants. (The Committee's selection shall be annually submitted to the Board for approval and to the stockholders for ratification.) The independent accountants are accountable to the Committee. The Committee shall approve the audit engagement and pre-approve any other services to be provided by the independent accountants.

■ Annually review reports by the independent accountants describing: their internal quality control procedures; any material issues raised by the most recent internal quality control review, peer review, or by any inquiry or investigation by governmental or professional authorities, within the preceding five years, respecting one or more independent audits carried out by the firm, and any steps taken to deal with any such issues; and all relationships between the independent accountants and GM.

- Ensure that rotation of the independent accountants' audit partner satisfies regulatory requirements, and set policies about hiring current or former employees of the independent accountants.
- Review and discuss with the independent accountants the annual statement required by the Independence Standards Board (ISB) Standard No. 1.
- Review and discuss the scope and plan of the independent audit.

Internal Audit

- Review the performance of the internal audit department including the objectivity and authority of its reporting obligations, the proposed audit plans for the coming year, and the results of internal audits. Review and concur in the appointment and dismissal of the General Auditor.

Legal, Compliance, and Risk Management

- Establish procedures for reviewing and handling complaints or concerns received by GM regarding accounting, internal accounting controls, or auditing matters, including enabling employees to submit concerns confidentially and anonymously, and review management's disclosure of any frauds that involve management or other employees who have a significant role in internal control.
- Review procedures and compliance processes pertaining to corporate ethics and standards of business conduct as embodied in GM's policy, *Winning With Integrity: Our Values and Guidelines for Employee Conduct.*
- Review policies and procedures with respect to officers' expense accounts and perquisites, including their use of corporate assets, and consider the results of any review of these areas by the internal auditors or the independent accountants.
- Review the assessment of management regarding compliance with laws and regulations designated by the Federal Deposit Insurance Corporation (FDIC) as being essential for safety and

soundness, compliance with regulations of the Office of the Comptroller of the Currency (OCC) relating to fiduciary activities, and compliance with other regulatory authorities.

- As the Qualified Legal Compliance Committee (QLCC), review and discuss any reports received from attorneys with respect to securities law violations and/or breaches of fiduciary duties which were reported to the General Counsel or the Chief Executive Officer and not resolved to the satisfaction of the reporting attorney.

- Discuss policies with respect to risk assessment and risk management, including GM's major financial and accounting risk exposures and the steps undertaken to control them.

The Committee may diverge from this list as appropriate if circumstances or regulatory requirements change. In addition to these activities, the Committee will perform such other functions as necessary or appropriate under law, stock exchange rules, GM's certificate of incorporation and Bylaws, and the resolutions and other directives of the Board. The Committee may obtain advice, assistance, and investigative support form outside legal, accounting, or other advisors as it deems appropriate to perform its duties, and GM shall provide appropriate funding, as determined by the Committee, for any such advisors.

Board Evaluation Tool: NACD Sample Board Self-Assessment Questionnaire*

Use this scale in your response:

1 = Strongly Disagree
2 = Disagree
3 = Undecided
4 = Agree
5 = Strongly Agree

	Evaluation Question		Recommendations for Improvement
	OVERALL		
1	The board is firmly committed to being held accountable.	1 2 3 4 5	
2	The board has critiqued, questioned, and approved management's corporate strategy.	1 2 3 4 5	
3	The board can clearly articulate and communicate the company's strategic plan.	1 2 3 4 5	

---

*Reprinted with permission from *Board Evaluation: Improving Director Effectiveness,* a publication of the National Association of Corporate Directors, Washington, DC (www.nacdonline.org).

	Evaluation Question		Recommendations for Improvement
	OVERALL		
4	The board ensures superb operational execution by management.	1 2 3 4 5	
5	The board focuses on management succession and aligns CEO leadership with the company's strategic challenges.	1 2 3 4 5	
6	The board and the compensation committee foster an aggressive value-driven and performance-oriented culture that aligns officer compensation with long-term performance and innovation.	1 2 3 4 5	
7	The board is knowledgeable about competitive factors, including customer satisfaction.	1 2 3 4 5	
8	The board ensures that the management team is responsive to market forces.	1 2 3 4 5	
9	The board is strategically involved in merger and acquisition discussions, and ensures management's execution in those areas.	1 2 3 4 5	
	THE RIGHT PEOPLE		
10	The board's independent directors have a wide range of talents, expertise, and occupational and personal backgrounds.	1 2 3 4 5	
11	The company's outside directors are independent-minded in dealing with company issues.	1 2 3 4 5	

	Evaluation Question		Recommendations for Improvement
	THE RIGHT PEOPLE		
12	The board is intolerant of mediocrity in management and board effectiveness.	1 2 3 4 5	
13	Directors do what is best for the corporation and shareholders regardless of countervailing pressure.	1 2 3 4 5	
	THE RIGHT CULTURE		
14	The board encourages a culture that promotes candid communication and rigorous decision making.	1 2 3 4 5	
15	Directors and managers work together to achieve "constructive interaction"—a healthy atmosphere of give and take.	1 2 3 4 5	
	THE RIGHT ISSUES		
16	The board focuses on activities that will help the company maximize shareholder value.	1 2 3 4 5	
17	The board consistently focuses on corporate strategy.	1 2 3 4 5	
18	The board and management act in concert, while showing fidelity to their respective roles.	1 2 3 4 5	
	THE RIGHT INFORMATION		
19	Directors study and understand relevant information in order to spend their time effectively and make informed decisions.	1 2 3 4 5	
20	Director requests for information are reasonable in amount and time frame, enabling thorough and prompt replies.	1 2 3 4 5	

	Evaluation Question						Recommendations for Improvement
	THE RIGHT PROCESS						
21	The board has composed a description of specific duties, goals, and objectives, and measures its performance against those responsibilities.	1	2	3	4	5	
22	The board has designated an independent committee to monitor board composition and operations.	1	2	3	4	5	
	THE RIGHT FOLLOW-THROUGH						
23	The board effectively follows through on its recommendations developed during the evaluation process.	1	2	3	4	5	
24	Evaluations lead to a clearer understanding of what the board must do to become a strategic asset.	1	2	3	4	5	
25	The full board agrees on and approves actions to address areas in need of improvement.	1	2	3	4	5	
26	The board initiates actions, plans with specific time lines for implementation of recommendations, and monitors progress.	1	2	3	4	5	

Champion Enterprises, Inc.
CEO Evaluation*

Scale:

0–3	Improvement needed
4–7	Satisfactory performance, meets requirements
8–10	Strong, superior performance, exceeds requirements

Chief Executive Officer Functions

_____1. Be responsible for the company's consistent achievement of its financial goals and objectives (growth, profitability, cash flow).

Comments:

_____

_____

_____

_____2. Make certain that the company's internal climate and policies are consistent with improving long-term quality.

Comments:

_____

_____

_____

*Reprinted with courtesy of Champion Enterprises, Inc.

_____3. Develop and motivate a strong top management team.

Comments:

_____

_____

_____

_____4. Make certain that the company's capital resources are suffi-
cient and properly allocated to provide returns.

Comments:

_____

_____

_____

_____5. Provide a positive internal and external leadership role for
employees, customers, shareholders, and suppliers.

Comments:

_____

_____

_____

_____6. Assure that the company implements a longer-term strategy
that maximizes opportunities and considers risks.

Comments:

_____

_____

_____

Key challenges in the coming year:

_____

_____

_____

_____

Major opportunities for further improvement:

_____

_____

_____

_____

Other thoughts and concerns relating to Champion and its Management:

_____

_____

_____

_____

During the past year, how would you evaluate the CEO on a 0 (lowest) to 10 (highest) scale.

Evaluation	Goals	Evaluation	Goals
	Overcoming industry/ economy concerns		Controls/internal audit
	Ramping up retail		Retaining, motivating, attracting management
	Consolidating manufacturing		Crisis management
	Upgrading quality		Spokesperson externally, communications
	Improving operations over next three years		E-Commerce integration
	Development		Overall marketing
	Retail		Over execution/ quality and speed
	Branding		Flexibility and listening
	Internet		Strategic visions

Evaluation	Goals	Evaluation	Goals
	Finance and insurance		Succession planning
	Analyzing trans-actional opportunities under changing environment		

Please list your three largest concerns:

_____

_____

_____

_____

_____

_____

_____

_____

_____

_____

_____

Statement of Values:
Johnson & Johnson Credo*

We believe our first responsibility is to the doctors, nurses and patients, to mothers and fathers and all others who use our products and services. In meeting their needs everything we do must be of high quality. We must constantly strive to reduce our costs in order to maintain reasonable prices. Customer's orders must be serviced promptly and accurately. Our suppliers and distributors must have an opportunity to make a fair profit.

We are responsible to our employees, the men and women who work for us throughout the world. Everyone must be considered as an individual. We must respect their dignity and recognize their merit. They must have a sense of security in their jobs. Compensation must be fair and adequate, and working conditions clean, orderly and safe. We must be mindful of ways to help our employees fulfill their family responsibilities. Employees must feel free to make suggestions and complaints. There must be equal opportunity for employment, development and advancement for those qualified. We must provide competent management, and their actions must be just and ethical.

We are responsible to the communities in which we live and work and to the world community as well. We must be good citizens—support good works and charities and bear our fair share of taxes. We must encourage civic improvements and better health and education. We must maintain in good order the property we are privileged to use, protecting the environment and natural resources.

Our final responsibility is to our stockholders. Business must make a sound profit. We must experiment with new ideas. Research

*Used with permission. Courtesy of Johnson & Johnson.

must be carried on, innovative programs developed and mistakes paid for. New equipment must be purchased, new facilities provided and new products launched. Reserves must be created to provide for adverse times. When we operate according to these principles, the stockholders should realize a fair return.

TIAA-CREF Principles for Fund Governance and Practices*

This statement reflects principles to which the TIAA-CREF investment companies aspire to conform, and which we intend to apply to other companies' funds that we offer to our customers. While TIAA-CREF recognizes that there can be good faith differences of opinion about governing structures and practices, we believe our industry should take steps to demonstrate that investment companies operate for the benefit of shareholders (the funds' investors), that their pricing and costs are open to scrutiny, and that they treat all investors fairly regardless of account size.

These principles should be read in conjunction with TIAA-CREF's Statement Regarding Fund Governance and Practices, which discusses our view of the opportunity that funds have to come together to restore the trust of individual investors. The principles are not a recitation of law, but rather a set of measures reflecting ways in which funds can put shareholders' interests first.

Principle One—We believe the following governing structures can help funds operate for the benefit of shareholders.

- At least three-fourths of a fund's directors, including its chairman, should be independent of the fund's investment management company (with serious consideration given to a board comprised entirely of independent directors);
- A fund's board should meet regularly in private, without management present;
- Directors should retain independent legal counsel;

---

*Reprinted with the permission of TIAA-CREF.

- Only independent directors should serve on the audit and nominating committees; and
- The audit committee should include one or more financial experts qualified to oversee the fund's independent auditor.

Principle Two—Regular elections of directors promote board accountability to shareholders.

- Shareholders should regularly have the opportunity to elect directors, whether via a public company-style proxy process or other means.

Principle Three—Fund directors should be highly qualified.

- Directors should be people of high character, experience and competence.
- To ensure that directors are dedicating sufficient time and attention to their board responsibilities, boards should develop guidelines governing the number of corporate board memberships their directors may have.

Principle Four—Fund advisers should provide shareholders with information on how the fund compensates portfolio managers.

- A fund's investment adviser should disclose the structure of portfolio manager compensation and the methodology used to determine such compensation.
- Shareholders have a right to know whether portfolio managers have incentives to focus on short- or long-term performance.

Principle Five—Funds should voluntarily cease the practice of directing brokerage in return for distribution.

- As an interim measure, funds should quantify the amount of brokerage business sent to brokers for distribution and include that amount in their 12b-1 fees.

Principle Six—Funds should be fully transparent with respect to fees, expenses and costs.

- Brokers should separate trading costs from research costs so that investment advisers can disclose them to investors.
- In the interim, the fund industry would do well to closely examine proposals to improve soft dollar disclosure, paying particular

attention to the preservation of high quality research and the goal of true transparency.

- Ultimately, advisers should pay for investment research from their own profits, thereby ending soft dollar arrangements.

Principle Seven—Funds should be fully transparent with respect to revenue sharing arrangements their advisers have with brokerage firms that engage in fund sales.

- Fund advisers should disclose the range of these payments and the brokers who received them.

Principle Eight—All fund shareholders deserve to be dealt with fairly.

- Certain distinctions in fees and discounts among groups of investors within a fund, depending on whether the fund is sold directly or through a broker, or the quantity of shares purchased, may be appropriate provided they are fully disclosed.
- No shareholder should get preferential treatment other than as fully disclosed.
- Funds should not share confidential information relating to holdings or trading strategies with certain shareholders who can then profit from that information at the expense of others.
- Funds should develop reasonable policies and procedures to address abusive short-term trading and market timing, and should apply these policies consistently.

Index